The Origins of the Developmental State in Taiwan

The Origins of the Developmental State in Taiwan

Science Policy and the Quest for Modernization

J. Megan Greene

Harvard University Press
Cambridge, Massachusetts
London, England
2008

Library of Congress Cataloging-in-Publication Data

Greene, J. Megan.
The origins of the developmental state in Taiwan : science policy and the quest for modernization / J. Megan Greene.
p. cm.
Includes bibliographical references and index.
ISBN-13: 978-0-674-02770-1 (alk. paper)
ISBN-10: 0-674-02770-1 (alk. paper)
1. Science and state—Taiwan. 2. Science and state—China.
3. Technology and state—Taiwan. 4. Technology and state—China.
5. Science and state—Taiwan—History—20th century.
6. Science and state—China—History—20th century.
7. Technology and state—Taiwan—History—20th century.
8. Technology and state—China—History—20th century.
9. Taiwan—Economic conditions. 10. Taiwan—Relations—China. I. Title.
Q127.T28G74 2008
338.95124'906—dc22 2007031715

Contents

Preface

Not long ago I was asked if the tale that I tell in this book is a story of success. This question gave me pause because it forced me to realize that at every turn, as I had researched, thought about, and constructed this book, I had been guided by a seemingly inescapable feeling that Taiwan, in spite of the various social, cultural, political, and economic traumas it has undergone, especially in the mid-twentieth century, represents a great success story and that this success is in many respects reflected in the transformation of the Kuomintang (KMT) from its mainland to later Taiwan period. My personal observations over the past nineteen years of Taiwan's rapid economic, social, and political transformation, my grounding in the dominant narrative of early KMT history, which has largely emphasized its failures, and my fascination with the concept of the developmental state all seem to have inexorably pushed me down the same path. The larger narrative of this volume, therefore, cannot help but be a narrative of success. It paints a picture of a state that, over time, built (or was pushed to build) a set of institutions to guide industrial development, institutions that have been important keys in Taiwan's industrial development (particularly its high-tech industrial development) over the past two to three decades. However, it was never inevitable that such institutions would be created, nor was it inevitable that they would work. Those who sought to create these institutions and patterns of interaction did not always have a very strong vision, and they frequently ran into obstacles. Among these stumbling blocks were the KMT's position vis-à-vis Japan and the Chinese Communist Party (CCP) in the 1930s and 1940s; Taiwan's very particular economic, political, and social circumstances in the 1950s and 1960s; and the continued existence well into the 1970s of the KMT's obstructionist political or perhaps institutional culture. Although the larger story is one of success, it is thus not at all true that each portion of this narrative is a success story. What we see, instead, is a party-state bumbling down a bumpy path toward development, encountering both successes and failures along the way.

My narrative is not intended as a full history of Taiwan's industrialization. Within this huge topic, I have only examined the evolution of industrial science policy under the KMT. Thus there is much that this narrative leaves out that a student of industrialization might wish to learn. The volume includes little to nothing, for example, on the role played by native Taiwanese industry or entrepreneurs in Taiwan's economic rise. Nor does it fully address the significance of the legacy of the Japanese colonial period. I leave these topics for other scholars to explore as they fill out the history of Taiwan's industrialization process and of the origins of the Republic of China's developmental state.

I gratefully acknowledge institutional and financial support for this project, which came in the first place from a research grant from the Chiang Ching-kuo Foundation. Further support came from the Institute of Modern History at Academia Sinica, the School of Oriental and African Studies Taiwan Studies Programme, and the University of Kansas New Faculty General Research Fund and General Research Fund. I could not even have begun this project without the help of the staff at the Archive of Academia Sinica's Institute of Modern History, who cheerfully made box after box of sources available to me and suggested other possible sources. I also wish to thank the Second Historical Archive in Nanjing for making available numerous sources on the 1927–1949 period. In this book I have drawn upon my own earlier explorations of some of these subjects that have been published in *Taiwan in the 21st Century*, edited by Robert Ash and myself (New York: Routledge, 2007), and in Terry Bodenhorn, ed., *Defining Modernity: Guomindang Rhetorics of a New China, 1920–1970* (Ann Arbor: Center for Chinese Studies, University of Michigan, 2002).

In addition, I want to thank Fritz Gaenslen for helping me to think about the "so what" question at various stages of this project; Bob Ash, for giving me the opportunity to spend time thinking and writing and for always taking the time to stop for an encouraging chat and a cup of coffee; Bill Kirby, for always being the most kind, supportive and helpful adviser and friend a person could have; Chang Jui-teh, for setting me on this path in the first place; Julia Strauss, for her advice, encouragement, and support; Kathleen McDermott, for supporting the project and for her editorial advice; the anonymous readers for Harvard University Press; John Donohue and Susan Badger for their editorial help; and the many participants in the various conferences and venues at which parts of this volume have been presented. I also thank the friends and family who have encouraged, advised, helped, and in some instances nagged me along the way, especially Morris Bian, Bill Bowman, Cheng Linsun, Chou Changjen, Luis Corteguera, Fan Meiyuan, Sara Friedman, Granville Greene, Jack P. Greene, Sue N. Greene, John Lie, Elizabeth MacGonagle, Magdalena Sanchez, Marta Vicente, and Kim Warren. And finally, I want to express my appreciation to my husband, Tony Melchor, and to my daughter, Azucena Melchor, for their love and patience.

Abbreviations and Note on Romanization

AEC	Atomic Energy Commission
CCP	Chinese Communist Party
CIECD	Council for International Economic Cooperation and Development
CUSA	Council for U.S. Aid
DPP	Democratic Progressive Party
ERSO	Electronics Research and Service Organization
IAEA	International Atomic Energy Agency
INER	Institute for Nuclear Energy Research
INS	Institute of Nuclear Science
IT	information technology
ITRI	Industrial Technology Research Institute
JCRR	Joint Commission on Rural Reconstruction
KMT	Kuomintang
MDC	Manpower Development Committee
MDP	Manpower Development Plan
MOST	Ministry of Science and Technology
NBIR	National Bureau of Industrial Research
NCSD	National Council for Scientific Development
NEC	National Economic Council
NGO	nongovernmental organization
NRC	National Resources Commission
NSC	National Science Council
NTU	National Taiwan University
PRC	People's Republic of China
R&D	research and development
ROC	Republic of China
S&T	science and technology
SMEs	small- and medium-sized enterprises

SRI	Stanford Research Institute
STAG	Science and Technology Advisory Group
TI	Texas Instruments
UIRL	Union Industrial Research Laboratory
UNESCO	United Nations Educational, Scientific and Cultural Organization
UNRRA	United Nations Relief and Rehabilitation Administration
USAID	United States Agency for International Development

I have used pinyin to romanize book and document titles originally in Chinese and for place and personal names except in cases where another spelling is most commonly used and likely to be more easily understood by the reader or in cases where I only know a name in an anglicized version. Thus place and personal names for Taiwan that are already well known by another romanization are not in pinyin. For example, Chiang Kai-shek, K. T. Li, Kuomintang (KMT), Taipei, and Hsinchu all appear as they are standardly romanized. Likewise, names that I have only found in English-language archival records that have not been fully spelled out are also romanized as I found them in the original documents.

The Origins of the Developmental State in Taiwan

Introduction: Science Policy in a Developmental State

Taiwan's mid-twentieth century is one of the great success stories in economic development. It is a story that has less to do with the Taiwanese themselves than with trends in scientific and technical development in China over the course of the twentieth century. Chinese modernizers since the 1920s have believed that economic development could be planned through scientific management and that it was the job of the government to plan and oversee development. Modern Chinese states, however, have not always successfully fulfilled this role, and modern Chinese political leaders have often failed to support the aims of modernizers. This book examines ways in which the Kuomintang (KMT) state planned and promoted science and technology (S&T) development both in mainland China between 1927 and 1949 and on Taiwan after 1949. It reveals a complex picture of interaction among technocrats, politicians, academicians, and outside advisers and shows that successful state leadership of the economy was not inevitable and the path to success not always apparent to the political leadership. Success came only after the political leadership combined forces with state planners, or technocrats, to push all relevant branches of the state as well as academicians and entrepreneurs to work together to promote S&T development. Today, as the Chinese state searches for new strategies to promote industrial development, Taiwan's S&T experience seems particularly relevant both as a model and as part of a long-term process that began in mainland China and that is now being taken up again by Chinese leaders.

The rapid growth of Taiwan's postwar "miracle" economy has most frequently been credited to the leading role of the state in promoting economic development. Of the abundant scholarship on the Republic of China (ROC) that describes it as a developmental state, little investigates its origins. In fact, Taiwan's developmental state is generally described as simply being, and few scholars appear to have given any thought to just how it *came into* being. This volume is about the origins of the ROC's developmental state. Its primary goal is to investigate how and why the ROC state built institutions and initiated policies of the sort that we associate with developmental states. It seeks answers to the following questions: Was it inevitable that the ROC would become a developmental state? Did the changes in circumstance that the ROC state encountered as it relocated from mainland China to Taiwan play a major role in helping the state to take on a developmental role, or did the state already have such tendencies in its early period? Was the state unified in its aims, or were there differences of approach between political and technocratic leaders? What internal and external pressures were brought to bear on the state as it constructed institutions and developed policy? To what extent did those institutions and policies reflect those pressures? Did the state always take a leading role in this process, and if not, how did it become *developmental,* a term that strongly suggests a leading role for the state?

This book uses the case of state-sponsored S&T policy as a lens through which to explore these questions. Though by no means the only significant facet of industrial development policy, S&T policy is especially important in Taiwan's case in large part because Taiwan's economic success in the last two decades has been built on high-tech industrial development.[1] There has been some scholarship on the ROC's S&T development in the 1980s and beyond, most of which describes ROC advances in these areas as unqualified successes.[2] No effort has been made, however, to consider the history of state-sponsored S&T development in the ROC, a history that, as we shall see, can teach us a great deal about how the state functioned and how it acquired the developmental role that has so often been attributed to it.

Taiwan's postwar industrial science policy grew out of a legacy from the mainland, a legacy now being revived in a new context by a different mainland Chinese government. However, it was not always the political leadership that kept this legacy alive. In fact, the interests of political leaders and technocrats were often at odds. Although the KMT government was committed to promoting industrial science policy on the mainland, it lost interest in this area of development in the 1950s and 1960s in Taiwan. Only under pressure from technocrats, academicians, and foreign advisers and aid givers, and in the face of external crises in the late 1960s, did the political leadership make a halfhearted commitment to promoting an industrial science policy. The political leadership's failure to lend its full authority to this project, however, caused the new policy to fail in the critical aspect of connecting the education and research sectors to the industrial sector. Without the enthusiastic support of Taiwan's authoritarian political leadership, Taiwan's "developmental state" was still not fully functional. It was only in 1978 that another set of external crises, political change at the top, and further pushes by technocrats and outside advisers converged to make the political leadership use its authority to take on the developmental role for which it has so often been praised. In the end, the success of Taiwan's developmental state was dependent on a marriage of technocratic expertise and political dictatorship.

This story shows that the state, even during its most authoritarian periods, did not function as a monolithic and unified entity. State interests as perceived by state planners (technocrats) and political leaders did not always coincide. State planners were most concerned with constructing strategies to maximize use of Taiwan's limited resources for industrial development. Political leaders, on the other hand, were more concerned with the ROC's political survival and before the 1970s did not always grasp the significance of economic development to survival. This narrative illuminates the complexities of Taiwan's developmental state and shows us that although actors from within the state (most notably technocratic state planners) may have promoted developmental strategies, these strategies could not be effectively implemented without the active support of the political leadership.

This book, therefore, offers a political history of Taiwan's scientific and technical development. It shows that although both success and strong state leadership did eventually come about, neither outcome was inevitable in a process that was more often characterized by failure and weak or ineffective state leadership. A coherent science policy evolved only haltingly and as the result of a complex interaction among eager technocrats, academicians, and foreign advisers and a shortsighted political leadership. At no time was it a direct result of top-down policy originating from the political leadership.

This story also has implications for our understanding of changes taking place in the past decade or two in mainland China. Like Taiwan under the KMT, the People's Republic of China (PRC) has considerable authoritarian power. Like Taiwan in the 1950s and 1960s, the PRC government under Mao Zedong failed over time to promote a coherent science policy to facilitate industrial development. Since the 1980s, however, the PRC has made a series of shifts that look very much like changes that Taiwan underwent in the 1970s. In spite of its major mid-century upheavals, China today appears in many respects to be following patterns that were established in earlier Chinese contexts, albeit with a significant difference, that the political leaders and the technocrats are the same people. In part because of this uncharacteristic overlapping of roles, Taiwan's successful combination of technocratic expertise and political authoritarianism, in particular, is a relevant model for China today.

The Importance of State Sponsorship of Science and Technology

A basic premise of this volume is that science and technology are important to economic growth and development. This premise has been shared by most modern states, technocrats, and economists since at least the close of World War II. Over the past half century state-sponsored scientific research conducted in many nations has yielded a wide array of new technologies, from atomic bombs to space rockets to antibiotics and vaccines to the Internet, and all of these technologies have contributed in one way or another to both national and global economic transformations. Of course, not all technologies have the far-reaching impact of those listed above, but that does not keep either states or private enterprises from investing in research and development (R&D) in virtually every sort of scientific field in the hope that they will produce something that will give them a competitive advantage in either the marketplace or the international political or strategic arena. Levels of investment in scientific and technical R&D have become important markers of development, and many states have invested in R&D in bids to elevate their levels of economic development throughout the postwar era.

Although Western states had begun to support some scientific research well before the twentieth century, it became especially apparent over the course of the twentieth century that scientific advancements and control over them were the keys to wealth and power in the modern world. As René Maheu, then director-general of the United Nations Educational, Scientific and Cultural Organization (UNESCO), noted in 1969, 90 percent of the world's scientific personnel were living in the industrialized world, and that meant that the remaining 10 percent were shared among the three-fourths of the world's population that lived in the nonindustrial world.[3] The developing world thus needed to gain access to and control of scientific and technical knowledge as well. The aim of UNESCO and other aid agencies such as the World Bank and the U.S. Agency for International Development (USAID) was to irrigate the world's vast scientific desert by urging states to develop science education; train personnel; plan research projects that would serve concrete national needs in industry, agriculture, and health; and foster an environment that embraced the ideals of scientific inquiry and the pursuit of scientific knowledge.

In writing on science policy, I share the fundamental assumption of international development agencies of the mid-twentieth century that a scientific infrastructure is an essential component of the overall economic and social development process. States interested in promoting development need, on the one hand, to encourage science education at all levels and, on the other hand, to foster an environment conducive to both applied and basic scientific research that can contribute to the advancement of general knowledge and the training of skilled technicians. Development agencies and social scientists were in substantial agreement in the mid- to late twentieth century that the most pragmatic way for a developing state with scarce resources to encourage scientific development was through the construction of centralized, state-administered scientific planning agencies. The ideal scientific planning organ would evaluate the economic state of the nation as well as the resources of the nation (economic, human, and natural) and would devise a plan to support a level of science education and research that would supply the nation with the amount of technically skilled and scientifically innovative manpower that its economy could absorb. It would also oversee the development of scientific and technical research that would have clear and direct social (public health and sanitation) and economic (industrial or agricultural) value.

This volume focuses on industrial S&T because over the long term industrial growth is and has been seen by the ROC state as central to Taiwan's economic success in a way that public health and agriculture have not. Separate books could be (and, to a certain extent, have been) written on the history of agricultural and medical science in the ROC.[4] It is undeniably true that the ROC state supported agricultural and medical R&D and manpower development both on the mainland and in Taiwan and that well-developed agricultural and medical sectors are essential to overall economic development. However, both the state and observers, including contemporary Western scholars, have placed considerably heavier emphasis (in the long run) on the role played by industry, and high-tech industry in particular, in Taiwan's economic "takeoff."

State Sponsorship of S&T in the ROC: A Bumpy Path to Success

Although the ROC state today assumes that highly developed S&T manpower and R&D capacity are essential for high-level industrial development, and there is ample evidence to suggest that the ROC state on the mainland during the war against Japan shared these assumptions, it has not been constantly the case that the ROC state has supported, or even seen the need to support, S&T. As Chapter 1 demonstrates, there are various indications that some among the KMT leadership understood the relevance of modern science and technology to the creation, in a broad sense, of a modern nation, as it was founding its new national government in late 1927. Certainly, through the creation of institutions such as Academia Sinica, a centralized, state-sponsored humanistic and scientific research institute, the KMT indicated that it sought to both promote and control the production of scientific knowledge. Moreover, during its first decade of rule, other centrally placed institutions such as the National Economic Council (NEC) and the National Resources Commission (NRC) undertook to sponsor various types of modern, scientific development projects and to catalog and make use of China's scientific and technical expert manpower. The Ministry of Education further sought to promote, albeit without much heart, the study of science, in particular among college students.

It was not until after the outbreak of war with Japan, however, that anything approaching a comprehensive science policy began to take shape in KMT-controlled China. Beginning in the early 1940s the Ministries of Education and the Economy, in coordination with the NRC, promoted a large-scale Movement to Promote National Defense Science that would encourage students to pursue scientific courses of study and increase the level of scientific awareness among the masses. In addition, institutions such as the NRC, the National Bureau of Industrial Research (NBIR), and Academia Sinica all implemented much more proactive efforts at training S&T talent than they had previously undertaken. All of these wartime efforts were described as having specific relevance to China's industrialization, and the shapers of these plans and movements all clearly saw industrialization as essential to China's future salvation. Already in the early 1940s, therefore, industrialization was a cornerstone of KMT development planning, and S&T manpower training and R&D had been clearly identified as essential building blocks for industrialization.

In spite of the KMT's interest in reviving industrial growth on Taiwan from 1945 on, however, in the wake of the KMT retreat to Taiwan in 1949, the earlier emphasis on S&T manpower and R&D development waned to the point that by the late 1950s the KMT government was implementing science education policies only to secure U.S. funding but not, it seems, out of any sense of commitment to S&T as an essential feature of industrial development. As we see in Chapter 2, until 1967 most efforts at construction of an apparatus for guiding scientific development in Taiwan were undertaken with the consent of the state, but the impetus for their construction came from the intellectual community, on the one hand, and U.S. aid agencies, on the other. Moreover, although the link between scientific and technical research and overall socioeconomic development was apparent to both U.S. aid givers and some ROC intellectuals, it does not seem to have become evident to the ROC government until after the cessation of U.S. aid in the mid-1960s. The one area in which the state took an active interest in promotion of science and technology at an early date (nuclear physics) had obvious military applications, and the political leadership, which sought above all to retake China, needed no convincing of the potential benefits of supporting academic research in that area. In the realms of S&T manpower development and R&D, therefore, the state neither initiated nor became involved in centralized planning (with the exception of nuclear physics) during its first twenty years in Taiwan. One might, therefore, question the degree to which there really was continuity between the KMT's mainland and Taiwan periods.

Beginning in 1965, state technocrats (not, however, the political leadership) began to take a more proactive approach to promotion of S&T manpower and R&D and to link it (as in the 1940s) concretely to the question of industrialization, and this is the subject of Chapter 3. To industrialize at a high level, these state planners argued, required innovation, creativity, and a workforce equipped to grapple with complex technical questions. To bolster this argument, state planners orchestrated opportunities for foreign advisers to push this message to the political leadership. As a result, between 1967 and 1969 the ROC state overhauled its institutions designed to direct S&T and began to make more active efforts to guide academic scientific research and science education. However, it does not appear that there was much more than a rhetorical commitment among the political leadership to the centrality of S&T to economic development until the mid-1970s, when a new set of plans and institutions were implemented that clearly assumed a close link between

S&T R&D and manpower development and industry. Chapter 4 examines the new efforts at constructing coordinated plans for S&T development in the period from 1969 to 1978 and considers their effectiveness.

In the late 1970s, yet another shift in institutional structure and approach to planning occurred, this time with the wholehearted support of a new political leadership consisting of the authoritarian but forward-looking Chiang Ching-kuo and his premier, the engineer Y. S. Sun. Chapter 5 examines the construction of the Science and Technology Advisory Group (STAG) and the Hsinchu Science Park. STAG institutionalized linkages between the state, industry, education, and foreign advisers and has functioned much more effectively than any of its antecedents. From the early 1980s, virtually all state ministries and institutions were held accountable to STAG. The Hsinchu Science Park, though it got off to a slow and rocky start, has become a resounding success as a single location within which both state-owned institutes and foreign- and domestic-owned private enterprise share technologies and work together to improve Taiwan's high-tech industrial capacity. Hsinchu has become a model, in fact, that Taiwan has sought to replicate in other locations since the mid-1990s.

By the early 1980s, therefore, promotion of S&T had become an essential element of the ROC's larger industrial development strategy and has remained so since. S&T was thus substantially empowered by the ROC state after 1979, and calls for S&T development became a hallmark of the state. By 1982 the basic institutions and structures were in place to enable the ROC state to direct an industrial science policy that would successfully coordinate industry, academia, and the state. I have thus chosen to end my narrative in 1982.

There is abundant evidence that Taiwan has benefited from these state-led development efforts, and in no sector is this more apparent than information technology (IT). Today Taiwan is one of the world's major producers and designers of computer components, and although there are undoubtedly numerous reasons for Taiwan's success in this area, there is no question but that the state's decision in the late 1970s to focus its educational, R&D, and other planning attention on IT was a good one. Taiwan has a highly developed and well-coordinated system of state and private investment in S&T manpower and R&D that contributes to Taiwan's overall economic growth and its international status. It is the ambition of this book to explain how this system came into being and, in the process, to uncover the story of how a state becomes developmental.

An Explanation of the State-Centered Narrative

Not all scholars attribute Taiwan's economic success to the KMT state. They point instead to the role of the market, the Taiwanese entrepreneurial spirit, the groundwork laid by the Japanese, and U.S. aid as explanations for Taiwan's rapid economic development.[5] Some argue that state policy hindered development in certain areas because it overemphasized particular sectors, thus leaving out parts of the economy.[6] Others argue that for certain sectors the state had no policy at all.[7]

While not wishing to deny the importance of forces other than the state in the ROC's economic development, I nonetheless agree with the numerous scholars who have emphasized the centrality of the state to the ROC's successful development. Tien Hung-mao, Robert Wade, Samuel Ho, Cal Clark, Ramon Myers, Tom Gold, William Kirby, and others have argued that the state played an important role in the promotion of economic development in Taiwan during the 1950s and 1960s. More recently, William Kirby and Morris Bian have characterized the early KMT state on the mainland as developmental, and this characterization is supported by the work of scholars such as David Pietz and Margherita Zanasi.[8] In addition, there has been an abundance of work by social scientists such as Chalmers Johnson, Linda Weiss, Stephan Haggard, Chien-kuo Pang, Alice Amsden, Chu Yun-han, and Meredith Woo-Cumings in the 1980s and 1990s that describes Taiwan's KMT-led state as a developmental state, most of which, however, fails to consider the origins of this pattern of state behavior.[9]

Like these works, this narrative is quite state centered. Although some scientific and technical innovation inevitably occurs in the private sector in any country, given the costs involved in research and development of scientific and technical ideas, little happens outside the public sector in an underdeveloped country, which is what Taiwan was in the 1960s. Moreover, S&T became a significant concern of state technocrats in the early to mid-twentieth century and of political leaders as well by the late 1970s. As a result of the state's interest in S&T, more planning and money were funneled into S&T education, manpower development, and R&D. Thus the story of S&T development in the ROC cannot help but involve the state. At the same time, a state-centered narrative of the history of S&T development in the ROC reveals quite a bit about the character and evolution of the ROC's developmental state.

I define a developmental state as a strong and proactive state that—armed with a meritocratic, efficient, and knowledgeable technocracy and institutions that provide it with highly embedded links to industry and society—imposes policies on the private sector that foster development.[10] Scholarly descriptions of developmental states in East Asia have often emphasized the importance of institutions designed to manage or guide the economy that are staffed by a cohesive and depoliticized technocracy.[11] The case study of S&T policy illuminates these two features of the developmental state (institution building and technocracy) to a considerable degree by showing how such institutions came to be created, on the one hand, and tracing the role of the technocratic leadership, on the other hand.

The history of S&T policy in the ROC is to a large extent the history of the construction and refinement of institutions to guide S&T policy. From the late 1950s until the early 1980s we see the development of a series of new institutions that functioned with varying effectiveness and with varying levels of state commitment or support. Although the ultimate aim of these institutions was fairly consistent, their ability to achieve this aim (the effective coordination of industry, academia/education, and the state to promote economic development) was not. Not all institutions designed to guide science policy, therefore, are equal.

The example of the ROC further suggests that technocrats alone cannot build a developmental state. And this raises the questions of just who the state is and how the state comes up with developmental policies. I propose thinking of the state in this context as being constituted of two groups that are not necessarily always operating with the same interests, political leaders, and technocrats.[12] In the case of the ROC prior to the first direct election of the president in 1996, the political leaders, by which I mean in particular the president and the premier, were not elected and governed using authoritarian strategies. They were primarily concerned with maintaining their own power, which after the move to Taiwan meant fostering economic and social stability, often, in the latter case, through coercive and dictatorial means. Chiang Kai-shek, in particular, also sought to enhance his military power to accomplish his goal of retaking the mainland. The technocracy, on the other hand, although clearly committed to maintaining stability, had a primary aim of nation building, which was not always a concern of the political leadership before the late 1960s or possibly even early 1970s. Moreover, although neither group operated in a vacuum, Taiwan's technocrats were clearly receptive to advice regarding nation building that came from both domestic and foreign sources. The policies and institutions for S&T development proposed and implemented by technocrats from the late 1960s on clearly bore the imprint of outside advisers.

Both Stephan Haggard, in *Pathways from the Periphery*, and Wu Yongping, in his more recent volume *A Political Explanation of Economic Growth*, have suggested that economic policy in Taiwan has only worked when technocrats and political leaders have acted in concert.[13] Wu has written that "the role and function of the economic bureaucracy in the formulation and implementation of economic policy hinge not on coherence but on mechanisms that can solve differences within the state."[14] The state, therefore, is not a monolithic entity that "supervises" both its own agents and the owners of capital.[15] Political leaders and technocrats, both part of the larger state, had to find common ground to make policy work. As we shall see, the case of industrial science policy in the ROC bears out this idea. The quest for a successful S&T policy was not undertaken by the political leadership but rather by a small group of technocrats who were heavily influenced by foreign advisers and local academics. It was only at the point at which the interests of the political leadership converged with the interests of the technocratic leadership, in the late 1970s, that the state wholeheartedly committed to the promotion of S&T and that new, more successful institutions could be constructed.

But what caused the interests of the political leadership and the technocrats to converge? The case of S&T development in Taiwan both supports and extends Haggard's idea that "international shocks and pressures, and the domestic economic crises associated with them, have been the most powerful stimuli for changes of policy."[16] Haggard focuses primarily on the role of external economic shocks, such as the oil crisis of the 1970s, and says little about political shocks, such as derecognition, in the case of Taiwan; however, his overall point holds true for external political crises as well as for economic shocks. As this volume will demonstrate, both political and economic crisis, generally coming from outside (although not always, as we see in the case of the Sino-Japanese War, which was certainly as much a domestic as an external shock), created opportunities, or propitious moments, during which new policies, institutions, and patterns emerged.

Neither science nor technology was the exclusive domain of the state either before or after the KMT established its government in Nanjing in 1927. The Chinese had historically engaged in various sorts of scientific investigation, and as the educational system was reformed and increasing numbers of young Chinese went abroad for study in the late nineteenth and early twentieth centuries, new, Western definitions of science and notions of scientific professionalism became popular among educators and within certain segments of society.[17] The KMT came to power, therefore, at a moment when command and production of scientific knowledge were already widely recognized as markers of modernity both in China and elsewhere.

There is ample evidence to suggest that the KMT party-state actively sought to lead a unified China into the modern era by strengthening it politically, militarily, morally, and economically. Its failure to do so effectively has been widely discussed and can be attributed to a variety of causes including excessive state bureaucratism, official corruption, poor planning, lack of popular support, appeasement of the Japanese, and an overwhelming obsession with eradicating communism above all else. Nonetheless, studies of some state institutions such as the NRC and NEC show that the KMT, or parts of it, was leading efforts in the 1930s and 1940s to construct a rational, technocratic bureaucracy, and these efforts all, to one degree or another, involved not only the adoption of techniques of "scientific management," a subject with which the NRC, in particular, appears to have been quite obsessed during this period, but also acquisition of control over scientific knowledge and its production. The state increasingly, especially during the wartime period, sought to harness China's scientific and technical manpower and to direct it toward certain goals.

During its first twenty years of rule, therefore, the KMT party-state sought to increase its command of both production and utilization of scientific knowledge. State economic planners attempted to put the state into a central role with respect to S&T in China in the 1930s and 1940s. After a multiyear hiatus on Taiwan, during which time the main advocates of S&T development in the ROC were scientists and foreign advisers, the same pattern was repeated, this time to much greater effect. There is no question but that the state, or at least certain technocratic elements within it, actively sought to guide and control S&T in China in the 1930s and 1940s and again on Taiwan in the 1970s and 1980s and to build institutions or patterns of institutional interaction to facilitate S&T development. Equally important, however, are the facts that in the 1960s and 1970s the political leadership was not consistently supportive of S&T development, and the ideas upon which the new institutions and plans were built often came from outside advisers.

This case study of state efforts at guiding and controlling S&T can help us better understand how the state evolved over time and how it sought to manage, develop, and utilize resources to promote industrial (and overall economic) development. These efforts indicate that highly placed state planners (technocrats) were eager to promote development and that they identified for the state a leading role in the development process. However, they also demonstrate that the KMT party-state was not wholly consistent in these efforts over time and that external circumstances as well as foreign advisers played an important part in shaping the ROC's developmental state. This case shows that states that are explicitly developmental are not necessarily constantly developmental in every respect. Moreover, such states may shut down elements of their developmental structure if external circumstances force them to. The case of ROC S&T policy shows us that the state—even in a developmental state—is not always the main agent of change or development.

— 1 —

Starts and Stops: The Kuomintang and Science and Technology

A fundamental premise of this volume is that scientific and technical education and, perhaps more important, research are essential to the development process. Any nation that hopes to gain economic independence and to achieve the status that is commonly referred to as "developed" must have as a part of its overall infrastructure a system for supporting scientific and technical research and strategies for producing scientific or technical manpower. Such systems and strategies are often, though not always, consolidated into state-run institutions and state-directed plans, although the degree to which the state itself controls scientific research and education varies widely. The belief that command of science and technology is essential to development has led to the construction of such institutions by most nations at some point during the nineteenth or twentieth century, and the KMT government of China and Taiwan has been no exception. It undertook to build centralized academic and industrial research institutions in its first decade and repeated the process after 1967 (though also in a very limited way after 1958) in Taiwan. At the same time, the ROC's Ministry of Education encouraged, at least through its rhetoric and policy, an emphasis on science education.

This chapter describes and evaluates the Chinese historical context for the emerging emphasis on science education and research and the construction of scientific research institutions (both academic and nonacademic) in Taiwan, focusing on the period from 1927 to 1958. By 1949 the KMT had a history of commitment to both applied and basic academic research and promotion of science education. Why, then, did the KMT, which supported scientific research and education in the Nanjing Decade (1927–1937) and was even more committed to it in the wartime period

(1937–1945), cease to do so in the 1950s in spite of the overwhelming international trend of that period toward state sponsorship of science education and scientific research institutions?

The International Context: R&D in the Mid-Twentieth Century

Scientific research is generally broken down into two categories: applied and basic. Although research with obvious industrial and agricultural applications can be of great economic value, basic research can also be important in terms of its contributions to general knowledge and the construction of an overall atmosphere of intellectual inquiry. States and industries benefit most from innovation, which leads to technological independence and is therefore an essential component of genuine economic development. But innovation, according to Nathan Rosenberg, requires "scientific research at a basic level. Occasional breakthroughs at this level lead to fundamental changes in the way we understand the physical world. This enlarged understanding, in turn, suggests applications in particular realms and therefore gives rise to research of a more applied nature. These more detailed findings eventually become embodied in the design of new products or processes, activities in which engineers and technologists play roles of increasing significance."[1] Both basic research and applied research, therefore, are essential for scientific—and, by extension, industrial and agricultural—innovation. States can promote national industrial, agricultural, and defense development by creating structures (such as plans, institutions, and financing) to encourage education and research in the right fields. In general, developed nations have well-funded national, and at least partly public, infrastructures to support basic and applied scientific research and a strong commitment to science education that can produce both a broadly skilled workforce and a more elite cohort of technicians and research scientists.

The idea that scientific research and economic development are intimately related originated in Enlightenment philosophy and the Industrial Revolution. Social scientists in the nineteenth century came to a fairly universal set of understandings about the evolution of human society, founded on the belief that society has progressed over time and that the most marked progress arose from the emergence of a middle class that supported the expansion of economic production and growth of science and technology. These developments, in turn, led to the Industrial Revolution and accompanying economic and political changes. The fact that this process of scientific discovery, industrialization, and economic and political development has taken place at different times in different places is what has led to the uneven development seen across the globe.[2]

If already by the nineteenth century it was generally assumed by social scientists in the West that science and technology were intimately related to political and economic development, it should come as no surprise that Western states, influenced by this theory, should have constructed institutions in which scientific and social scientific research could be conducted that would both explicate this theory and facilitate the continuation of the process. Scientific studies had, in fact, been conducted in European institutions that received official patronage (such as the British Royal Society and the French Academy of Science) since the mid-seventeenth century. By the early nineteenth century the French state, for example, was employing the scientific knowledge being produced by a highly professionalized scientific community to promote industrial, agricultural, and medical development. In other words, economic and social development plans were being formulated and implemented with the assistance of scientific knowledge and personnel.[3] Similarly, tsarist Russia also patronized science and scientists from the time of Peter the Great in the seventeenth century. However, at least one scholar has suggested that the tsarist government, fearing the emergence of a middle class that might exert political or economic pressure, "was ambiguous in its attitudes toward the development of industry and industrial research."[4] So though not all European models of state sponsorship of science led inexorably to state employment of scientific research institutions for the purposes of promoting economic or social development by the end of the nineteenth century, that model certainly did exist, and it was taken up with increasing fervor in the early to mid-twentieth century by emerging powers such as the new Soviet Russian state, the German state, and the United States.

By the end of World War II, it had become patently clear to virtually all observers that scientific advancements, and control over them, were increasingly the keys to wealth and power in the modern world. The wealthiest, most industrially advanced, best-fed, and most militarily powerful nations in the postwar era were those with established and productive scientific research communities that had clear links to industry, agriculture, and the military. As a plethora of new nations emerged in Africa and Asia in the wake of imperialism, each seeking to put itself on a solid economic footing, new postwar and postcolonial institutions such as the United Nations, the World

Bank, the various commonwealth structures, and the U.S. Agency for International Development (USAID) all began to offer advice and funding for economic development. By the late 1950s a key element of their programs was the promotion of scientific education and research across the globe.

Over the course of the 1950s and 1960s, the United Nations Educational, Scientific and Cultural Organization (UNESCO), in particular, became increasingly oriented toward the promotion of plans to improve the scientific and technical self-sufficiency of developing nations. From 1963 UNESCO's recognition of the importance of scientific development gained greater international attention through the UN-sponsored United Nations Conference on the Application of Science and Technology for the Benefit of Less Developed Countries. As one author has observed, "This conference stirred the conscience of the world, and . . . a period of accelerated expansion of activities began, involving assistance to member states in the formulation of scientific development policies and institutionalizing decision-making for th[is] . . . purpose."[5] From this point on, UNESCO sponsored a series of conferences on the application of science and technology to development. These conferences resulted in the articulation, over the course of the 1960s, of a particular approach to identifying a role for science and technology in development characterized by an emphasis on science education at all levels, the cultivation of technical manpower, the promotion of both applied and basic research, and the construction of centralized state institutions to guide science policy and ensure that science education and research remained relevant to development.[6]

At a conference in Israel in 1969 René Maheu, director-general of UNESCO, observed that "the industrialized countries have at their disposal 90 percent of the world's scientific personnel. The developing countries have a percentage of scientists and engineers in the population twenty times less than that of the industrialized countries; among the scientists, the proportion engaged in research and therefore contributing to scientific and technical innovation is four times smaller in the developing countries than in those that are already developed. The non-industrialized countries have been said to be a desert as far as research is concerned; three-quarters of the world's population live in that desert."[7] UNESCO's aim, therefore, was to irrigate the scientific desert by offering financial aid, advice, and technical assistance and setting up international cooperative programs. Most essential, though, according to Maheu, was the need for each nation to establish its own national science policy. "This policy," he said, "constitutes the indispensable system of data and targets, which, established in the light of material and human resources on the one hand, and of social and economic needs on the other, makes it possible both to form the required potential, by planning the training of scientific and technical personnel, and to schedule the work, by assigning priorities to the different sectors of research."[8] UNESCO advocated science policies that outlined specific strategies for developing education, training personnel, and planning research projects that would serve concrete national needs in the areas of industry, agriculture, and health but that would also foster an environment that embraced the ideals of scientific inquiry and the pursuit of scientific knowledge.

Over the same period, the U.S. government, pursuing a policy of containment and a strategy of encouraging economic stability and growth in states in Asia and Europe that bordered on the Soviet bloc, adopted a similar approach to promoting development in the regions with which it was concerned. U.S. advisers in Taiwan encouraged scientific development in almost exactly the same terms that UNESCO did there and elsewhere. In the late 1950s, for example, USAID encouraged the ROC government to implement a science education plan at the primary and secondary levels so as to improve the basic scientific capacity of Taiwan's population.

By the 1960s, both the United Nations and the United States were clearly promoting a development model that had as one of its central features an emphasis on the role that scientific education and research could play in promoting the modernization of both the economy and society. Development had become equated with command of scientific knowledge, and the acquisition and creation of such knowledge were thus touted as constituting the best path for developing countries to pursue. As we shall see in the next chapter, the United States and the United Nations both promoted this model to the KMT from at least the late 1950s, but the KMT was not especially receptive, at least in the beginning. One might expect that the KMT's reluctance to pursue this model of scientific development was due in some way to a failure to comprehend the relevance of science to modernization. However, both China in general and the KMT in particular already had a considerable history of concern over this very question.

The Chinese Historical Context

The imperial Chinese state had a long history of support for education through its civil service examination structure and for academic research through scholarly academies. Direct state support for active scholars (as opposed to bureaucrats) came through institutions such as the Hanlin Academy. The sort of scholarship that the state sought to encourage, however, was mostly historical, philological, and philosophical, and state support for any kind of scientific research was rare. In the late imperial era, to the extent that the imperial state supported S&T it was mostly in the realm of astronomy and production of the calendar, areas that had significant symbolic import. Late Ming and Qing emperors even employed Jesuit priests to undertake this work, as they were deemed to have superior astronomical and mathematical skills. By the mid-eighteenth century, under the Qianlong emperor, the Qing state was demonstrating considerable interest in science and technology relevant to the Qing's military and expansionist aims, in particular, artillery and cartography.[9]

In the second half of the nineteenth century, China made more tentative steps toward adoption of Western-style approaches to scientific education (in the fields of mathematics, engineering, and shipbuilding) as debates occurred at court over the kinds of general modernization efforts (if any) the Qing government should promote as it faced both large-scale domestic rebellion and increasing military and economic aggression from the West and Japan. These early expressions of interest in modern, Western science emerged in the context of discussions over the quality of Qing civil servants, and for some critics, this meant the merits of the educational emphases of the civil service examination system. As during earlier times of crisis, Chinese officials of the 1860s and 1870s were quick to blame the Qing government's failures against the British and the Taiping rebels on a lack of talented officials in government. The Tongzhi Restoration of 1862–1874 aimed at restoring the Qing government to its earlier position of strength, and strengthening the government meant improving the quality of its officials.[10]

While the underlying assumption of the early Restoration was that neo-Confucian learning was the best kind of learning to prepare government officials, the Qing government and in particular its provincial officials nonetheless gradually implemented reforms that—although they were not aimed at transforming conventional ideas about qualifications for government—did have the effect of promoting some practical (Western) learning. Many of these early reforms were the result not of official policy but of personal decisions on the part of leading provincial leaders. In the 1860s, necessity led some men in positions of power to recruit and promote officials according to their practical abilities rather than their moral qualities.

Zeng Guofan, who led the fight against the Taiping Rebellion, for instance, had a "pragmatic interest" in recruiting technical talent and populated his personal staff with men skilled in finance, military planning, foreign affairs, engineering, and science, many of whom had chosen not to pursue classical educations.[11]

Also in the mid-1900s, as a result of the opening of treaty ports, China saw an influx of Western missionaries. These missionaries brought with them Western ideas about health, hygiene, and medicine, which they spread through mission hospitals and orphanages, as well as different ideas about science education, which they spread through mission schools. Some of these schools eventually became new universities as the Chinese educational system was transformed in the early twentieth century. In addition to establishing such institutions, nineteenth- and early-twentieth-century missionaries also set up numerous publications in which they introduced Western ideas about science and technology to China. These publications ranged from the *Society for the Diffusion of Useful Knowledge in China,* which was founded in 1834 to introduce works on various subjects including, but not limited to, geography, natural history, medicine, and mechanics, to almanacs and serials, such as the *Shanghae Serial,* published in the late 1850s, and the *Chinese Scientific Magazine,* published in the late 1870s.[12]

In the 1870s, provincial leaders in particular began to support the creation of new armies, new government institutions, and new schools for Western learning, and many of their advisers in these endeavors were missionaries. All of these changes demonstrated a new concern with practical learning as something necessary to government. Shen Baozhen, a protégé of Zeng Guofan, was one of many officials concerned with pragmatic government. Shen's particular worry was that high officials should have practical training in administration or should at the very least be assisted by such people.[13] In addition, Shen advocated changes in the way officials were educated. He "called upon the scholar-gentry class to study science (ke-chih), 'learn what is useful, apply it, and become useful persons.'"[14] In 1871 Li Hongzhang and Zeng Guofan proposed an educational mission to the United States that would be designed to produce students educated in both the Chinese and Western traditions who would become "men of useful abilities."[15] The expectation was that they would study subjects such as engineering and mathematics.

Much of this growing interest in Western scientific learning had resulted from China's mid-nineteenth-century military crises. The new armies that had been created in the 1860s to put down the Taiping Rebellion spawned a new class of modern militarists who found it expedient to appropriate Western military strategy and Western armaments to achieve their military goals. The successes of these new armies not only against the Taiping but also in subsequent campaigns against the Nian and Muslim rebellions led the new-style militarists to take their Western military learning quite seriously. By the 1880s and 1890s Li Hongzhang, Zhang Zhidong, and Yuan Shikai were leading the way in creating Western-style military academies and modern armies.[16] These new academies and armies were often formed under the guidance of German and, later, Japanese advisers and trained their pupils and troops in the latest Western military techniques and strategies. Nonetheless, these modern academies, which on the surface appeared to promote a very different approach to education than had been seen previously in China, were still loathe to abandon traditional standards. Zhang Zhidong's academy, for instance, had specific regulations that applicants "be civilian or military degree-holders, expectant officials, or members of established official or gentry families."[17]

The new policies *(Xinzheng)* of the last decade of Qing rule also attempted to introduce a new system of education aimed at finding a balance between modern and traditional learning. The first attempt to create a modern educational system in 1902 would have "a Confucian Academy at the apex" and a university system, with a series of universities below it, devoted to different studies, such as classics, the arts, politics and law, commerce, science, engineering, agriculture, and medicine. This system, which combined Chinese and Western learning, was never implemented.[18] In spite of such attempts at constructing a national education system that would promote Western scientific learning, many bureaucrats continued—even after the abolition of the examination system—to assume that "officials would continue to be trained according to traditional norms."[19]

While certain individuals in the mid-nineteenth century and even the Qing state, by the early twentieth century, were clearly cognizant of the role that scientific and technical studies, on the one hand, and studies in the Western-style social sciences and humanities (like law and foreign languages), on the other hand, could contribute to the national modernization project, the Chinese failure to construct research institutions until the early decades of the twentieth century indicates that the late Qing Chinese state had no particular sense of the potential value of scientific and technical innovation or nation-specific research (geological, agricultural, economic, sociological) to the overall development process. Though scientific studies were increasingly finding their way into the curricula of modern educational institutions in the first decades of the twentieth century, it took until the 1920s and 1930s and the return of the first groups of Western-educated scientists and social scientists before modern Western-style research began to take off and China saw a veritable explosion of scientific studies and attempts to apply a scientific method to nearly every facet of life. Most of the impetus for this academic development came from individual scholars and intellectuals who built science and social science departments at existing institutions of higher learning and created new institutions and groups to support scientific learning.[20] Significant facets of this scientific development were a trend toward the pursuit of China-specific field research (in the fields of geology and archaeology, for instance) and also a growing interest in laboratory sciences.

As this brief narrative demonstrates, prior to 1927, although Western science and technology had been the subject of considerable and ever-increasing interest on the part of China's educated elite, Chinese states had given limited support to S&T education and research. Moreover, even though scientific education and research was being undertaken in government-funded institutions of higher learning by the mid-1920s, China's lack of a unified national government during that period made it impossible for China to have anything approaching a national science policy between 1916 and 1927.

S&T under the KMT: The Nanjing Decade

Beginning in 1927, various factions within the new KMT government undertook a series of efforts at institutionalizing China's S&T development. To this end, in 1927 the KMT's Central Executive Committee, urged forward by Cai Yuanpei, president of Peking University, approved the creation of Academia Sinica, an institution designed to bring a centralized order to the existing education and research-oriented institutions that had sprung up in the last decade of the Qing period and during the early Republic. In the early 1930s different factions within the same government created two more institutions—the National Economic Council (NEC) and the National Resources Commission (NRC)—that explicitly attempted to coordinate the relationship between S&T research and economic development. In addition, over the course of the Nanjing Decade, the KMT's Ministry of

Education increasingly emphasized science over social science or humanistic education.

The first of these new institutions was Academia Sinica, established on the same day that the government was inaugurated.[21] Academia Sinica was a state-funded research academy that was to be staffed by the best-trained and brightest of China's academicians and independent researchers. As part of a larger pattern of constructing centralized institutions, the early Nationalist government designed Academia Sinica as a sort of umbrella institution that would absorb several preexisting research institutes and locate them in a single spot. The Nationalist government also anticipated that Academia Sinica would eventually take on the role of coordinator of academic research across China.

Academia Sinica was a government institution under the direct control of the Executive Yuan. It had a highly centralized structure and was organized hierarchically. At the head was the president, and under him were the original nine institutes (meteorology, astronomy, physics, chemistry, geology, engineering, psychology, history and philology, and social sciences) and two museums. Each institute had its own internal hierarchy, with a head and a series of research associates, including both full-time and part-time investigators. At an intermediate level between the president of the Academy and the various research institutes, there was intended to be a *Pingyihui* (advisory council) "consisting of thirty members selected from among the scientific experts of the whole country together with a certain number of ex-officio members."[22] This council was not actually formed until 1935 under Ding Wenjiang's leadership as secretary-general of the Academy.

As can be seen from the original nine research institutes of Academia Sinica, there is no question but that the architects of the Academy expected it to put most of its emphasis on the natural and physical sciences. Only two of the original institutes were dedicated to the humanities and social sciences, the Institute of History and Philology and the Insitute of Social Sciences. Moreover, during the 1930s the number of scientific institutes continued to grow and included institutes for botany, zoology, and psychology by the end of the decade.

The new KMT party-state had several motives for establishing Academia Sinica. First, it offered the government access to the latest scientific and social scientific knowledge without having to train its own people to engage in academic research. Second, it could be a link between the central government and those members of China's academic community who would be willing to participate in Academia Sinica. By creating what was quickly to become the most prestigious institution of higher learning in China and by rapidly recruiting some of the best-known and most widely respected of China's intellectuals to staff the Academy, the Nanjing government initiated a long-term process of nonpolitical cooperation with China's scientific elite. The establishment of a cooperative intellectual-state relationship could have the dual effect of pacification of a potential source of criticism of the state and creation of an intellectual resource that could prove useful to the practical needs of nation building. It also enabled the government to exert an informal control over those intellectuals who joined the Academy. An additional benefit of such an institution was the positive effect it could have on the Nanjing government's domestic and international image. The Academy's creation represented an international propaganda effort, a means by which the KMT could prove to Europe and America that China was, indeed, a modern nation, concerned with both domestic development and intellectual experimentation like the Western powers. China now had a government-funded institution for scientific, social-scientific, and humanities research that could facilitate international contact on an equal footing, contact that could at best result in transfers of technology and know-how and at the very least lead to China's increased stature in the international world of academia.

Although it was a state-sponsored institution, the Academy was designed to appear intellectually independent, and its research agenda was developed by the academicians themselves, only some of whom had connections to the government. According to the Academy's charter, these intellectuals would allocate funds, organize new research projects, and design cooperative projects to integrate research-oriented organizations throughout the country. Allowing the Academy's members to play a leading role lent credence to the idea that the Nationalist government's scientific research agenda had intellectual integrity and also allowed intellectuals themselves to feel that they had a hand in determining the direction of state-sponsored research. Given that the budget for the institution came almost entirely from the legislature and that the president of the Academy was a political appointee with close ties to the KMT, however, it is clear that the government hoped to exert some influence over the Academy.[23] Interestingly, the state made very little effort during the Nanjing Decade to capitalize on its investments in Academia Sinica in terms of pushing it to do applied research. Moreover, little effort was made prior to 1936 to coordinate the research undertaken at Academia Sinica with larger national economic needs.

Academia Sinica was not the only state-funded academic research institute. The state also financed research in the graduate schools of the national universities and the Beiping Research Academy, as well as institutes that conducted investigations in geology, agriculture, and industry. In addition, the KMT government created two new nonacademic institutions in the 1930s to organize and oversee various applied scientific modernization projects, the creation of which further underscores the notion that, from the perspective of the state, academic and applied research were not necessarily linked and not all research organs were intended to directly serve the immediate economic needs of the nation. Through the National Economic Council *(Quanguo jingji weiyuanhui)* the government financed specific projects in infrastructural development and agricultural and livestock production.[24] The National Resources Commission *(Ziyuan weiyuanhui)* served more to organize the utilization of the nation's resources (natural and human) for purposes of nation building and national salvation. Both the NEC and the NRC fell under the jurisdiction of the Executive Yuan, but neither functioned as a regular branch of the civil government. Unlike Academia Sinica, which focused much of its energy and resources on research in basic science, both the NEC and the NRC targeted specific applied questions of immediate agricultural, industrial, and military relevance.

The NEC was created first. It was established in the spring of 1931 by a group of reform-minded KMT leaders headed by Wang Jingwei. Its initial success, according to Margherita Zanasi, was largely due to the high level of financial independence it had from the state and its "development vision based on a joint leadership of the political and economic coastal elites."[25] The NEC was empowered to plan and implement projects for economic reconstruction and development, especially in coastal areas. It sought, in particular, to end China's dependency on foreign manufactures and to encourage domestic manufacture of raw materials for domestic markets. The projects undertaken by the NEC included highway construction and improvement of the transportation infrastructure; water conservancy and flood prevention; expansion of public health facilities and care; and agricultural development projects to promote the growth and export of tea, improve livestock production, expand the use of new sericulture techniques and hence the manufacture and export of silk, and improve cotton crops and the manufacture of cotton goods. As Zanasi's work on the NEC's Cotton Control Commission and David Pietz's work on Huai River Management clearly demonstrate, the NEC did in some cases effectively reform and modernize both industry and infrastructural development.[26]

A second KMT institution that promoted scientific economic modernization projects was the advisory council that Chiang Kai-shek formed in 1932—the National Resources Commission. Originally known as the National Defense Planning Commission, this initially secret group was designed to make plans for China's economic and industrial development in the face of possible war with Japan. It was intended as a nonpolitical organization through which China's scientific elite could aid the process of nation building.[27] However, according to Zanasi, its very existence was the result of political discord within the KMT. The NRC was constructed by Chiang to compete with the NEC, over which he had virtually no control during the 1931–1936 period. As Chiang regained full control of the central government in 1936, however, he oversaw the dismantling of the NEC and the transfer of its assets and functions to the NRC.[28]

The role of the NRC was to build and oversee state-owned enterprises, in particular industries and mines. It was divided into eight departments—military, international, cultural, economics and finance, raw materials and industry, transportation and communications, population, soil and foodstuffs—and technical experts. These various departments, staffed by personnel with considerable technical expertise, managed the KMT's newly developed state-owned enterprises.[29]

One important institution that came under the control of the NRC was the National Bureau of Industrial Research (NBIR). The NBIR was established in July 1930 in Nanjing and later brought under the direction of the NRC. The NBIR conducted S&T research designed to serve the needs of the various state-owned industries guided by the NRC. Its particular purposes were to conduct research into industrial materials and to improve industrial technology.[30] Within this single institution, we can see an effort to link the research world (though not the academic research world) with the industrial world and a recognition that state-sponsored research and development activities could serve the larger goal of industrial development.

The NRC also sought to identify and manage national resources that could be employed as the nation industrialized. To this end, beginning in 1934 the NRC's department of technical experts undertook surveys of expertise to identify the nation's technical experts *(zhuanmen rencai)*. These surveys were made (or at least attempted) of all educational institutions, government administrative organs, and engineering and management organs, including both state-owned and private enterprises. The intent was to identify experts in a wide range of S&T fields, including mining, chemical industry, water management, spinning and weaving, forestry, aviation, pharmacy and public health, and so on. Once a basic name list of such experts was secured from the institutions in which they were employed, the NRC would follow up with survey forms and even, in some cases, interviews. By 1937 the NRC had located and cataloged the skills, work experience, and educational backgrounds of 18,000 industrial technical experts.[31]

Undertakings of this sort leave little doubt that even before the outbreak of war against Japan the KMT was interested in utilizing its skilled manpower resources to promote industrial development. This interest in S&T manpower is also evident in the realm of education. In 1929 the Ministry of Education began to push a new emphasis on scientific and technical education. Its first step was to restrict the development of humanities departments and promote the establishment of new science schools and departments. The Ministry of Education accomplished this by promulgating a new organizational law for universities and technical schools in 1929. The new law ordered universities to establish at least three colleges or divisions, one of which had to be a science division. Science, according to the law, included natural sciences, agriculture, engineering, and medicine.[32]

Over the course of the early 1930s, the Ministry of Education took further steps to encourage science education and discourage students from pursuing studies in the humanities and law. One such method was to reapportion resources away from the humanities and into science and technology. As one 1936 report noted, "Those colleges and departments of arts and social sciences which are considered inadequate and inefficient have been instructed either to discontinue their existence or to stop admitting new students, so that the money could be used for the development of the colleges and departments [of] applied sciences."[33] In 1930 the Ministry of Education began to limit the number of students who could matriculate in the humanities and law. It enacted a new regulation, under which the number of entering students in the humanities and law was not permitted to surpass the number of entering students in the sciences.[34] The Ministry of Education was reacting to a real preference among students for humanities and law over the sciences. In 1930, 36.6 percent of university students studied law and political science, and 22.5 percent studied liberal arts, whereas only 11.5 percent studied engineering, 9.7 percent studied natural sciences, 6.1 percent studied education, 3.7 percent studied medicine, and 3.1 percent studied agriculture.[35]

The new regulations appear to have yielded results, as by 1936 the Nationalist government was claiming that "according to the recent statistics . . . the number of new students admitted to the courses on technology is now ranking first, with that for pure science ranking second. This proves that the scheme of the Ministry is achieving a very satisfactory result."[36] Government statistics indicate, however, that although more students were indeed matriculating in the sciences over the course of the Nanjing Decade, scientific fields were still not growing at the same rate at which legal studies were declining. The overall effect of the reforms seems to have been only a modest increase in the number of young scientists and engineers.[37]

From the examples above, we can see that by the Nanjing Decade (1927–1937) Chinese leaders were beginning to recognize the importance of both command and production of scientific knowledge to domestic economic, industrial, and social modernization, on the one hand, and to international representation of China as a modern or developed nation, on the other hand. Although KMT rhetoric often suggested that the social sciences and the humanities, and especially fields in those areas that involved the study of Confucian traditions, would also form an important foundation for China's future development, actual education and research policy indicates a heavier emphasis on scientific education and research and a deep faith in the value of such endeavors to the nation-building process. From at least 1928 the KMT actively promoted scientific research and education through the construction of institutions and the implementation of policies. The question is, Why?

The leaders of the Nationalist party-state were undoubtedly influenced by China's late-nineteenth-century experiences, the KMT's own experiences, and the overall early-twentieth-century Chinese intellectual environment to have a strong faith in science. The most successful late-nineteenth-century leaders had all advocated utilization of Western scientific learning to strengthen the nation. Moreover, the KMT itself came to power with the strength of Western-trained armies using modern weapons and with an ideology aimed at overall economic reconstruction, industrialization, and the repeal of the unequal treaties, all of which would require Western scientific and social scientific learning.

At the same time, the general intellectual environment from the mid-1910s on had increasingly been one of enthusiastic advocacy of science as a panacea and rejection of tradition as an albatross around China's neck. As Chen Duxiu wrote in the journal *New Youth*, "In order to advocate Mr. Science, we have to oppose traditional arts and traditional religion."[38] Chen's "Mr. Science" became a popular figure among May Fourth intellectuals who sought a new direction for China's future development and rejected China's traditions as obstacles to progress. For these young thinkers, science represented a path to progress and modernity. As Richard Suttmeier has noted, for May Fourth scholars a " 'modern' society is one in which the way and spirit of science predominates."[39] At the same time, science offered a way of making the modern world intelligible and accessible. John Buck has observed that

> the appeal of science in modernizing societies has rested on its promise to provide a "systematic ideology" capable of making sense of changes that traditional "cultural resources" could no longer explain. In early twentieth-century China this systematic vision was a vision of the future. For those who became scientists, that was precisely what made science attractive. In their view the scientific community stood as a model for the good society; and the norms and values of the scientific enterprise promised to be the source of a distinct discipline for those willing and competent to accept them . . . If China as a whole were to model itself on those communities (Western ones), then it would also be able to function effectively in the modern world.[40]

In 1920s China this scientific perspective permeated much of the larger intellectual and political environment, as scientists insisted "repeatedly that science and its methods could constitute a new 'strong center' for Chinese society and provide the 'minds of the people' with 'exact and profound studies to fasten onto.' "[41] This phenomenon has come to be known as scientism. Scientism has been defined by Daniel Kwok as "the tendency to use the respectability of science in areas having little bearing on science itself. In China, the desire for national growth was accentuated by the weakness in technology, and it is thus not surprising to find among her Western-educated intellectuals great enthusiasm for science."[42] Against this backdrop, it seems only logical that the new KMT government also implemented policies that emphasized the primacy of scientific research and education and an overall scientific approach to life.

KMT leaders in the 1930s developed their own brand of scientism, one that advocated Western science but not at the expense of traditional values. Chiang Kai-shek's New Life Movement exhortations to physical exercise and injunctions against opium use, consumption of alcohol, and spitting in public places, for instance, although clearly influenced by Western scientific views on health and medicine, were presented within a framework of self-cultivation that was shaped above all else by Confucian traditions.[43] Likewise, in mid-1930s speeches to students, Chiang made frequent mention of the relevance of a scientific spirit and a scientific method to the overall modernization goals of the party-state, but his definitions of scientific spirit and scientific method were littered with references to the Confucian classics.[44] On the other hand, Chiang remained consistent with May Fourth scientism insofar as he argued that the scientific spirit and method were broadly applicable, and his discussions of science, therefore, were not limited to a narrow definition of modern, Western-style laboratory sciences.

In a 1935 speech, Chiang proposed the idea that the scientific method was nothing new to China and that the Chinese had had a scientific method and a scientific spirit for thousands of years. Unfortunately, the Chinese had lost this method and as a result had become weak and corrupt. To elevate the nation back to its former greatness, according to Chiang, China needed to revive its scientific method.[45] Even as he sought to build this historical argument that identified the scientific method as an essentially Chinese, rather than Western, phenomenon, however, Chiang's definition of the scientific method sounded very modern and Western. It consisted of (1) determining scope and structure; (2) planning ahead; (3) cooperative effort; (4) research and experimentation; (5) analysis and compilation of data; and (6) improvement and innovation.[46]

Scientism, as an approach to everyday life and the process of constructing a modern nation, can be found in the development strategies of the KMT's ministerial-level bureaucracy as well as the thinking of the political leadership during the Nanjing Decade. If considered as a modernizing discourse, this scientism appears to lack depth. References to science and scientific modernization in the speeches of Chiang Kai-shek have little substance and seem, like much of what he had to say, to fall into the category of moral maxims by which to live life. On an institutional level, however, we can see that at least parts of Chiang's government were committed to implementing concrete scientific and technical strategies for industrial and overall economic development. Not all of China's scientific institutions were being utilized for economic ends, but certainly the NEC, NRC, and NBIR were all very clearly focused on making real use of scientific and technical manpower and research and development to promote China's economic modernization even before the outbreak of war with Japan.

S&T under the KMT: The Wartime Period

By the late 1930s the KMT government's approach to the promotion of S&T was almost entirely dictated by the needs of the war. In his book *China's Destiny* (originally published in 1943), for example, Chiang emphasized the importance of the study of both basic and applied science that could serve concrete national needs: "Mechanical and civil engineering, mining and metallurgy, medicine, and other applied sciences cannot be thoroughly mastered without physics, biology, mathematics, and other natural sciences as their basis. Therefore, besides the training of industrial personnel, the schools must also emphasize natural sciences to provide the basis for applied science. We must, therefore, in the remaining years of the war, speed up the strengthening of education and expand the schools."[47]

In fact, Chiang was simply reiterating a point that his economic planners had been making for some time. By 1941 Weng Wenhao, head of the NRC, was concerned that postwar China might not have the kind of scientific talent it needed to enable it to rebuild its industrial base unless it began preparing for the future.[48] To this end, the NRC, in cooperation with the Ministry of the Economy and the Ministry of Education, promoted a National Defense Science Movement *(Guofang kexue yundong)*. The aim of the movement was to "make the whole nation fully recognize the importance of national defense science and the importance of building national defense industries."[49] To achieve this goal the mass education branch of the Ministry of Education would lead the way by promoting science lectures, publishing science magazines, putting on science expositions, and staging performances of scientific experiments, all of which were intended to improve the scientific literacy of the people. Additional government and party organs, such as the Ministries of Education, Defense, and Propaganda, the New Life Movement Committee, and the Three People's Principles Youth Corps, would be called upon to promote the movement through similar measures.[50]

In the early 1940s a Science and Technology Planning Committee *(Kexue jishu cejinhui)* was set up by the Ministry of Education to oversee implementation of the new National Defense Science Movement. The committee was headed up by Weng Wenhao and included among its participants heads of numerous ministries and research institutes. It required that county- and city-level governments set up their own science organs that would be devoted to promoting science among the masses and in elementary and middle schools. There is ample archival evidence to suggest that on paper, at any rate, these organs were created by around 1943, and some wrote in to the Ministry of Education to report on activities they were sponsoring, suggesting that they actually did exist in some areas.[51] A further push to promote science was made by the Ministry of Education beginning in 1945, when all elementary and middle schools and colleges were required to hold National Defense Science Movement activities on national holidays such as the National Day, Children's Day, and Youth Day. Schools were required to show movies about science, host educational lectures, hold speech contests with science themes, and open up laboratories and libraries to the general public. The intent of the activities was to lure the public into the educational arena and to demonstrate to them various ways in which science and technology could be used to defend, save, and reconstruct the nation.[52]

The aim of the National Defense Science Movement was not just to get the public thinking about science and its role in modern life; it was also specifically to add to the number of scientifically competent people in China with an eye to preparation for postwar reconstruction. State planners therefore encouraged science education, particularly in engineering and physics, and developed strategies to funnel as many students as possible into these fields. The "Resolution to Promote the National Defense Science Movement" laid out a plan to train 39,000 engineers and 11,000 natural scientists in the decade between 1941 and 1951. With these numbers, state planners believed that China's industrial development prospects would greatly improve. The plan also targeted vocational education and short-term training, through which it estimated that it could give scientific and technical training to a total of 89,662 people over a ten-year period, most of them students in vocational schools. Implementation of the plan was overseen by the Science and Technology Planning Committee. Within a year or two the ten-year manpower projection figures had been substantially refined so as to include projections for virtually every technical field that might be of interest to the Ministries of Defense, Finance, Communications, Economy, Agriculture, and Forestry and the NRC.[53]

Statistics from the Ministry of Education show that numbers of students enrolling in the sciences did increase dramatically during the wartime period, and so the Science and Technology Planning Committee must have come close to meeting its goals by the late 1940s (Table 1.1). It is difficult to tell, however, whether the rising number of students in the sciences was a direct result of efforts by the National Defense Science Movement or whether

Table 1.1 Numbers of students in the sciences at the vocational level and above

Year	Total number of students	Physical sciences	Engineering	Medicine	Agriculture
1932	42,710	4,159	4,439	1,852	1,557
1935	41,128	6,336	5,514	2,977	2,163
1940	52,376	6,090	11,227	4,271	3,675
1945	83,498	6,480	15,200	6,291	6,380
1947	155,036	10,060	27,579	11,855	10,179

Source: Di er ci zhongguo jiaoyu nianjian (The second China education yearbook) (Nanjing, 1948), 7: 1403, 1412.

Note: The huge jump in numbers between 1945 and 1947 is due to the inclusion of students in previously occupied areas. Worth noting is that the numbers of science students in college only did not increase quite as dramatically as the numbers in this table. Vocational education in the sciences was rapidly expanded during the 1940s, and some of the growth in science education was taking place at that level.

it resulted, instead, from a general feeling among China's youth that practical studies would be more sensible, given the political and military climate of both the wartime period and the subsequent civil war period.

In addition to the education, popular education, and propaganda facets of the movement, its promoters also made a much clearer effort to link scientific research to national industrial and defense needs. The "Resolution to Promote the National Defense Science Movement" called on the nation's existing research institutes—in particular, Academia Sinica's engineering, physics, and chemistry institutes; Beiping's physics and chemistry institutes; and the graduate schools of the nation's universities—to engage in defense-related research. To further encourage them along these lines, so-called national defense institutions would have their funding doubled if they constructed research plans and passed them along to the Science and Technology Planning Committee for approval.[54]

Such financial incentives would have been especially meaningful to China's research institutes during the 1940s, although it was generally already the case by the early 1940s that they were conducting war-related research. Following the 1937 outbreak of war with Japan, most of the KMT's scientific institutions had relocated inland, along with the government. By and large, they ended up in Sichuan and Yunnan provinces, where they set themselves up as best they could in what were generally ill-equipped circumstances to perform tasks relevant to military aspects of the war effort, as well as those related to the agricultural, medical, and industrial development of China's hinterland.[55] Even Academia Sinica, which had always had a stronger commitment to heavily academic, basic research than applied science, sought to support the war effort. As Ren Hongjuan, then secretary-general of Academia Sinica, noted, "Most of our work has a direct bearing on the war."[56] And Zhu Jiahua, then president of Academia Sinica, argued that the Academy's attention needed to be shifted away from basic sciences: "In the current period of war against Japan," he said in March 1941, "the nation and society need applied science."[57] Zhu raised the same theme again two years later when addressing the Three People's Principles Youth Corps: "We want to make sure the nation rapidly receives the usefulness of science and that society gets its benefits; during this period of war against the Japanese there is an even greater need for so-called 'applied learning.' "[58]

On the whole, Academia Sinica was responsive to calls for applied scientific research. During the war, nearly all of the institutes of the Academy were engaged in projects that had concrete applications in wartime China, often at the request of the NRC. The NRC, for example, asked the Institute of Sociology "to study the problems of wartime economy." In response, the institute conducted surveys of industry and currency conditions and estimations of war losses[59] The Institute of Geology, which relocated to Guilin, in Guangxi province, during the war, surveyed the mineral resources of China's southwest and discovered deposits of tin, tungsten, gold, antinomy, lead, zinc, mercury, iron, and coal ore. These deposits provided mineral resources that could replace sources to which the landlocked KMT no longer had access. Other institutes at Academia Sinica took on the important work of figuring out how to use these mineral resources to manufacture weapons, develop industry, and modernize China's southwestern provinces. The Institutes of Physics, Engineering, and Chemistry all conducted important applied research that led, among other things, to the manufacture of tungsten magnetic steel, other kinds of steel, and purification of chemicals. The engineers also experimented with glassmaking and tested timber, working, in particular, with materials that could be found in Yunnan province.[60] These projects were of critical importance if the KMT was to have any hope of fighting back against the Japanese.

Like Academia Sinica, the NBIR also became absorbed by war-related development concerns and shaped its research agenda accordingly. The NBIR's work plan for 1939–1940 particularly emphasized the need to build industry in southwest China, where there had previously been relatively little modern industry. The bureau thus conducted surveys of natural resources and their utilization and began developing industries aimed, in particular, at producing items that had previously been imported to the region and serving the needs of the military.[61] The NBIR itself undertook research related to whatever industries needed to be developed, including ceramics, forestry, glass refraction, fermentation, combustion engineering, plastics, and leatherwork. When it could, it worked together with academic researchers who had also relocated to southwest China.

As the KMT sought to promote scientific development during the wartime period, it looked abroad for assistance of several varieties. Foreign aid, training, and models all played a role in shaping China's approach to the promotion of science. As Qian Changzhao, vice-secretary of the NRC, observed in a 1942 speech, China would be dependent on foreign cooperation to effectively build its industrial base in the postwar era.[62] With this in mind, the NRC and the Ministry of the Economy, in particular, actively sought ways to capitalize on foreign alliances, especially with the United States, to further enhance their S&T capacity. Such strategies ranged from simple requests to the U.S. government for foreign publications and microfilms for educational purposes to negotiation of agreements with the French government for technology transfer and use of foreign advisers in the construction of new power plants.[63]

In addition, the NRC's NBIR undertook a less formal strategy of sending engineers to the United States in 1943–1945 to learn new techniques, get training, engage in technology transfer, and presumably also establish potentially beneficial relationships with American firms. As Weng Wenhao wrote in a letter to the U.S. ambassador, "Although the Bureau has succeeded to some extent in helping to solve some of the technical problems arising in our industry, yet they are handicapped by limited equipment and technical resources at their disposal . . . The . . . Bureau has chosen twelve technical experts along twelve different lines to be sent to the United States to visit factories and research institutions to study specific technical problems."[64] The training program appears to have come about somewhat haphazardly, as a result of a chance letter from S. D. Ren, the Chinese American vice president of the Universal Trading Corporation in New York, who, having read a piece in the *New York Times* about the NBIR, wrote to the head of the NBIR, Y. T. Ku, in September 1942, offering whatever help he could. Ku immediately took Ren up on his offer by asking him to find placements in

American industries for a group of NBIR engineers whom he hoped to send for further technical training. After nearly two years of planning, the first group of twelve engineers landed in the United States, where they took up positions in various private industries and academic research laboratories. Interestingly, in their first letter back to Ku, the thing the engineers appear to have found most worthy of emulation in the American system was not any specific technology but rather the pattern of long-term employment of skilled laborers in particular industries. "We can see," they wrote, "that China's greatest difficulty will not be in the initial training of men, but in creating for them a sense of political and economic security, which will allow them to continue along one line, in one plant for decades on end."[65]

The Science and Technology Planning Committee was also looking at foreign models for how it, or some similar umbrella organization designed to promote S&T for economic development, should be constructed. Archival evidence suggests that the committee was interested in modeling itself after the U.S. Office of Scientific Research and Development, established in 1941 by Franklin Roosevelt to coordinate, initiate, and support research related to national defense. Information on the U.S. Office of Scientific Research and Development was solicited by Vice-Minister of Education Gu Yuxiu.[66] Along similar lines, in 1943 the Ministry of Education hosted a visit to southwest China by Britain's Professor A. V. Hill and Sir Shant Bhatnagar from India, both of whom were there to talk to representatives of the NRC, NBIR, Academia Sinica, Ministry of the Economy, and Ministry of Education about British and Indian models for similar institutions.[67]

Foreign aid was also critical to the continuing emphasis on scientific research and education during the war. The China Foundation, which had helped to finance Chinese higher education for some time prior to the war, spent over $2 million financed by bank loans on science teaching and research professorships during the war.[68] In addition, during the wartime period, the Nationalist government learned to capitalize on new foreign aid opportunities that could help it support science education and research. Both the United Nations and the U.S. government offered support in the form of technical assistance, grants, equipment, and books. The United Nations Relief and Rehabilitation Administration (UNRRA) supported education and research in science and technology in China between 1944 and 1947. Foreign advisers in fields such as medicine, engineering, and agriculture were sent to China during this period, many of whom offered courses and seminars at Chinese universities. After 1946 UNRRA also supplied educational equipment and books to universities and technical colleges doing work in areas relating to medicine, agriculture, and engineering.[69] The U.S. State Department also financed educational fellowships for Chinese students and scholars to train in the United States and sent American experts to work in Chinese educational institutions and government organs.[70]

The 1940s were a boom time for S&T development in China. The exigencies of war led both political leaders and economic planners within the KMT to develop a coherent and multifaceted set of strategies to promote S&T development, particularly as it pertained to industrial and military needs. On a propaganda level, the Ministry of Education and the Ministry of the Economy used the National Defense Science Movement to push students toward the study of science and expand the scientific awareness of the general public. The Science and Technology Planning Committee pushed Academic researchers to make their research more relevant to immediate national needs. And the NRC and NBIR developed a series of strategies to improve China's industrial capacity through training programs, manpower projection, manpower development planning, and pursuit of cooperative S&T relationships with foreign states and organizations. In addition, it appears that there was some interest on the part of the state in construction of a permanent organ to guide S&T development, possibly along the lines of the U.S. Office of Scientific Research and Development. By 1945, therefore, the KMT state was engaged in S&T manpower development through regular and mass education as well as expert technical training, support for industrial research and development in state-sponsored organs, and construction of a new organ to guide these processes—precisely the sorts of strategies pushed by the United States and United Nation in the postwar era. The state, during the 1930s and 1940s, became increasingly developmental in its approach to S&T and undertook a set of institutional and policy initiatives that bore remarkable similarities to those undertaken by the same state in the late 1970s in Taiwan. Over the course of the following decade or longer, however, these trends were all reversed as a result of the new circumstances that the KMT faced as it lost the civil war to the Communist Party on the mainland and retreated to Taiwan.

Continuity and Change on Taiwan

When the ROC took control of Taiwan at the close of World War II, it acquired a territory that had a legacy, albeit one that was damaged by the war, of scientific research and education. The Japanese had made considerable progress in modernizing Taiwan's agriculture, industry, communications, and sanitation and in educating its subjects in fields such as forestry and medicine. To this end, they had established a university as well as an agriculture and forestry college in Taiwan, although both of these institutions were made more available to Japanese colonialists living in Taiwan than to the Taiwanese themselves.[71] Taihoku Imperial University was established in 1928, and by 1944, it had faculties of science, medicine, agriculture, and engineering.[72] Taihoku's mission was not purely educational, however. It was designed in large part as a research-oriented institution where Japanese could conduct research about Taiwan and things Taiwanese. As a result, the university had a very high faculty-to-student ratio. Although there was clearly a tradition of high-level scientific study that developed under the Japanese in Taiwan, it appears that by the time the KMT removed its center of government from the mainland to Taipei, with the exception of the large number of medical doctors among elite Taiwanese, the Japanese scientific legacy had been largely reduced to an infrastructural and behavioral one.[73] Infrastructurally, the KMT had been lucky to find in 1945 the facilities of Taihoku that could soon thereafter be given over to the new National Taiwan University. In other respects, the Japanese promotion of scientific learning in Taiwan could be best seen in terms of the significant medical, agricultural, engineering, and sanitary improvements that had occurred under Japanese rule across the island.

Upon retrocession, Taiwan rapidly became a locus of scientific inquiry for some mainland scientists. Both the NRC and Academia Sinica were immediately interested in investigating Taiwan's industrial and agricultural potential. The NRC rushed to set up a Taiwan bureau and nationalize any remaining industries immediately after retrocession in 1945, and Academia Sinica quickly sent botanist Li Xianwen to Taiwan to conduct research on sugar. Li ended up staying there, and although still fairly junior, as the only botanist from mainland China in Taiwan after 1949, he eventually became the first head of Academia Sinica's reconstructed Institute of Botany in Taiwan.

After the retreat of the Nationalists to Taiwan in 1949, many of the institutions created on the mainland remained in place, in a formal sense, but in reality science and the encouragement of science were not initially a high priority for the KMT on Taiwan.[74] Although the government actively promoted economic and educational development in the 1950s, there is little evidence to suggest that the state continued to promote scientific development during that same decade.

The NRC was the only government organ that continued to demonstrate anything near the same level of concern over S&T after the KMT retreat to Taiwan.[75] In 1950 it conducted yet another survey of scientific manpower with, again, particular emphasis on identifying talent that could contribute to industrial development and bolstering development related to national defense. It also sought to identify scientific talent, laboratories, factories, and libraries. The purpose of the survey was simply to get a sense of the scientific resources, human and otherwise, in Taiwan. The survey results showed that there were 464 scientists working in twenty-one labs and twenty-nine factories (some of which overlapped). The survey also showed how rapidly mainland technicians had taken over Taiwan's industrial sector. Of the respondents, roughly one-fourth were Taiwanese; all others were from the mainland. Some of the Taiwanese had clearly had experience working in the mining industry or in fertilizer plants under the Japanese. All of the respondents had college educations or beyond, and some had studied in the West.[76]

Interestingly, the survey was only made of state-owned enterprises (and in this respect it differed from earlier NRC manpower surveys). The intent of the survey was to identify human and other resources that would help with national defense, and perhaps it was assumed that only NRC-directed enterprises could contribute to that goal; but even so, one has to imagine that there were skilled technicians working elsewhere in Taiwan who went unnoticed. In addition to the NRC's failure to collect data on whatever native S&T manpower or non-state-owned industry there might have been, the NRC also did not survey academic institutions or laboratories for talent, although, as we have seen, the NRC had worked closely with the Ministry of Education in the past. These omissions were undoubtedly responses to Taiwan's actual conditions (or mainlander perceptions of them) and as such might tell us something about the complicated relationship between mainlanders and Taiwanese in the late 1940s and 1950s, but for our purposes they are most meaningful for what they tell us about changes in state attitudes toward S&T development. The survey demonstrates a move away from the NRC's previous tendency to see industry and education as linked. This new tendency (not to link the two) would characterize industrial development policy for at least the next decade.[77]

In fact, the KMT's approach toward education underwent a marked shift after 1949, and in an apparent reversal of its 1930s strategy, the KMT increasingly emphasized the preservation of Chinese culture over the promotion of science throughout the 1950s. After 1949 the KMT was most concerned with constructing rationale to support its claims to being the legitimate government of China. To fail to make this claim would certainly lead to its demise, and so the quest to demonstrate that KMT-controlled Taiwan represented the true China in a cultural sense became much more fundamentally important to KMT survival than S&T development appeared to be at the time. Once again, the exigencies of the immediate political and military situation guided state policy. In this case, however, little thought appears to have been given to long-term development concerns.

To the extent that the state appears to have valued Academia Sinica in the 1950s, for instance, it was not for the contributions it could make to science but for those it could make to the preservation of Chinese culture. Zhang Jiyun, minister of education, wrote in 1949 that "so long as the culture of a nation exists, it is always possible to effect the revival of that nation."[78] At the opening meeting of Academia Sinica's first Council of Members *(Yuanshi huiyi)* in April 1957, Chiang Kai-shek gave a short speech urging the academicians to preserve and continue Chinese cultural traditions. The only one of Academia Sinica's institutes to move to Taiwan intact was the Institute of History and Philology, which coincidentally was the only institute that focused specifically on Chinese studies. The KMT leadership clearly saw Academia Sinica as playing a cultural role but no longer viewed it as a scientific resource or a tool to be used in any modernization projects.

Through most of the 1950s, Academia Sinica, under the leadership of Zhu Jiahua, acquiesced to the government's limited vision of the institution's role, putting substantial resources into the construction of facilities to house both old and new institutes for the study of Chinese history, literature, and culture. Furthermore, it only sought outside funding from foundations such as Ford and Rockefeller for projects related to Chinese cultural studies.[79] The Institute of History and Philology and the newly created Institute of Modern History formed the core of the new Academia Sinica on Taiwan, but even so, the experience of the Institute of History and Philology, which had moved almost wholesale to Taiwan, was not especially encouraging, as most of its books, archival materials, and artifacts were left to mildew for nearly a decade in a warehouse in Yangmei.[80] The Institute of Mathematics, which had also sent some of its library to Taiwan, did nothing in the early years in Taiwan. It took until Academia Sinica's move to Nankang in 1957 for the Institute of Mathematics to begin to work and train some young people and start to do research.[81] At the same time, the Academy also began laying plans for new institutes for the study of ethnology and modern history and began to revive old ones that had existed on the mainland—chemistry, physics, zoology, and botany.[82] However, scientific development did not again become a significant focus at Academia Sinica until Hu Shi became president of the Academy in 1958.[83]

Conditions at Taiwan's institutions of higher learning were not much better than those at Academia Sinica during the 1950s. Faculty in all disciplines complained well into the 1960s about poor pay, bad facilities, and lack of materials. The sciences were supported mostly only in the realm of agriculture, which did receive considerable assistance from the U.S. government, much of which was funneled through the Joint Commission on Rural Reconstruction (JCRR). Research was done in both academic and actual agricultural settings on rice, sugar, tea, and a variety of fruits.[84]

Why did the government not support the same sort of industrially relevant scientific research and S&T manpower development in the 1950s as it had in the 1940s on the mainland? By the 1950s it had become self-evident that, in order for a modern nation-state to survive militarily and economically, it needed to have command of the latest military, industrial, and agricultural technology and that this could only be done with a strong community of scientific researchers. The leadership of the KMT had been at least somewhat aware of this state of affairs as early as 1927, when Cai Yuanpei spearheaded the movement to improve the national system of higher education and create a state-sponsored academy of scientific and humanistic research (Academia Sinica). By the early 1940s this notion was firmly entrenched among KMT economic planners and educators, and even political leaders made reference to it in speeches and publications. Surely the KMT had not completely lost sight of the value of science to a state by 1949?

More likely is that a series of circumstances converged in the 1950s that made science not appear to be the most profitable investment for the KMT's scarce resources. First, relatively few highly trained scientists and technicians had fled to Taiwan with the KMT.[85] Of those who had chosen not to remain in China after 1949, most had moved to Europe or the United States. Moreover, from the perspective of the KMT, at any rate, few Taiwanese were sufficiently educated, skilled, or politically reliable to participate in either applied or basic science research efforts.[86] Taiwan had (or appeared to the KMT to have) limited skilled scientific manpower, therefore, in which to invest, and to create a new body of manpower would require a substantial, long-term investment in both education and research.

Second, investment in scientific facilities and manpower development not only was costly but also represented a permanent or semipermanent commitment to the island. If, as Chiang Kai-shek and the KMT leadership continued to assert well into the 1960s, Taiwan was merely a brief resting place from which the KMT would launch its mainland recovery efforts, then of what significance would be large-scale state investment in long-term scientific projects?

Third, the KMT had constructed a sort of state S&T planning organ in the form of the Science and Technology Planning Committee during the 1940s. This organ was not reconstructed on Taiwan after the KMT's 1949 retreat. Moreover, the previous leadership of the NRC, Ministry of the Economy, and Ministry of Education, who had constituted the leaders of the Science and Technology Planning Committee, had also not continued in their positions (most had not gone to Taiwan with the KMT). This lack of institutional and personnel continuity appears to have contributed to the shift in priorities of the KMT on Taiwan.

Fourth, the level of industrial development in Taiwan was relatively low during the 1950s, and there was still a limited need for a broad base of highly skilled S&T manpower. As Taiwan's industrial base broadened and deepened during the 1960s and 1970s, Taiwan's economic planners became increasingly interested in expanding manpower training programs and encouraging industrially relevant R&D. In the 1950s, however, these were not yet central concerns even of state economic planners.

Fifth, the academic scientists affiliated with Academia Sinica, National Taiwan University (NTU), Qinghua University, and other such institutions seemed confused about how to proceed with their research. At the very least, scientists attempting to establish new institutes of botany and chemistry at Academia Sinica, for instance, did not employ a wise strategy for selling themselves and their work to the government. In repeated government publications of the early to mid-1950s the preparatory institutes for research in the natural sciences boasted of their pursuit of basic rather than applied research. It took until the late 1950s and early 1960s for the focus to begin a slow shift to applied research.[87]

Sixth, the KMT government in Taiwan in the 1950s was not wealthy. Its resources came mostly from agriculture, fledgling industry, and foreign aid. U.S. aid was the only likely source of funding for scientific research through most of the 1950s, but it was not forthcoming. When Zhu Jiahua reported on the miserable condition of Academia Sinica to the Educational Committee of the Legislative Yuan in 1953, they asked if he had tried to get U.S. aid. His pessimistic response was that Academia Sinica had considered asking for it several times, but because they would only be likely to get matching funds at best, and since they were getting so little from the government, they felt it would be meaningless even to ask. Also, Zhu's understanding was that the United States emphasized the military, industry, and agriculture. Scientific research and schools were less important and therefore harder to get money for.[88] In 1955 Academia Sinica finally did make a request to the United States for "$1,179,000 for building construction, procurement of books, and manuscript printing costs."[89] The request was denied on the grounds that U.S. aid was to be used to increase agricultural and industrial production and to support the military. To the extent that aid could be used for education, it was only to support vocational, industrial, and teacher training. Academia Sinica, according to George St. Louis of the U.S. aid mission, was not doing enough applied research to be able to fall into the first category or enough training to fall into the second category.[90] Conditions were not favorable for any significant foreign investment in industrially relevant science research or education in the 1950s unless, as we shall see below, that science also had obvious potential military benefits.

Nuclear Science: The Exception to the Rule

In the area of nuclear physics, the ROC government took a more proactive approach to building both academic and nonacademic research programs than it did in any other scientific field. By the mid- to late 1950s the state was promoting nuclear research in a variety of ways: it created an Atomic Energy Commission (AEC), it helped to finance a nuclear science program at Qinghua University, it established the Chungshan Institute of Science and Technology, it sent delegates abroad to a variety of international meetings on nuclear science, and it petitioned the U.S. government for various nuclear technologies.

The AEC was created in 1955 subsequent to the signing of the atomic energy agreement between the United States and the ROC. It was placed alongside institutions such as the Council for U.S. Aid (CUSA) under the Executive Yuan. The first head of the AEC was Zhang Xiaofeng, who subsequently established Qinghua's Nuclear Science graduate program.[91] Taiwan's

AEC was responsible for negotiating agreements with the International Atomic Energy Agency (IAEA) and the U.S. Atomic Energy Commission; it also solicited financial and technical assistance for Taiwan's growing research programs in nuclear science. The 1955 atomic energy agreement paved the way for nuclear research in Taiwan by establishing procedures through which the ROC could lease uranium and other nuclear and reactor materials from the United States.[92] Building on that initial agreement, in 1957 Taiwan's AEC negotiated the U.S. sale of a swimming pool reactor to Taiwan for $750,000, half of which was paid as a gift by the U.S. Atomic Energy Commission. The reactor was given to Qinghua University and formed the basis for its research program in nuclear physics.[93]

The Qinghua University Institute of Nuclear Science (INS) was established in 1957, and even though its swimming pool reactor was not functional until 1961, the program began accepting and training graduate students as early as 1957.[94] By 1959, according to Paul R. Byerly Jr., USAID was financing the research of a number of Qinghua scientists.[95] Through the early 1960s Qinghua's nuclear science program received a substantial amount of the ROC's fledgling National Council for Scientific Development's available funds, and this trend continued into the 1970s under the National Science Council (NSC). As noted above, the founder of Qinghua's nuclear science program was also the first head of the AEC. Subsequent AEC heads also had close ties to the Qinghua program.[96] Although both organizations claimed to promote only the peaceful use of nuclear energy, the AEC—and, by extension, Qinghua—had connections to the military's nuclear program, which was almost certainly engaged in nuclear weapons research.

The Chungshan Institute of Science and Technology was established as a secret institute for the study of military science and technology. It is not clear just when the Chungshan Institute became involved in nuclear research, or precisely what sort of nuclear research program it ran, but in 1968 a new Institute for Nuclear Energy Research (INER), ostensibly under civilian control, was established next door to the Chungshan Institute.[97] INER was placed under the direction of the AEC, but at the same time the AEC was reorganized so that the second-ranking member was the director of Chungshan.[98] Moreover, some of INER's staff members were in the military.[99]

In 1957 the ROC was already actively sending scientists to international nuclear conferences. According to the *China Yearbook 1958–59*, "Representatives were sent from China to the International Conference on the Application of Radioisotopes in Scientific Research held in France in September 1957, and to the Chicago Atomic Energy Exhibition and Nuclear Conference in March 1958."[100] The funding for researchers to attend international conferences appears to have come from either the ROC government or the U.S. government by way of CUSA.

Clearly, much of the support for Taiwan's nuclear research program came from the United States, but the ROC appears to have been fairly aggressive in its solicitation of this assistance. Taiwan's willingness to sign agreements on the peaceful use of atomic energy, and the island's obvious lack of other energy sources, must surely have helped the ROC make a good case with the U.S. Atomic Energy Commission for its interest in exploring the possibilities of atomic energy.[101] According to David Albright and Corey Gay in the *Bulletin of the Atomic Scientists,* however, "Some U.S. officials date Taiwan's first interest in nuclear explosives to the 1950s or even earlier. In their view, Taiwan's early involvement in the IAEA and its interest in the 'Atoms for Peace' program was intended to obtain equipment and vital nuclear training for both civilian and military purposes."[102] Perhaps ROC officials really did have to resort to subterfuge to acquire nuclear technology. Even though the Taiwan Straights crises of the mid- to late 1950s gave the ROC government an excellent excuse to ask the U.S. government for more direct nuclear weapons assistance, their requests yielded no results. In 1958 the ROC government apparently requested that the United States arm the ROC military with nuclear warheads and provide training in nuclear weapons operation for ROC military personnel. The U.S. Department of State was unwilling to comply with either request.[103]

The state's various institution-building efforts in the AEC, at Qinghua, and at Chungshan demonstrate that there were exceptions to its general lethargy with respect to the promotion of scientific research. If science could be shown to have a direct application to important national goals, such as military development and mainland recovery, then it had a better chance of getting attention and funding from the government. Nuclear physics was already well under way by the late 1950s because it could sell itself. Economic and industrial development of Taiwan took longer to become important national goals, however.

During its first two decades of rule in China, various factions within the KMT state actively encouraged S&T education and manpower development as well as R&D for industrial purposes. Although these efforts were not well coordinated, they nonetheless demonstrate a significant level of awareness on the part of the KMT leadership that state promotion of S&T development could benefit the state and the nation. During the Sino-Japanese War, KMT economic and education administrators and planners worked together to promote a coordinated and multifaceted approach to S&T development that strongly resembles the set of strategies that the KMT on Taiwan implemented after 1978 and that the PRC has promoted since the 1990s. There is little question but that the KMT state during the wartime period should be described as developmental, at least in terms of its approach to promotion of S&T for industrial development. It proactively assisted industrial development by constructing centralized institutions and plans to promote research in strategically important areas and also sought to train skilled manpower to serve future industrial needs.

After its 1949 retreat to Taiwan, however, the KMT failed to maintain anything approaching a similar level of interest in scientific development. To the extent that the KMT did promote scientific and technical education and research, it was solely in areas related to agriculture and nuclear physics. The state was impaired by real economic and infrastructural conditions but was also reluctant to commit to building Taiwan, preferring to garner its resources for its imminent retaking of the mainland.

The KMT position on state-supported S&T development in the 1940s was broadly consistent with the dominant approaches of the major Western powers of the time, such as the United States, Britain, Germany, and France. By the early 1950s, however, the KMT state had fallen behind in this respect, and Taiwan's lack of scientific and technical development strategies in the late 1950s and early 1960s was a cause for concern on the part of foreign observers, as we shall see in Chapter 2. Beginning in 1958, Taiwan's academic researchers and foreign advisers worked in concert to persuade the KMT state to construct an institution to oversee developments in S&T research and to improve S&T education.

— 2 —

The First Push: Domestic and Foreign Advocates

Numerous studies have been done on the role of the state in Taiwan's economic and social development since 1949. Some of these works have noted the state's involvement in scientific and technological development in Taiwan, but none have looked closely at the origins of this involvement. Although Taiwan's successful S&T development is generally attributed to strong state leadership, in fact the impetus for most kinds of scientific development came from Taiwan's intellectual community and foreign advisers. In the late 1950s, at the urging of the intellectual community, the government and the academic community worked together to construct the National Council for Scientific Development (NCSD), a council designed to guide and promote scientific and technical development in Taiwan. Although it received some government support, the NCSD was funded mostly by the U.S. government for its first several years. Moreover, its program for the promotion of scientific and technical research and development was heavily influenced by U.S. scientists and advisers. In spite of the existence of this institution and the U.S. support for it, still, in the mid-1960s, one visiting U.S. scholar characterized Taiwan as a "scientific desert."[1] Not until the late 1960s did the ROC state (in part because it was urged to by U.S. advisers) begin to take a more active role in promoting science and technology by taking formal control of the NCSD, initiating other programs, and increasing funding for scientific and technical research and development.

It was not the political leadership but outside advisers, including academicians and foreign aid givers, who initiated the process through which Taiwan developed its first institutions and plans for scientific and technical development. To what extent should the state be accorded credit for successful centralized planning schemes when, in fact, the schemes originated elsewhere? The very fact that the state's early involvement in scientific and technical development was essentially accidental, rather than planned by the state, suggests that much of the existing literature on state-led development and state planning in Taiwan may have been shaped by some problematic assumptions. Positive interpretations of state-led development should, perhaps, be reevaluated in light of these findings.

The State as Leader?

Social science literature has generally characterized the state as the leading agent for development in Taiwan. Tien Hung-mao, Robert Wade, Samuel Ho, Cal Clark, Cheng Tun-jen, Ramon Myers, Tom Gold, and William Kirby have all argued that the state played an important role in promotion of economic development in Taiwan during the 1950s and 1960s. These authors have all focused their work on the KMT's economic personnel, institutions, and policies, although their studies have, for the most part, been confined to the state's overall economic policies. The thrust of their argument is that the state has played a central and leading role in the promotion of economic development in Taiwan. As Robert Wade has said, when the Nationalist government "came to Taiwan it took over the preexisting centralized structure built by the Japanese and reinforced it. From the beginning powers of policy formation and social control were vested in a well-trained bureaucratic cadre, within which authority was concentrated at the top. Still today economic policy-making is intensely centripetal; it is carried out entirely in Taipei and almost entirely within the executive branch, with some input from the top of the party."[2] Similarly, Cheng Tun-jen has written of the ROC's move toward a policy of export orientation that "the party state organized and more importantly 'supervised' a loose developmental coalition, consisting of technocrats and local and foreign capital."[3] From these descriptions, one gets the impression of a highly centralized, state-led process that was governed by pragmatic economic concerns and was in place from the moment the ROC took control of Taiwan, or at least from the moment at which the United States started offering economic development assistance.

Not all scholars ascribe such a leading role to the state, however. Wu Yongping, in his case study of the development of small- and medium-sized enterprises in Taiwan, for example, argued that the state's decisions to implement policies that supported small- and medium-sized enterprises were dictated by political rather than economic concerns. He writes that "it is insufficient to view the role of the state in economic development solely in terms of its economic goals. In fact, it is often difficult to distinguish clearly between political and economic goals."[4] Wu, Stephan Haggard, and Alice Amsden all observe that both technocrats and political leaders needed to find common ground to make policy work.[5]

As noted in Chapter 1, S&T is an important facet of economic development, and its role in Taiwan's development has not been ignored by scholars. Constance Meaney, Paul K. C. Liu, Walter Arnold, and Jennie Hay Woo have addressed the state's encouragement of science and technology as a subset of state-led economic development. For the most part, however, their studies ignore the early period of KMT rule on Taiwan and focus instead on the period beginning in the early 1970s and ending in the late 1980s. In her article on Taiwan's semiconductor industry, Constance Meaney argues "that the state was indeed the decisive actor in the development of Taiwan's semiconductor industry."[6] She observes that "within the state apparatus, there was a relatively autonomous cluster of actors committed to an idea of national development that favored building a competitive semiconductor industry."[7] Meaney dates the state's involvement in the semiconductor industry to 1974, when the National Science Council (NSC) and other government organs began to promote the growth of the industry. Although her conclusions are sound, she nevertheless fails to consider how it came to be that the state promoted the semiconductor industry and does not address the question of whether there were any precedents for this cooperative relationship between the state and industry. Paul K. C. Liu's article "Science, Technology and Human Capital Formation" also virtually ignores the 1950s and 1960s.

Like Meaney and Liu, Walter Arnold has focused his work on state-sponsored science and technology in the 1970s and 1980s. Arnold has observed that "over the past two decades the developmental bureaucrats of . . . Taiwan . . . have attempted to foster the development of science and technology through the creation and use of some type of institutional structure."[8] To the extent that he addresses the preceding decades, it is only to observe that little was being done. He says, "In the 1950s and 1960s economic growth was spurred primarily by labor intensive industries and the export of processed goods; very little scientific research and development was actually carried out except in the field of agriculture where improved varieties of crops and animals were quite successfully developed."[9] Arnold does note the creation of the NCSD in 1959 but suggests that it did little in the way of promoting science and technology in the 1960s. In fact, Arnold observes, it was not until "the early 1970s" that "the role and significance of the NSC increased," and the state began to play a more important role in science and technology development.[10]

Only Jennie Hay Woo, in her article "Education and Economic Growth in Taiwan," says much about the 1960s, noting that the state played a significant role in the cultivation of a skilled labor force in the 1960s, thereby at least indirectly promoting scientific development. Woo states, "From 1966 onward, educational expansion in Taiwan has been guided very explicitly by a Manpower Development Plan (MDP)."[11] Woo notes that under the MDPs the growth and development of the education system was planned according to the needs of the economy.[12] Woo also observes that "an important feature of these plans was that they were actually implemented."[13]

The existing literature thus leaves the reader with no conclusive picture of the role of the state with respect to scientific development in the 1950s and 1960s. If one were to extrapolate from the literature on economic development, one might assume that the state took an active role in promoting scientific development in the 1950s. To judge from the literature on scientific and technical development, on the other hand, one might assume that the state played virtually no role in promotion of science (except in the area of education) prior to the 1970s.

To be sure, although recent works on Taiwan's development have tended to emphasize the guiding role of the state, scholars have noted other forces that were also at work in the 1950s and 1960s. Foreign governments, most especially the United States, played a significant role in assisting the Nationalist government in formulating economic and military development strategies. In addition, some foundations and nongovernment organizations also promoted development in areas related to science and technology, not always in close coordination with the government.

Thomas Gold has noted the significant role played by the United States in Taiwan: "In the critical 1950s, the KMT regime, guided and supported by the United States, institutionalized the structure within which Taiwan's economy, society, and politics would evolve." Gold has observed that "the main leverage held by Americans, and consequently the regime's prime constraint, was U.S. assistance." Gold goes on to observe that some of Taiwan's "economic transformation . . . can be traced to American insistence and the threat of withholding aid."[14] To a great extent, as William Kirby has noted, "American influence [was] applied through the extra-ministerial Council on US Aid, whose funds were administered outside the government's regular budget."[15]

CUSA was created in 1948. It was chaired by the ROC premier and was staffed by representatives from ten ministries but "was semi-autonomous in nature and functioned outside of the regular ministries."[16] It coordinated the relationship between the ROC and the U.S. mission in Taiwan and was responsible for planning how U.S. funds would be used. To a large extent, it served as a central planning agency to oversee economic development in Taiwan.[17]

Organizations such as the Joint Commission on Rural Reconstruction (JCRR) and U.S. private foundations such as the Rockefeller and Ford foundations provided some support for academic research in Taiwan during the 1950s. These organizations and foundations were quite specific about the kinds of research they were willing to fund, however. JCRR, which "played a leading role in the formation and coordination of Chinese agricultural policy," was closely tied, though not subordinate to, the Executive Yuan.[18] It was financed for the most part by U.S. aid. The research programs funded by JCRR were mostly applied agricultural projects, and few involved the personnel or facilities of Taiwan's academic institutions in any way. Beginning in the mid-1950s the Rockefeller and Ford foundations provided funding for Chinese cultural studies being conducted at Academia Sinica's Institute of History and Philology and Institute of Modern History.[19] Through the funding of research on Chinese history and culture, U.S. foundations and scholars exerted a significant influence on Taiwan's academic environment.[20] Thus scholars have provided us with ample evidence that the U.S. government and private foundations played a role in Taiwan's economic development in the early 1960s. But, with the exception of Chang Peng-yuan in his study on scholarly relations between Taiwan and the United States, none have evaluated the overall impact of U.S. assistance on scientific and technical research.

This chapter shows that although the state rapidly constructed an apparatus for guiding scientific development in the 1960s, the impetus for the construction of this apparatus came not from the state itself but from the intellectual community, on the one hand, and U.S. aid agencies, on the other. Moreover, although the link between scientific and technical research and overall socioeconomic development was apparent to both U.S. aid givers and some ROC intellectuals, it does not seem to have been evident to the

ROC's political leadership until after the cessation of U.S. aid in the mid-1960s. In the realm of promotion of industrially relevant R&D or manpower training programs, therefore, the state neither initiated nor became involved in centralized planning (with the exception of nuclear physics, as discussed in Chapter 1) during its first twenty years in Taiwan.

Science and the State in the 1950s

Although the government actively promoted economic and educational development in the 1950s, there is evidence that the state lacked interest in promoting scientific development during that same decade. The state did essentially nothing during the 1950s to create a climate that would encourage those capable of performing scientific research to engage in research. Extensive resources were pumped into primary and secondary education, but almost nothing was invested in higher education or research.[21]

Institutions of higher education and research such as National Taiwan University (NTU), Qinghua University, and Academia Sinica existed, but as research institutions they existed in little more than name. Universities, such as NTU and Qinghua, received earlier and more ample funding to support the education of the populace, but even that funding was not forthcoming until the late 1950s and early 1960s, and very little of it was intended to support scientific or other research.[22] Moreover, of the academics who had accompanied the KMT to Taiwan, few were scientists, as noted in Chapter 1, and so even when academicians talked about the need to fund research in the 1950s, they were as often as not thinking about humanities and social science rather than scientific research.

Accounts by academicians affiliated with Academia Sinica, NTU, and other institutions of higher learning show the low pay, poor living conditions, and lack of adequate research facilities of scholars in 1950s Taiwan. Wu Dayou, a physicist and later president of Academia Sinica, noted that "the Government did not pay enough attention and support to [Academia Sinica]."[23] According to Chang Peng-yuan, "Academia Sinica never had enough staff members or a large enough budget . . . [and] that is why there were never any academic achievements made by the Academia Sinica during those years."[24] Historian and then ambassador to the United Nations Jiang Tingfu wrote in a September 1957 diary entry that Li Ji, an archaeologist and the head of Academia Sinica's Institute of History and Philology, told him that "for his institute on modern history, he needs trained men. All his staff needs better pay."[25] A year and a half later Jiang met with a group of scholars from Academia Sinica's Institute of Modern History who, he noted, "are very unhappy because their Institute does not pay anybody enough to enable them to work steadily at research, because it lacks books and documents, etc."[26] Conditions for nearly all scholars in Taiwan, natural and social scientists alike, were bad. The problem of inadequate pay was critical to the question of promotion of research. Scholars were not paid enough for their work as teachers at the island's few institutions of higher learning and had no choice but to look for other sources of income. Required in this way to spend most of their time working at nonscholarly endeavors just to make ends meet, these scholars had little or no time to devote to any kind of research at all.

The government also failed to construct facilities in which research could be performed. Academia Sinica had a fairly typical experience in this regard. In a 1953 speech to the Educational Committee of the Legislative Yuan, Zhu Jiahua, then acting president of Academia Sinica, complained that the Academy could not afford to rebuild. Academia Sinica had no facilities, not even library space for existing books. In 1953 all of the Institute of History and Philology's valuable texts and archival sources were still being housed in an old garage in Yangmei. Zhu further lamented that the Academy was losing good scholars to the United States and elsewhere because it could not pay competitive wages. He went on to say that he could not really blame scholars for going abroad, given the horrible working conditions in Taiwan. At least they had a chance of some success abroad where they had the facilities they needed. The punch line of Zhu's speech was a plea to the Legislative Yuan to be more supportive of scientists.[27]

From the moment it moved to Taiwan, Academia Sinica was engaged in a constant struggle to find resources to build new facilities and to reestablish the various scientific institutes it had left behind on the mainland. According to an Academia Sinica publication, "Although requests for appropriation of funds were submitted to the Government in the winter of 1950, the first appropriation of NT$1,510,000 was only released in installments between the winter of 1953 and summer of 1954. A second grant of NT$1,580,000 was received in two installments between the end of 1954 and the summer of 1955."[28] By the early 1960s, Academia Sinica was receiving considerably more money from the government than it had been, NT$9,045,024 (U.S.$226,125) in 1962–1963, but it was still not enough to enable the Academy to construct new facilities and pay for research projects simultaneously.[29]

The National Council for Scientific Development

In the unencouraging atmosphere of the 1950s, academicians were forced to take matters into their own hands and push the government to provide more support for higher education and research and target science education and research as a particular area of development. Hu Shi, the newly appointed president of Academia Sinica, proposed the creation of the NCSD *(guojia changchi fazhan kexue weiyuanhui)* in 1958, and it was established on February 1, 1959, as part of the Long-Range Science Development Program that was adopted at the 599th Session of the Cabinet.[30] The NCSD was to be jointly administered by Academia Sinica and the Ministry of Education, but academicians always played a more dominant role. It was divided into three committees: physical sciences, natural sciences, and social sciences and humanities. Each committee was made up of seven to eleven members who served for one year. The committees performed a variety of duties, including screening applications for grants, fellowships, and subsidies. Not surprisingly, the aims of the NCSD were clearly intended to serve the immediate needs of Taiwan's small community of research scientists and included improvement of equipment and facilities, creation of research chairs and visiting professorships, provision of housing for visiting professors, and subsidies for scientific publications.[31]

Almost from its inception, the NCSD placed much heavier emphasis on the support of research in the physical and natural sciences than on the humanities and social sciences, thus signifying, at least insofar as the NCSD can be considered a true state organ, a minor shift in the state's approach to academic research. According to the *China Yearbook* of 1960–1961, it was the government that had decided that "the aids and grants from the Long-Range Science Development Fund shall be temporarily concentrated on the natural sciences, the basic sciences of medicine, the basic sciences of engineering, the humanities and the social sciences. The allocations to the natural sciences, basic medical sciences and basic engineering sciences shall not be less than 80 per cent of the total amount."[32] The fact remained, however, that the ROC government itself made only minimal financial contributions to the NCSD.

In 1967, the NCSD was elevated in status, and its name was changed to the National Science Council, as we shall see in Chapter 3. It was simultaneously removed from the joint control of Academia Sinica and the Ministry of Education and placed under control of the Executive Yuan (cabinet).[33]

The NSC continued to be mostly staffed, however, by representatives of Academia Sinica and the Ministry of Education, and even now it performs only a slightly expanded set of functions, most of which were already being performed by the NCSD by 1965. The NSC has acquired substantial clout in the realm of academic research and now supports untold numbers of research projects with huge grants. As Walter Arnold observed in the late 1980s, the NSC "has been Taiwan's most ardent promoter of science and technology research and development for two decades now."[34]

The NCSD as a Vehicle for Soliciting U.S. Aid

The NCSD was tailored to fit the requirements for U.S. aid. By the late 1950s Academia Sinica's leadership was much more closely connected to the United States and the international political community than had been the case in the early years of the decade. Hu Shi, who took over the presidency of Academia Sinica in 1959, had been ambassador to the United States immediately prior to becoming head of Academia Sinica. He was therefore in a good position not only to solicit U.S. aid but also to shape the NCSD as an organization that would fit American aims and funding strategies.

In 1958 the U.S. government began to disburse funds to promote science education in Taiwan through a "6-year science education program by making grants to educational institutions for the improvement of their physical facilities for teaching science. The program also provides money for sending Chinese scientists to the United States for advanced study and the invitation of American consultants to Taiwan."[35] The science education program had two original objectives: "to create in a six-year period a minimum necessary corps of high level scientists to operate successfully the laboratories and research units of The Republic of China" and "to provide adequate equipment and facilities to the already established institutions of education and research." In a general sense "the instructional phase coupled with research improvement is expected to provide China with the tools necessary to promote scientific and industrial growth."[36] Although the KMT was not, as we saw in Chapter 1, pushing a scientific development model in the 1950s, the United States was.

The science education program was intended to be a development-oriented program quite consistent with the UN approach discussed in the previous chapter. Shortly after the program was put into effect, the United States initiated what it called an accelerated development program for

Taiwan that would make Taiwan into an "attractive 'showcase' of [the] achievements [of a] free society" and "maximize sound economic growth [in the] next 4–5 years[,] attaining [a] condition where future growth would be self-generating, thus eliminating [the] need [for] foreign aid except military items and surplus agriculture products."[37] On the ground, however, the science education program did not aspire to such grand ambitions, and most of the science education money appears to have gone to construction of laboratories in schools across Taiwan.[38] In 1961, following the implementation of the new accelerated development program, USAID revised the goals for the science education program. It now aimed to "promote the expansion of industry and agriculture towards economic self-sufficiency." To accomplish these ends the science education program "would concentrate on upgrading science facilities to produce graduates with better science background to fit into the economic expansion. At the research level the aim would be to promote 'directed research' of both an applied and basic nature to solve problems related to industrial and agricultural expansion."[39]

At the same time, private foundations such as Fulbright and the Asia Foundation began to grant research subsidies and sponsor studies abroad. Unlike the funds that other foundations had been disbursing to promote research in Chinese culture, much of the Asia Foundation money was directed into science. Funding from the Asia Foundation, however, was also tied, albeit covertly, to the U.S. government. As Nancy Tucker has written, the Asia Foundation, established in 1956, "enjoyed secret funding from the Central Intelligence Agency. Openly, it carried on programs of scholarly exchange, providing support for research at the Academia Sinica; for instructional programs in science, sociology, and agriculture; and for the distribution of thousands of volumes to several academic institutions . . . At the same time, there were also covert efforts to recruit agents, provide cover for underground operations, disseminate anti-communist propaganda, and fund the research of sympathetic academics."[40]

Overall, the United States granted Taiwan roughly $100 million in nonmilitary assistance between 1950 and 1965.[41] As soon as it became clear to a handful of elite ROC academicians that some of this funding might be able to go into scientific development, the NCSD was created. The NCSD came into existence only a year after U.S. aid agencies branched into financing scientific education. The mission of the new organization, while rooted in Academia Sinica's history, was also shaped by the kinds of funding that could come from U.S. aid.[42]

Only one year after the creation of the NCSD, members of the council were invited to participate in the Sino-American Conference on Intellectual Cooperation in Seattle. Members of the NCSD participated in the conference in order to advertise the state of affairs for academic researchers in Taiwan, solicit ideas on how to improve those conditions, and let some of their concrete material and financial needs be known. Although Li Xianwen, a botanist at Academia Sinica, has suggested that the conference was "all thunder and lightning but no rain," the conference did serve as a good informational source for members of the NCSD.[43] The stated purposes of the conference, according to George E. Taylor, head of the Far Eastern and Russian Institute of the University of Washington, were "to discuss the scholarly and professional problems of international intellectual communication and cooperation in general [and] . . . to make recommendations concerning the intellectual relations between Free China and America."[44]

In addition to NCSD members and other academicians from Taiwan, attendees included American academicians, Chinese academicians located at U.S. institutions, representatives of U.S. foundations and funding agencies (such as Ford, Rockefeller, Fulbright, and Asia), and representatives of U.S. and ROC government organs. Virtually every participant in the meeting had some suggestions to make on how Taiwan's academic environment could be improved. Even Jiang Menglin, former minister of education of the Nationalist government in Nanjing and chairman of the Joint Commission on Rural Reconstruction, issued a statement on "JCRR as an Example of Effective Sino-American Cooperation." In his statement, Jiang offered suggestions on how similar cooperative efforts might learn from the past as they constructed plans for the future. Jiang's advice on what not to do included admonitions against "putting up big impressive buildings" and competing with local enterprise.[45]

The conference was not merely a long series of individual presentations, however. It divided into three working groups of scholars representing the humanities, social sciences, and natural sciences. Each group concluded its discussions with a report in which it made concrete proposals on how to improve intellectual communications between the ROC and the United States.[46] The "Report of the Committee on Natural Sciences" produced a number of proposals for improving conditions in Taiwan, most of which focused on training of elite scientists and improvement of research facilities. Included among the committee's suggestions were sending Chinese faculty abroad for study, bringing American faculty to Taiwan, improving conditions in Taiwan so as to entice Chinese scientists to return, and establishing graduate programs at universities in Taiwan.[47]

Relatively few new ideas for improving Taiwan's scientific community surfaced at the meeting, but even so, the meeting gave Taiwan's intellectuals ample opportunity to impress the other conferees with Taiwan's academic and research potential, on the one hand, and the island's need for more resources, on the other hand. For the most part, the American conferees were eager to suggest small ways in which the U.S. scientific community could assist that of Taiwan. One Chinese American participant, for instance, proposed that American research laboratories ship their surplus equipment to Taiwan.[48] Ultimately, however, Taiwan's scientific research community suffered from one major problem, which was addressed in the statement by the natural sciences group when they suggested that Taiwan's academicians should explore all "available sources of support from foundations and from the United States government."[49]

As the experience of the 1960 Sino-American Conference suggests, the NCSD was unabashed in its solicitation of foreign aid of all sorts. As Wang Shijie, new president of Academia Sinica, said in 1963, "While we in China are striving to bring our country to a 'scientific take-off,' we sincerely hope for and welcome the assistance of, and cooperation with, institutes and foundations in foreign countries. The dispatch of scientists and scholars to free China for teaching or research would be of great help to us."[50] Money was clearly a constant worry for the NCSD and Taiwan's academicians in general until at least the mid-1960s.

While the NCSD was undoubtedly designed to take advantage of potential opportunities for U.S. aid, it did also receive funding from other sources. From its inception, funding for the NCSD came from three sources: government funds, U.S. aid, and donations from foundations such as the China Foundation and Asia Foundation. In his "A General Report on the National Council on Science Development," written in 1964 or 1965, Qian Siliang, then president of National Taiwan University and a member of the NCSD, indicated exactly where the NCSD's funding had come from during its first five years (Table 2.1).

By 1964 it appeared that the NCSD was beginning to receive increased support from the state. In the NCSD's December 1964 four-year plan, the council proposed a budget of NT$50 million per year (total of NT$200 million),

Table 2.1 Funds received by the NCSD, 1959–1964

Source	NT$ received	U.S.$ received
a. U.S. aid		
Science Education Program—Part B	NT$103,394,325	U.S.$1,194,600
b. KMT government	NT$107,400,000	
c. Foundations		
China Foundation		U.S.$91,700
Asia Foundation		U.S.$59,400
Total	NT$210,794,325	U.S.$1,345,700

Source: Qian Siliang, "A General Report on the National Council on Science Development," As-Qian, Box 41, p. 5.

Note: U.S. aid came from the science education program, which was divided into Part A, for educational purposes, and Part B, for research spending. The NCSD only received funds from Part B.

of which half would come from the NCSD's existing revenue sources and half would come from an NT$100 million lump-sum allotment from the Executive Yuan.[51] In 1965 Wang Shijie announced that the NCSD's funding was going to become more regularized and that the NCSD would henceforth be getting 2 percent of net earnings of provincial enterprises from the Taiwan Provincial Government as well as additional money from the Central Government for a total of between NT$20 million and NT$30 million a year.[52] These numbers sound good, but in fact they are quite low.

The NCSD used its budget to support the establishment of national research chairs and visiting professorships and to finance research grants to faculty and researchers, fellowship programs for faculty and researchers, institutional grants for facilities improvements and faculty housing, and publication of technical journals.[53] As Qian Siliang reported, during the NCSD's first five years, roughly 80 percent of the NCSD's budget had gone to construction of research facilities; 13 percent to construction of residences for scholars, research professorships, and grants; and 7 percent for sending scientists abroad.[54]

Most important among the NCSD's early accomplishments, according to both Qian and Wang, was the headway the NCSD had made with respect to improving the standard of living of scientific researchers. From 1959 to 1964 the NCSD established 121 research professorships, provided 94 fellowships for study abroad, and made 2,441 research grants. As Qian observed, "We do realize the importance of having research facilities in the development of science, but more important is the men who would utilize these facilities. Due to the low pay-scale here scholars and research workers used to worry constantly about making a subsistence living so much that they had scarcely the energy nor the mind for, and interest in, scientific research . . . The grants and subsidies provided by the Council not only enhanced the aptitude and interest for the scientists and scholars to carry on with their research work but also constituted a sort of morale booster to the intellectual community as a whole."[55]

It should be noted, however, that not all of the NCSD's plans for improving the quality of life of Taiwan's scientists met with unqualified success. The research professorships were particularly problematic, as they were designed to be staffed by established researchers, and there were simply not enough such scholars in Taiwan in the early 1960s. Not only had a relatively small number of China's elite scientists accompanied the KMT to Taiwan, but an equally small percentage of students who had left Taiwan to pursue graduate studies in the United States and Europe were actually returning to Taiwan. In a 1961 address on the status of scientific research and education in Taiwan to the Taipei Rotary Club, Qian Siliang addressed the issue of returned students. The rate of return was so miserable that Qian was literally able to count out the number of Ph.D.'s in the sciences who had returned to take positions in Taiwan: he noted six chemists, one mathematician, one geologist, and one botanist who had either already returned or were on the verge of returning to take up academic positions in Taiwan.[56] A second problem was that the academic atmosphere of Taiwan was plagued by a tendency toward cronyism and infighting. According to Jiang Tingfu, Qian Siliang told him over a September 1962 lunch that the "National Research Professorships, financed by China Foundation, have been left 50% unfilled. He said mutual jealousies caused the deans to refuse to recommend: the same old story."[57] The research professorship program, therefore, was at least as problematic as it was successful.

A second important role the NCSD played during its first years of existence was to provide funding for the improvement of research facilities. During its first five years the NCSD funded the construction of forty-four major buildings. According to Qian Siliang, by 1962 "research facilities in local universities and academic establishments [had] been substantially strengthened and the living condition of scientists and scholars [had] been more or less improved."[58]

By 1964 the NCSD had also initiated a series of strategies for training or retraining of scholars in Taiwan. One method, as noted above, was to provide fellowships for study abroad. A second strategy was to recruit scholars from abroad to come to Taiwan as short-term visiting scholars. To this end, the NCSD had financed the construction of forty-three visiting scholars' residences. A third approach to training scholars on Taiwan was the summer seminar, the implementation of which was the result of a new set of proposals for the role of the NCSD, which will be discussed below.

Overall, the leaders of the NCSD were relatively self-congratulatory by the mid-1960s. As Wang Shijie noted in a December 1963 address, "The National Council on Science Development with the full support of Academia Sinica is playing a significant role in the maintenance and promotion of research work in Taiwan."[59] USAID, on the other hand, was considerably more reserved in its evaluation of the accomplishments of the NCSD. From the perspective of Paul R. Byerly Jr., USAID's education adviser in 1963, the NCSD and USAID did not at all share the same aims; the NCSD was content to pursue limited goals, whereas USAID was hoping to link scientific research to Taiwan's larger development process. As Byerly noted, "The opinion of many of the people in the long range science council [NCSD] has been that the emphasis should be on academic research and that there need be little relation to economic development. While this was partially possible under the original description of the project, the change of AID support [in 1961] required close relationships between research project [*sic*] and economic development. This has been difficult for the Council to accept." Byerly went on to note that "the members of the long range science council [NCSD] play a passive rather than an active role in the development of a long range science program. Attempts to persuade the Council to take an active role have so far not been successful."[60] Byerly's critical assessment of the NCSD came near the end of USAID's science education program, which lasted only through 1964.

In fact, Byerly's criticisms of the narrow focus of the NCSD were right on the mark. All evidence suggests that the main function of the NCSD prior to 1964 had been to advocate for Taiwan's beleaguered scholarly community. Virtually all of its budget was spent on improving the physical situation, in terms of both research facilities and standard of living, of elite scientific researchers in Taiwan. Little to no attention had been paid to the bigger picture. The NCSD made no particular effort to explain to the state or the broader public why it was important to have research scientists or what role they might play in the larger nation-building or economic development process. Moreover, members of the NCSD, who were actively competing for science education money from USAID, must surely have understood that USAID, at any rate, did see research science and national economic development as linked. The academic community in the late 1950s and early 1960s, therefore, appears to have been just as myopic as the KMT. Neither made much, if anything, of the larger development role to be played by S&T until after 1964.

The Sino-American Committee on Science Cooperation

In 1964, with the end of the science education program and USAID's involvement in Taiwan's scientific development, a new mechanism for ROC-U.S. scientific communication was needed. What had, up to that point, been an aid-driven relationship was formalized into a strategy for intellectual cooperation with the establishment of the Sino-American Committee on Science Cooperation, the creation of which had originally been proposed at the 1960 Sino-American Conference on Intellectual Cooperation.[61] The collaboration was formally established between Academia Sinica and the U.S. National Academy of Sciences and was formed during a visit of a delegation from the National Academy of Sciences headed by Dr. Joseph Platt, president of Harvey Mudd College in Claremont, California. The aim of the committee was to promote cooperative ventures.[62] It is clear that one of the principal concerns of the delegation was to push Taiwan to start thinking about S&T in terms of its economic significance.

Almost as if the NCSD did not exist, delegates suggested that the ROC government establish "a mechanism for planning on a national scale in the domains of science and technology."[63] In fact, a discussion took place between Joseph B. Platt and ROC premier "C. K. Yen on the question of setting up an Office for Science and Technology under the Premier's Office." Platt's proposal suggested "the establishment of an Office for Science and Technology with appropriate supporting staff, funding, and power to convene a Science Advisory Council and an Intergovernmental Coordination Committee."[64] The fact that Platt, who did meet with NCSD members, could have made such a recommendation, utterly disregarding the existence of the NCSD, is further proof that the NCSD was failing to play a leading role in terms of guiding S&T development or considering its relevance to nationally pressing needs.

By August 1964, however, Platt had identified the NCSD as the national scientific planning organ and was recommending that its functions be expanded. In a letter to Wang Shijie, Platt suggested that the NCSD be placed under the Executive Yuan and given "the power to receive funds from governmental and non-governmental sources, to disburse these funds to advance science and technology in the Republic of China, and to conduct such studies as it finds necessary for the determination of effective policies." He further suggested a reorganization of the NCSD into a council of twenty-one members, one-third of whom would be from Academia Sinica, one-third of whom would be from the Ministry of Education, and one-third of whom would be appointed from the general scientific and technical community by the premier.[65]

The American delegates also made several additional recommendations. They suggested that Taiwan undertake surveys of research projects and manpower resources, find further ways to promote institutional cooperation between universities in the United States and Taiwan, establish a set of new research centers in Taiwan, look for ways to promote collaboration between researchers and industry, and continuously work to identify research priorities based on economic need.[66] The American delegates were therefore pushing Taiwan's academic research community hard to streamline itself and make its work industrially relevant. They also urged the ROC to make the most of its limited resources by investing only in research with industrial or other development applications.

Immediately following the creation of the Joint Committee, a China Committee for Sino-American Science Cooperation, made up mostly of members of Academia Sinica, was established. Many of the members of the China Committee were also members of the NCSD. It was only logical that the organ selected to oversee the implementation of these recommendations would be the NCSD.

The NCSD's 1964 Four-Year Plan and the Shift in Priorities

In direct response to the recommendations of the April 1964 conference, the NCSD announced its new four-year plan for the "Promotion of Science and Technology in Taiwan" in December of that same year. This plan identified three major problems that the NCSD should target between 1965 and 1969: the exodus of talented youths from the country, the increasing need of science and technology for economic development, and furthering Sino-American cooperation in promoting scientific and technological programs.[67] For the rest of the decade, and into the 1970s, these concerns dominated the NCSD and its successor, the NSC. The plan was necessary for three reasons: "the need for a general elevation of the standard of science research and training; the requirements of future economic development; and the need for strengthening Sino-American cultural ties."[68] These new aims, and in particular the second of them, represented a substantial change from those articulated by the NCSD at the time of its creation. The NCSD had clearly taken the U.S. advice to heart and was beginning to justify scientific research in terms of the ROC's economic development.

To alleviate the three problems mentioned above, the plan proposed the expansion or continuation of some of the programs it had already undertaken, such as increasing the number of national research chairs, visiting professorships, and fellowships for foreign study. The plan also proposed several new initiatives that were clearly constructed in direct response to the suggestions made by the National Academy of Sciences delegation, for example, increasing the number of, and improving the quality of, graduate schools; promoting more extensive cooperation between universities and research institutes in the United States and Taiwan; and most important, "organizing research and training centers to answer the scientific and technological needs of industrial and economic development."[69]

Implementation of the program began immediately with the inauguration of the summer science seminar program in the summer of 1964. During the summer of 1964 the NCSD sponsored a large summer seminar that was held at NTU, Qinghua, and Academia Sinica. Twelve Chinese scholars working in America in mathematics, physics, and biology were brought to Taiwan to lead the seminar, during which they spoke to participants about recent developments in the field and new techniques. The seminars included labs and were run at the places with the best facilities in each area: math at NTU, physics at Qinghua, and biology at Academia Sinica. The funds for the event came from the China Foundation and the Asia Foundation. The seminar had two aims: expanded training of Taiwan's scientists and improvement of communications between scholars in Taiwan and those abroad.[70]

Even more important, however, the NCSD's 1964 four-year plan aimed at finding solutions for the two major problems of the exodus of talent and the increasing need of science and technology for economic development.

Exodus of Talent

Immediately after the creation of the China Committee for Sino-American Science Cooperation in May 1964, a seven-member subcommittee was established to conduct a survey of research facilities and projects and scientific manpower. In conjunction with the work of the China Committee's subcommittee on manpower, the U.S. Committee initiated its own survey of Chinese scientists in the United States. It sent out 1,500 surveys to Chinese-born or Chinese American scientists residing in the United States to find out how many of them would be available for short- or long-term assignments in Taiwan.[71] Of course, a by-product of this survey was a thorough list of Chinese scientific manpower in the United States who might be enticed to go (or return) to Taiwan at some point in the future.

The most pressing problem for Taiwan was the increasing number of university graduates and skilled scientists departing for the United States and elsewhere in search of advanced degrees or job opportunities. The ROC walked an uncomfortable tightrope with respect to the exodus of talent. On the one hand, the only real way for the ROC to increase its scientific and technological manpower was to send students abroad. Between 1957 and 1961, 8 percent of university and college graduates in Taiwan went abroad to study. From 1962 to 1963 the percentage of students going abroad jumped to 16 percent. On the other hand, as an NCSD report observed in 1964, "of the large numbers of the graduates who left the country, very few have returned."[72] Only 7 percent of those who left between 1957 and 1963 had returned by 1964. In spite of efforts to lure young scholars back to Taiwan, Taiwan was simply not able to compete with the United States in terms of salaries and research infrastructure. Moreover, other than KMT members or devout anti-Communists, mainlanders living abroad had little incentive to go to Taiwan, a place to which they had no particular ties. Many Taiwanese, on the other hand, were alienated by the KMT's authoritarian regime and the low probability that they would advance in any sort of civil service position (including university appointments) and were also not likely to return. For numerous reasons, then, Taiwan was not likely to attract talent from abroad or reverse its brain drain in the 1960s.

The most obvious solution to the problem of departing talent was to attempt to keep students in Taiwan. This only made sense to the extent that there were adequate graduate training programs in Taiwan, but as the NCSD admitted in late 1964, "The Council has been fully aware of the seriousness of the situation and has made considerable efforts to improve facilities for graduate studies and encourage more trained scientists to return to serve the country. However, the outcome has not been particularly successful. There are many factors responsible for the current trend of events, but lack of adequately equipped and supported graduate schools and research institutes is a major problem with which the Council must deal."[73]

In January 1965, as part of its overall four-year plan, the NCSD proposed a four-year "Scientific Manpower Development Program"; the program described itself as "a proposal to establish a four-year program for strengthening the development of the scientific manpower which is urgently needed for social and economic development in the Republic of China."[74] The program's objectives were "to build up highly qualified scientific and technological manpower by establishing efficient and well-equipped research centers; . . . To reduce the exodus of talented youth and scientists from the country; . . . To provide the country with a steady supply of competent scientists and highly trained technological manpower."[75]

The U.S. influence on the Scientific Manpower Development Program was heavy and overt. The document makes frequent reference to the work on the exodus of talent of Dr. Charles V. Kidd of the National Institutes of Health in Bethesda. Kidd was a clear advocate of the UNESCO approach to S&T development discussed in Chapter 1. Kidd's report noted that "the development of an adequate supply of scientists, engineers, and technicians is a basic problem in the application of science and technology in developing areas . . . The strategy of manpower development is as significant as any other facet of policy for science and technology in developing areas."[76] The report went on to suggest how developing countries might work to keep or attract scientists. Patriotism, Kidd observed, was one important way of bringing scientists back to serve the nation. He also pointed out that

> the attention paid to science by national governments is significant. The place given to matters of science in the councils of state will influence the decisions of scientists to remain at home or to migrate. Tangible evidence that the activity in which they are engaged is worthy of specific attention by government tends to influence scientists, and this is true whether they are engaged in fundamental or applied research. Such actions as the establishment of a science section as part of a national planning body, or the establishment of a national research council, can symbolize the significance of science and tend to hold scientists at home. Such forms are significant,

> over the long run, only to the extent that the form of attention to science and scientists is followed by action . . . The line of policy directed at keeping scientists at home is simply the line of policy directed at strengthening science in a country.[77]

Science policy, Kidd argued, was the domain of the state, and S&T would only grow with direct and energetic state involvement. The Scientific Manpower Development Program, however, made much of the need for cooperative effort between Taiwan and the United States and less of Kidd's recommendations that developing nations call on patriotism and increased state involvement.

Using Kidd's recommendations as general guidelines, while still not pushing for greater state involvement, the NCSD proposed an extensive series of measures, most of which were identical to earlier initiatives including those made in the plan for the "Promotion of Science and Technology in Taiwan" that had been published a month earlier. The main new initiative in the Scientific Manpower Development Program was the proposal to establish five new research centers in the fields of Mathematics, Physics, Chemistry, Biology, and Engineering. These five new research centers were created in such a way as to take advantage of existing resources. Each one was built at the academic institution that was strongest in that field.

Science and Technology for Economic Development

A second issue tackled by the NCSD in its 1964 four-year plan was that of the role of science and technology in economic development. Up to this point Taiwan's promoters of scientific development had not made the rhetorical link between their argument for increased attention to science and the larger question of economic development—this, in spite of USAID's early 1960s insistence that scientific research was a key ingredient in the overall development process. In NCSD documents, the relationship between scientific and economic development had merely been implied. Now, for the first time, at the urging of U.S. advisers such as Platt and Kidd, the NCSD was playing up the relevance of scientific development to economic development. As the NCSD's four-year plan stated, "Another problem of national importance . . . [is] the increasing need of science and technology for the advancement of [the] national economy." The NCSD also hinted in the "Promotion of Science and Technology" that the impetus for this new emphasis came in large part from the government, which was (at the urging of Joseph Platt) reviewing the structure and role of the NCSD with an eye to investigating "how the work of the Council can be expanded to meet the technological requirements of national economic development." The Executive Yuan's subcommittee to study the NCSD had, in fact, "proposed to enlarge its membership from 35 to 45 members to include wider representation presumably from agriculture and industry as well as from economic and other administrative agencies."[78] It appears, therefore, that the Platt and Kidd visits not only helped the NCSD reconceptualize its role but also catalyzed the state into at least a small degree of action with respect to S&T development. Chapter 3 will explore this re-involvement of the state in promotion of S&T in the mid- to late 1960s.

Further evidence of the NCSD's new approach to articulating the developmental role of science and technology was its new emphasis on the link between basic and applied research. According to the four-year plan, "There is much to gain through increased interchange and cooperation among scientists and specialists working in academic institutions and in applied fields." The plan explicitly identified scientific research as an essential component of agricultural, industrial, medical, and economic progress. It also acknowledged the interdependence between institutions of higher education and research and overall economic progress: "No country can be industrialized without well staffed, equipped and supported centers of higher learning to prepare scientists, specialists and leaders for industries. Nor will there be any adequate means of supporting the academic and research institutions without prosperous industries and a growing national economy."[79]

Science's New Image

In contrast to Zhu Jiahua, who had pleaded ineffectively in the 1950s for state support for academic research, the leaders of Taiwan's scientific community in the early to mid-1960s were, with U.S. guidance, defining an identifiable set of goals for the development of the academic community and a clear rationale for the pursuit of research. Academic research had been redefined, as early as 1959, as *scientific* research, and scientific research, by 1964–1965, was being further defined as a combination of basic and applied research, pursuit of which could and should be justified in terms of national needs. As one scholar noted in 1963, "Scientific research and science education are prerequisites for any nation aspiring to make progress."[80]

Not willing to view early attempts by academicians to promote scientific development as failures, Wang Shijie began, in the early 1960s, to construct a rationale to explain the late blooming of research. He argued that Taiwan had had to concentrate on the development of education during the 1950s and could not afford to focus on research until the 1960s: "In the late 1940s, the high point of our task was to put every school-age child in elementary schools. In the fifties the major battleground was centered on secondary education; that is, to set up more and better middle schools . . . We are now faced with the tremendous demand for more and better institutions of higher learning."[81] In a December 1966 speech to the Chinese Agricultural Association *(Zhonghua nongyehui)* Wang articulated his views on the pattern of scientific development in most nations, Taiwan included. According to Wang, a nation's scientific development typically underwent two stages: first, a period during which college-level education was improved and, second, a period during which research was promoted. Taiwan in 1966, according to Wang, should be entering the second stage. Two things needed to be done to accomplish this goal: first, the government needed to determine a way to pay scientific experts; second, graduate programs of all varieties needed to be established at Taiwan's universities.[82] Construction of graduate programs would become a big point of emphasis for Taiwan's academicians.

The state made a tentative and limited commitment to scientific and technological development in 1959 with the creation of the NCSD. The impetus for the creation of the NCSD, however, came not from the state but from Hu Shi, from other academicians, and less directly from an increased availability of U.S. funds for scientific research in Taiwan. Throughout the early to mid-1960s, the NCSD received guidance and direction not from the ROC government but from the U.S. government and other funding agencies. This guidance came through the stipulations the United States and various foundations put on funding and also from U.S. advisers acting, most typically, as delegates of U.S. government–sponsored missions. Other than sanctioning the creation of the NCSD, in fact, the state seemed entirely disinterested in the promotion of academic (or almost any other sort of) scientific and technical research.

In the early 1960s, U.S. observers remained skeptical about the extent of the ROC's commitment to scientific development. They felt that the ROC had not grasped the relevance of scientific research to overall economic and social development. The state's commitment to nuclear physics at a time when it was offering next to nothing to scientists for research in other fields underscores the point that it was only interested in supporting science with obvious, and preferably militarily beneficial, applications. It was not just the state that failed to identify the potential importance of scientific research. It took until 1964 for the NCSD, an organization committed to the promotion of scientific research, to begin to describe and even to a limited extent market its work in terms of economic development, and the state followed quickly on its heels.

— 3 —

The State Gets Interested: The Lure of Economic Development

In 1965, ROC economic planners and political leaders began to demonstrate a new awareness of the role that science education and research might potentially play in economic development, leading to an important turning point in the evolution of state sponsorship of S&T in the ROC. This turning point occurred over the course of 1967 and 1968, during which time the NCSD was reconstructed, a new organ to supervise science policy under the National Security Council was created, the Ministry of Economic Affairs invited a group of Western scientific and technical advisers to evaluate and make recommendations on Taiwan's S&T situation, and—to cap off all of these changes—a twelve-year plan for science development (which will be described in Chapter 4) was promulgated. During the same period of time, the rhetoric of S&T became increasingly popular among Taiwan's political leaders, who began a low-level propaganda campaign that would boost interest in S&T in Taiwan and also serve their domestic, regional, and global political interests.

There is institutional and rhetorical evidence that between 1965 and 1969 the state was beginning to internalize many of the earlier suggestions of the United States and UNESCO regarding the importance of science and technology to economic and social modernization. It is important to note, however, that not all parts of the state absorbed or acted upon these ideas to an equal degree or in the same way. As we saw in Chapter 1, these ideas had already been adopted to a considerable extent during the wartime period, but they had subsequently become less important to the KMT state. This shift in the attitude of various parts of the state toward S&T in the 1965 to 1969 period, therefore, represents a revival of practices and perceptions that the same state had already experimented with in somewhat, yet not wholly, different circumstances and suggests that the KMT state was most likely to take on a proactive and developmental role with respect to S&T development during times of comparative crisis.

Industrial Development and the Increasing Importance of S&T

Until the mid-1960s, Taiwan's economic bureaucracy under the KMT had focused most of its efforts on improving agricultural output, rebuilding the Japanese transportation infrastructure, and encouraging the growth of essential industries, all with the aim of making Taiwan truly self-sufficient. The time had, perhaps, not been right for concerted state efforts at developing S&T. As K. T. Li, minister of economic affairs, and himself a physicist by training, noted in a 1964 speech to the Sino-American Conference on Scientific Cooperation, "The immediate and deepest concern to the Government and industry in the early years of Taiwan's postwar economic reconstruction was increased production, rather than increased productivity through know-how, in order to enlarge the flow of goods into the island economy suffering from severe shortages of goods of every description and mounting pressures of inflation. Under such circumstances, the producer had no urge to improve the quality of his products or raise the operating efficiency of his plant."[1] By the mid-1960s, these early goals had been reached. At the same time, the large influx of U. S. aid that had sustained Taiwan's economy through the 1950s and early 1960s was petering out. Given these circumstances, it was only logical that Taiwan's economic bureaucracy should, in the early 1960s, start encouraging the development of an export economy that could help to replace the foreign income that would be lost with the end of U.S. aid. This meant giving "increasing attention to quality control, cost reduction, technical changes and other factors making for higher productivity."[2] Work along these lines was supported by the Ministry of Economic Affairs' Industrial Planning and Coordinating Group, which, as a part of this shift in economic goals, began subsidizing some limited industrial research in the very early 1960s.[3]

At first, Taiwan's exports were mostly surplus products from existing industries that had already saturated Taiwan's market. Before long, however, economic planners were identifying new opportunities to invite foreign capital into Taiwan to develop new industries. The presence of new multinational industries not only would mean an influx of foreign capital but also might lead to technology transfer and the emergence of indigenous industries in the same sectors. Certainly low labor and other costs as well as low environmental protection standards made Taiwan an appealing venue for construction of new plants by large multinational corporations such as Dow Chemical.

However, as Taiwan's economic planners were to realize, to be truly attractive to multinational corporations and well placed to take advantage of the spin-off benefits of these industries, Taiwan would require a larger pool of skilled S&T manpower and a more advanced scientific and technological environment than it had at that time. In fact, evidence that economic planners were cognizant of the potential relevance of S&T education and planning to economic development can be found as early as 1961, when K. T. Li delivered a speech to the Joint Commission on Rural Reconstruction on human resource development in which he observed that "with the intensification of industrial competition in the post-war years, scientists, engineers and other professional personnel capable of bringing about changes and improvements in technology have become the most wanted of all human resources."[4] It was imperative, he continued, for Taiwan to "become self-sufficient in human resources to absorb and adapt the technology already imported, in order to be able to eventually stand firmly on our own."[5] It took until 1965 for even Taiwan's economic planners to begin to take the first steps in this direction, however.

By 1965 the Ministry of Economic Affairs, headed by K. T. Li, had become interested in proactively promoting scientific and technical development in Taiwan and began to encourage and participate in government efforts to improve S&T education, research, and overall science policy. As Taiwan's industrial trajectory began to shift in the mid- to late 1960s, the state's economic planners became increasingly conscious of the role that S&T manpower, knowledge, skills, and innovation would eventually play in Taiwan's economic development and began to place more and more emphasis on the construction of institutions and plans that could improve Taiwan's S&T education and research environment and make it as relevant as possible to industrial development. As a result, in the 1965–1969 period, we can see the gradual emergence of an overarching science policy in the ROC on Taiwan that neither the academicians nor the foreign advisers of the early to mid-1960s had managed to implement.

Taiwan's economy needed to reach a certain level of development before state planners were willing to begin encouraging the state to invest in S&T. However, industrial development was not the only catalyst for the shift that took place in the late 1960s. Unlike the economic planners, ROC political leaders appear to have been motivated much more by regional and international political concerns than by the notion that to press for further investment in S&T was simply the next logical step on the road to development.

1965: A Turning Point for the State

The year 1965 was an important turning point in terms of the evolution of the ROC's commitment to support of S&T development, but not because it had reached a level of economic development that required more S&T manpower or research in order to continue growing and also not because it had finally decided to start listening to the advice of American advisers or Taiwan's academic community. The major catalyst for the shift in state priorities was the PRC's test of a uranium bomb in October 1964, an act that was followed two years later by, first, a guided-missile test in October 1966 and, then, a test of a thermonuclear device in December 1966. The initial news of the atomic bomb test stimulated a series of new initiatives by the Ministries of Defense, Education, and Economic Affairs over the course of 1965.

Taiwan's military establishment immediately created the new Chungshan Institute of Scientific Research "to promote scientific research for national defense."[6] The institution was initially given three research tasks: peaceful uses of nuclear energy, study of rockets and missiles, and application of electronics.[7] In the same year, the Ministry of Education began to articulate a new interest in reshaping education to better suit the needs of the economy by encouraging the development of vocational education. According to the *Free China Review,* C. H. Yen, minister of education, said in the spring of 1965 that education in the ROC still had not been adapted to the economy and this needed to be rectified. His plans for this included the move from six to nine years of compulsory education and the construction of a five-year vocational school program.[8]

In late 1965, in a first effort to unite various parts of government to discuss the development of S&T, the Ministries of Economic Affairs, Education, and National Defense jointly convened the ROC's first national science conference. Specific sessions were held over four days on research and development, mobilization of manpower, national defense, and industrial expansion, and the conference yielded a series of specific recommendations including making science training more relevant to defense needs, finding solutions to the shortage of science teachers, pay increases for scientists, and the construction of a national science policy committee. Both President Chiang Kai-shek and Premier C. K. Yen spoke at the conference, Chiang urging "the training of more scientific personnel . . . [and that] schools and industry . . . close ranks for a full utilization of science in the national cause."[9] Though somewhat vague, Chiang's remarks are clear enough to show that by late 1965 the ROC's political leadership was aware that there was a link between science and industry and that development of that relationship might in some way contribute to nation building.

C. K. Yen gave shape to Chiang's remarks in the opening address of the conference on November 2, 1965, in which he posed the question, "How can we improve and strengthen our research in science and technology so as to best suit our nation-building and military development needs?" In the same address, Yen made it clear that he hoped that the conference participants would use the conference to come up with "a set of policies that will become the future direction and plan for the development of science and technology."[10] The conference was clearly conceived of as an opportunity to group government officials and scientists together to create policy with respect to coordination of education, defense, and industry.

Yen went on to observe that this was the first meeting of its kind and to lament that China (by which he clearly meant both the mainland and Taiwan) was not keeping pace with other nations in terms of scientific development. Scientific development, he argued, would be important for both rebuilding the mainland, after retaking it, and building Taiwan. His speech was infused with an urgency about the development of S&T rooted in the sense that Taiwan had just not made enough effort and that if it could not keep up with other nations, the consequences might be dire, especially with respect to national defense. Not only was national security at stake, Yen argued; it was also the case that inadequate efforts were being put into developing science for industrial and business purposes.[11] As Yen stated, "All farsighted industrialists will certainly increasingly emphasize the development of research and happily support it. But the big problem now is how to advance the relationship between industry and science and technology."[12] The new and intense urgency with which Chiang and Yen spoke of the need to improve S&T can only be read as a somewhat panicked reaction to the PRC's acquisition of nuclear weapons. Suddenly the realm of S&T had become a battleground in a way that KMT political leaders, at any rate, had not previously understood it to be. The First Science Meeting was held to identify a battle plan.

Though many of the topics of discussion at the meeting were the same ones that the NCSD had been discussing for years (improvement of research facilities, better pay, etc.), two important new directions emerged from the First Science Conference. First was the recognition that the government had the power to influence S&T development through policy. Attendees observed that economic growth resulted from scientific development of new knowledge and was the benefit of investment in scientific research. Long-term national economic plans, therefore, needed to take into account the impact of technical progress and to consider the need for increased investment in S&T.[13]

Second was the acknowledgment that science and technology formed an essential foundation for both the military and economic strength of a nation and that science policy should therefore be planned by a specially designated body of people equipped to understand and develop the linkages between these diverse areas.[14] There was considerable debate over just what this science policy body should look like and where it should be placed. Conferees discussed both a comprehensive restructuring of the NCSD and the possible implementation of foreign models. Platt's suggestions (discussed in Chapter 2) appear to have been taken seriously by this group; in addition, both the Japanese and British models of centralized science policy construction were discussed as alternatives.[15] In the end, a new body was created a little over a year after the conference in the form of the National Security Council's Supervisory Committee for Science Development.

The First Science Meeting took place in late November 1965. Over the course of the following two years a series of major and minor linked initiatives to promote S&T were taken by the ROC government. Among the minor initiatives was one that resonated with the sorts of science activities that the KMT had promoted in the 1940s. In the summer of 1966 a summer youth program on science was created by the China Youth Corps.[16] Of somewhat greater import was the autumn 1966 establishment by the Executive Yuan of the Zhongzheng (Chung Cheng) Science and Technology Research Chairs Foundation, whose aim was to endow eighty research chairs at ROC colleges and universities.[17]

The Creation of the Committee for Science Development

By far the most significant among the state's new science initiatives was the creation, in accordance with the recommendations of the First Science

Meeting, of a new science planning committee under the control of the National Security Council. This new committee, the Supervisory Committee for Science Development of the National Security Council *(kexue zhidao weiyuanhui)*, was created in March 1967 and was given the responsibility of making S&T policy recommendations to the president.[18] The placement of the new committee under the National Security Council suggests that its first priority would be matters of national defense, as does the fact that its first head, Wu Dayou, was a physicist. While defense-related S&T was clearly among the concerns of the new committee, it is telling that the first series of recommendations that Wu Dayou and the Committee for Science Development made to the government were centered on the same kinds of practical issues that had theretofore plagued the NCSD, such as improving the salaries of academics.[19] On the one hand, the basic problems still needed to be addressed before any big plans could be considered. On the other hand, perhaps the Committee for Science Development was not, at least at first, much more farsighted than the NCSD had been.

In fact, in spite of its name, according to the *China Yearbook*, the National Security Council itself was intended to be a planning organ. It was "in charge of research, design, coordination, supervision and evaluation in the formulation of major policies."[20] Likewise, the Committee for Science Development was also intended as a planning committee. In addition, the membership of the Committee for Science Development also suggested that it would not be exclusively concerned with defense matters. Members of the committee included Minister of Economic Affairs K. T. Li, Minister of Education C. H. Yen, Minister of National Defense Chiang Ching-kuo (Chiang Kai-shek's son and the future president of the ROC), and a number of highly placed scientists, several of whom were physicists and two of whom were at Qinghua University, home of the ROC's only academic program in nuclear physics.[21] The presence of both K. T. Li and C. H. Yen on the Committee for Science Development signaled the expectation that the new committee would produce comprehensive science policy that truly engaged both academia and industry as well as national defense.

By June 1969, if not earlier, the Committee for Science Development had expanded its role well beyond anything that the NCSD had ever managed. Wu Dayou was by that time making statements that clearly showed the broad planning role of the Committee for Science Development and that moved it beyond the small issues it had started out with. At the same time, the Committee for Science Development was operating in the coordinating role that both Academia Sinica's *Pingyihui* and the NCSD had been intended to perform, helping to construct plans to link the economy, defense, and education. From the state's perspective, it made sense to have a more state-oriented organ play this role (just as it had when the Science and Technology Planning Committee was created for similar purposes in the early 1940s). As Wu noted in the spring of 1969, science from the perspective of a nation is a different thing than science from the perspective of scientists. From a national perspective, science is important insofar as it relates to the needs of society in areas like education, the economy, and national defense. Within the structure of the National Security Council, according to Wu, larger plans for nation building *(guojia jianshe)* came under the purview of the Building and Planning Committee *(Jianshe jihua weiyuanhui).* The role of the Committee for Science Development was to come up with S&T plans that would be consistent with the larger plans constructed by the Building and Planning Committee. The Committee for Science Development was not actually under the leadership of the Building and Planning Committee, but the most important function of the Committee for Science Development was planning, and the plans that it constructed had to fit into larger national development plans.[22]

The ROC had thrice before created organs designed to coordinate S&T education and research and link them to national development needs. Of these, the most effective had been the temporary Science and Technology Planning Committee of the 1940s. Academia Sinica's *Pingyihui* had experienced only a relatively brief period of meaningful service along these lines in the mid- to late 1930s, and its national planning function had more or less been taken over by the NCSD upon its creation in the late 1950s. As we saw in Chapter 2, however, the NCSD had been so ineffective as a national S&T planning organ that foreign experts like Platt, Byerly, and Kidd hardly recognized it as such. Their calls for the construction of a science planning committee in 1964 clearly influenced the ROC's executive branch in its decision to construct the Committee for Science Development. The very prominent placement of the Committee for Science Development within the government structure, moreover, indicated that this new committee would be taken more seriously and would thus be able to construct more meaningful plans than its more academic predecessors.

When the new committee was formed, neither the *Pingyihui* nor the NCSD was abandoned, though both were rendered meaningless in terms of any planning or coordinating functions that had originally been intended for them. Just what to do with the NCSD was in fact an early agenda item for the Committee for Science Development, which was given the authority to restructure the NCSD and take over responsibility for guiding it. According to Wu Dayou, who seemed to be trying to find face-saving rationales for why the NCSD should be substantially restructured and placed under the new committee, society had progressed to the point that the NCSD was no longer relevant in its current form. Moreover, he went on to say, the resignation of Wang Shijie as head of the NCSD at a time when Wang was retaining his position as president of Academia Sinica was forcing a revision of the bylaws of the NCSD. While praising the NCSD for its contributions to the development of science in the ROC in terms of support for institutional development and individual scholars, overseas training for researchers, and invitation of visiting professors, Wu also noted that several criticisms could be made of the way in which the NCSD had operated. For instance, it had been criticized for overemphasizing basic science and underemphasizing social sciences, humanities, and applied sciences. This tendency, he rationalized, was partly due to the mission of the institution that had—as a long-range program—aimed to build a foundation, and basic sciences can be seen as foundational, but it could also be explained by a lack of resources. The NCSD had also been criticized for being too heavily controlled by Academia Sinica. Wu's solution to these problems was to allow the NCSD to continue to administer and develop the programs that it had already implemented but to place it under the Committee for Science Development. In August 1967, as a result of these discussions, the NCSD was restructured and renamed the National Science Council (NSC). It was also given a substantial budget increase, NT$92 million for 1967–1968.[23]

With the creation of the Committee for Science Development and the restructuring of the NCSD, the ROC now had a clearer and more streamlined institutional strategy for guiding science policy and building the science infrastructure. The first line of policymaking would be the Committee for Science Development, which would construct and oversee long-range and large-scale S&T plans that would be coordinated with other sorts of national development plans coming out of the National Security Council or other government organs. The concrete implementation of specific recommendations of those plans might be carried out by a number of institutions, but the most likely would be the Ministry of Education and the NSC. Less clear, however, was just what the new national science policy should look like and how it would be connected to economic development.

The Hornig Mission

To assist in the exploration of this question, K. T. Li and the Committee for Science Development collaborated through the spring and summer of 1967 to organize the Hornig Mission of September 1967. This mission was made up of a group of S&T experts from the United States. The participants were expected to evaluate Taiwan's level of S&T development and to make recommendations on how, in particular, to improve on the integration of S&T into the educational and industrial sectors. The Hornig Mission helped to define the shape of the new relationship between the United States and the ROC in the post-aid era. It also offered advice that in many respects shaped ROC science policy for the coming years. In addition, it served as a prototype for what would in the late 1970s become the Science and Technology Advisory Group (STAG), thus establishing an important pattern of interaction between ROC planners and the international business community that eventually led to the direct involvement of ROC businessmen in S&T planning.

The Hornig Mission was the direct result of a May 1967 discussion between American president Lyndon Johnson and ROC premier C. K. Yen on "the need to strengthen science and technology in the ROC as a vital force in national and regional development."[24] Its role was to evaluate universities, research institutes, and industries (and it thus had a broader scope than the earlier mission by Joseph Platt). Its participants were drawn from both the private and the public sectors and, in addition to mission head Dr. Donald F. Hornig, special assistant to the president for S&T, included: Dr. Raymond Bowers, science adviser, Office of Science and Technology, Executive Office of the President; Dr. James B. Fisk, president of Bell Telephone Laboratories; Dr. Daniel F. Margolies, science adviser, Office of Science and Technology, Executive Office of the President; Dr. Albert H. Moseman, associate, Agricultural Development Council, New York; Dr. Bruce S. Old, of Arthur D. Little; William W. Thomas, economic officer, China Desk, U.S. Department of State; and Dr. Robert T. Webber, regional science attaché.

Prior to the mission, the Committee for Science Development had done a great deal of preparatory work, especially in the production of a series of highly self-critical briefs for mission participants. These briefs provided background information but also offered a preliminary set of evaluations of the state of education, particular types of industry, and so on. As such, they undoubtedly influenced the way in which mission participants approached their tasks. It is difficult to know precisely what the Committee for Science Development intended as it constructed such openly critical reports. The most likely possibility, however, is that Wu Dayou and his committee were hoping to guide the Hornig Mission toward conclusions that they, themselves, had already drawn and solutions that they were hoping to implement but for which they perhaps needed the backing of external evaluators.

The main concern of the Committee for Science Development was the failure of industry and academia to find ways to interact with each other. As one brief observed, "There is practically no interchange or coordination between the academic and the industrial activities. For this state of affairs, both the academic and the industrial men are responsible. There is a lack of understanding of the problems by both sides."[25] The reasons for this lack of understanding, according to Wu Dayou, were: "Firstly, our science was and still is so weak that we tended to emphasize the basic sciences, both in teaching and research. We did not believe we had sufficient foundation in the basic sciences to really step into the modern research in the industries yet. Secondly, the kinds of light industries developed so far in Taiwan did not call for much research studies of an advanced nature. Thirdly, the industries have not yet appreciated the long-term benefit of supporting some research themselves. Lastly, there has been a lack of positive directions from our government."[26] More simply put, neither government nor industry was ready to sponsor or participate in such a relationship. Money, according to the Committee for Science Development, was the biggest obstacle to the development of a positive relationship between industry and academia, and the committee offered several suggestions, such as government subsidies and assistance from nongovernmental organizations (NGOs) and developed countries for jump-starting the process.[27]

In his welcoming remarks to the Hornig Mission, K. T. Li followed up on the self-critical tone of the Committee for Science Development's briefs and openly invited mission participants to engage in frank discussion of Taiwan's S&T situation. Echoing NCSD statements of the previous five or more years, he said, "Our efforts toward the development of science and technology are just beginning. They are, however, scattered, poorly organized, ill equipped, and understaffed." He went on to observe, "It is clear . . . that we will have to step up our efforts in the field of science and technology if we are to sustain our economic growth, or ever hope to narrow the income gap. This is especially true in consideration of the scarcity of natural resources on Taiwan."[28]

Like the Committee for Science Development, Li also pushed mission participants to think about the relationship between academia and industry, but his concern was over education's failure to meet industrial manpower needs rather than the academic research community's failure to connect to industry. The next economic plan, he observed, would promote development in electronics, petrochemicals, machinery and steel, and export processing, and as these industries grew, so would demand for technicians and engineers. To meet this demand, Li said, "the government has decided to upgrade manpower at three different levels. First, public schooling will be extended from six to nine years beginning next year. Second, technical training at both the universities and vocational schools will be further strengthened . . . Thirdly, the facilities and personnel of the research institutes will be effectively improved."[29] Li may have been boasting about what the ROC had already accomplished in the educational sector, but he was unquestionably also inviting participants to offer advice on manpower development as well as the topics that the Committee for Science Development had already laid out in the briefs.

The Hornig Mission addressed the questions of manpower production, coordination of academia and industry, and more, going well beyond the scope of these important but still rather superficial guidelines that Li and the Committee for Science Development had laid out. Hornig's initial comments indicated that he was prepared to approach the problem of how to further develop S&T in the ROC from a perspective very similar to his hosts'. "What's needed," he said, in a statement to the press, "is the dynamic situation in which one has the complete spectrum from pure scientists, applied scientists and engineers, economists and industrialists—all in close contact with each other, all in close communication with each other, and all working together toward national goals."[30]

Although all of the mission participants made useful suggestions, not all of them operated on precisely the same set of assumptions. Some, Hornig most prominent among them, advocated a highly centralized and planned approach to S&T development that would be characterized by strategic use and development of resources. Other mission members saw the looser approach that the United States had developed as an appropriate model. How, for instance, should the ROC best link S&T education and research to the real world? As Dr. Raymond Bowers pointed out, "One of the problems to which we must particularly address ourselves is how to stimulate here the involvement and interaction which exist in the US (although not always successfully) between universities, research organizations, and industry."[31] Bowers was clearly hoping to, in effect, reconstruct in Taiwan the sorts of patterns and processes that already existed in the United States. Hornig, on the other hand, clearly felt that however the ROC met this challenge, it could not do so in a manner identical to the United States because, for one thing, "smaller industries are typical here."[32] Applied research could not, therefore, be conducted within the industrial sector as easily as in the United States because few industries had the resources to support it.

Instead, Hornig argued that in the ROC S&T had to develop along planned lines and toward a set of very specific and clearly laid out objectives. As he observed, "A 'general' buildup without such objectives will not be very helpful." Hornig envisioned for the ROC a strategy of S&T development that would depend heavily on a well-informed S&T planning group with the capacity to identify concrete and attainable development goals. As he said, "Applied research and its relationship to industrial development must be considered as a response to specific needs and focused on problems which can be identified and delineated. The success of such research must be measured by its contribution to the solution of these problems."[33] From Hornig's perspective, the ROC would be unlikely to succeed in its attempts to further develop S&T that would serve the industrial sector without a coherent and centralized planning group to evaluate the specific needs of industry, to identify and delineate the problems, and to encourage applied research in appropriate areas.

As K. T. Li had hoped, members of the mission did give considerable attention to the question of manpower and offered advice on a wide range of matters relating to manpower development. Hornig, still following the line that the ROC needed a centralized planning organ, argued that it only made sense to funnel resources to the people who could do the most with them and that it was a waste of time and effort to attempt to spread them around fairly. Another suggestion was that the vocational education system needed to train more low-level technicians. The ROC's hierarchical civil service structure (used in government but to a limited extent in academia as well) also came under fire for failing to promote real talent.[34] These strategies all aimed at pushing ROC educators and bureaucrats alike toward a more innovative approach to valuing ability over age, seniority, or position.

Mission participants were especially critical of the education system, which Bowers said overemphasized rote memorization and suffered from an excessively rigid curriculum, and Hornig saw as having especially underdeveloped systems of technical and vocational education.[35] Not only did the education system itself need an overhaul, but a plan needed to be devised that would build connections between education and industry and help (or perhaps force) the educational system to train the sorts of manpower that industry actually needed. To remedy this situation, both Dr. Bruce Old and Dr. James Fisk suggested that the ROC develop a cooperative education program "with six months or so of academic education each year, followed by two months of direct industry experience, either during the school year or the summer."[36] In response, C. H. Yen, minister of education, noted that although people had been talking about establishing cooperative structures between education and industry for years, little had been done to realize the plans.[37] The problem, from his perspective, seemed to be in figuring out a way to actually implement such a program.

In addition to their evaluation of S&T in the ROC, and their suggestions for strategies for improving it, the Hornig Mission also pointed out that none of this could be done without a substantial investment. As some of the participants observed, developed countries usually spend 2 percent or more of their national income on research. According to Hornig, Taiwan should have been in a position to devote 1 percent to 2 percent of its national income to research in universities and industry.[38] Of this sum, only 10 to 20 percent should be devoted to basic research, Hornig said. The rest, he argued, needed to support industrial and other applied research, and for that to happen, the ROC clearly needed a new system to coordinate both public and private S&T research.[39]

At the end of the mission, participants met with Chiang Kai-shek, and Hornig took the opportunity to drive a few points home. The people he had met were thinking along the right lines, and saying the right things, but in the end, he said, success would depend on resources. The ROC's political leadership needed to start finding ways to finance S&T development. "The time," he said, "is right now to take new, forceful steps and the United States is prepared to assist. However, such steps will require a new commitment of resources by the Republic of China."[40] With the right sort of commitment from the state, however, a new post-aid cooperative relationship might be built between the ROC and the United States that could facilitate the ROC's S&T development.

The Hornig Mission brought to a head a set of processes that had been under way for at least the two years prior to it. It did so by clarifying in a very public way an argument that foreign observers and Taiwan's academic scientists had been making since the late 1950s. Hornig and his colleagues made every effort to state both for the benefit of the press, who reported widely on the mission, and the ROC's political leadership, with whom the mission met, that the moment had come for serious investment in S&T development. The mission also helped to position both the Committee for Science Development and K. T. Li to take a more proactive role in fostering S&T development in Taiwan.

The Hornig Mission yielded abundant advice for ROC economic and education planners on how to proceed with respect to S&T development, but perhaps the most important points made by Hornig and others were about the need for a substantial budget and the importance of constructing coordinated plans that considered the relationship between education, research, and industry. By the end of 1967, Wu Dayou was clearly showing that he had refined his earlier thoughts on S&T planning and assimilated the perspective articulated by the Hornig Mission. On New Year's Eve 1967, he laid out his "New Plans for Developing China's Science." In it, he wrote, "Planning scientific development from the perspective of national construction isn't just a matter of doing things like establishing one research institute, but is a matter of planning a whole system of science, technology, and application. The primary consideration in a discussion of this kind of problem is to decide upon the clear and definite policies and aims of the nation and to determine the scope and budget of scientific development in accordance with these policies and then concrete plans can be made." He went on to observe that one of the greatest obstacles to constructing a science development plan in the ROC was the uncertainty of its fiscal situation and the small size of the government budget. Projecting ahead, Wu outlined the likely distribution of resources for science development. He anticipated that roughly half of the money for science development would go to research in nuclear science, engineering, and technology, all of which were especially important to facilitate the rapid development of industry and the increasing demand for electricity. He projected that the other half of the money would go to university and technical school science education, research, research for national defense, and the NSC.[41] Thus we can see that both industry and national defense were important concerns for the new Committee for Science Development, though other than nuclear science, Wu still does not appear to have had a very specific set of sciences or technologies into which he planned to funnel funds.

Nonetheless, Wu clearly recognized that S&T development might happen in a number of sectors. To this end, the Committee for Science Development was working in cooperation with the Ministry of the Economy, the Ministry of Defense, the Farmer's Association *(Nongfuhui)*, and other groups to figure out exactly how to develop S&T in coordination with their particular plans. Wu was also clearly thinking in a way that the NCSD never had, about the larger planning and coordinating role that could be played by the Committee for Science Development. Planning, Wu understood, required coordinated effort involving a wide variety of government ministries, educational institutions, and research centers. Influenced by the Hornig Mission, Wu even went one step further and expressed his hope that the ROC business community would also involve themselves in this planning process.[42]

The mission also provided a potential new model of interaction between the ROC and the United States in the post-aid era, though one that would not be seriously utilized again (at least in the case of S&T development) until the late 1970s. Both the ROC and the United States seemed to be searching for a new pattern for their relationship, and as Hornig said, the United States was ready to help the ROC in this new period of its development. In the short run, K. T. Li certainly used Hornig's observation that a new cooperative structure needed to be worked out to facilitate technology transfer from the United States to Taiwan as a sort of leverage, as he wrote to Eugene R. Black, also a special S&T adviser to President Johnson, to request further U.S. attention to this point.[43] In fact, as mentioned in Chapter 2, a Sino-American Science Cooperation Program had been initiated in 1964 with an eye to establishing a structure to facilitate scientific cooperation in the post-aid era. This program became more formalized in 1969, owing almost certainly, to Hornig's advice, with an agreement between the ROC and the United States to establish a bilateral program administered by the ROC's NSC and the U.S. National Science Foundation designed to increase academic contacts and cooperation and facilitate the exchange of "information, ideas, skills and techniques."[44] As C. K. Yen observed of the new program, "I personally believe this science cooperation program between our countries is the logical follow-up after the discontinued American economic aid. The aid program enabled us to heal the war ravages in Taiwan and start our economic buildup. The science cooperation program, I am sure, will help preserve the economic achievements and further expand the fruits of the economic aid."[45]

The Hornig Mission was important for several reasons. First, as we have seen, it facilitated direct communication to Chiang Kai-shek and the KMT political leadership of the message of just how important S&T was to economic (and not just military) development. Chiang and Yen were probably more likely to take that message seriously if it were coming from elite U.S. scientists, some of whom had direct connections to the White House, than if it came from Taiwan's own economic planners. In addition, the timing of the mission could not have been better, coming as it did at a point when Chiang and Yen were already beginning, for other reasons, to become convinced of the need to promote scientific development. The Hornig Mission thus served an essential domestic propaganda purpose for economic and science planners who needed to convince political leaders of the importance of S&T. Second, the Hornig Mission helped to expand the vision of Taiwan's S&T leadership by giving them a broader and deeper set of goals toward which to work. Third, it helped to establish a basis for continued cooperation between the ROC and the United States in the post-aid era. Fourth, and this will be further explored in Chapter 5, it provided a model for later S&T development that involved solicitation and utilization of foreign advice. This model was used to great effect by K. T. Li in the late 1970s and beyond.

The Political Rhetoric of Science: Additional Motives for Promoting S&T

Thus far we have seen that the state was, indeed, becoming increasingly involved in the promotion of S&T through the mid-1960s. From the perspective of economic and education planners the principal underlying rationale for this shift appears to have been concern with promotion of rapid industrial and economic development. Planners such as K. T. Li and Wu Dayou, as we have observed, saw S&T as playing an indispensable role in the overall economic development process, and this sense of the interrelatedness of the two shaped their approach to the construction of plans and policies for the promotion of S&T in both the educational and industrial sectors. However, pragmatic economic concerns were not the sole reason that the state became an active promoter of S&T research and education. The ROC's political leaders were also developing an interest in S&T in the mid- to late 1960s for a rather different set of reasons.

Beginning in 1965, two of the ROC's leading political figures, President Chiang Kai-shek and Premier C. K. Yen, began consistently articulating political arguments related to their quest to strengthen their position vis-à-vis mainland China as important motivations for their support of science. Science, therefore, was taking on a new rhetorical significance at precisely the same moment that it was being identified by economic planners as an essential cog in the industrial wheel. Science became increasingly well defined and carefully considered by ROC development planners in the Ministry of Economic Affairs and the Committee for Science Development in the late 1960s, but it remained ill-defined even though often mentioned in the public utterances of the ROC political leadership. Just as one branch of the state was beginning to grasp precisely how important S&T was for economic development and modernization, the political branch began to employ a rhetoric that made science appear to be little more than a vague code word for *modern* and that turned S&T development into a political weapon to be used in propaganda battles against the PRC.

Like the other, more concrete state-sponsored S&T developments of 1965, this rhetorical development was triggered by the PRC's publicization of its development of nuclear weapons. With this event, the scientific arena suddenly became a contested space between PRC and ROC, and the ROC began to wage a propaganda war to demonstrate to the world that it was not only modern but responsible in its use of S&T.

In the spring of 1965, Chiang Kai-shek proclaimed, "Youths of the nation! Peiping's attempt to employ nuclear weapons as a means barbarously to extend aggression, to blackmail the whole world, does not stand for scientific progress. It only further attests to Mao Tse-tung's brute crimes of oppressing our mainland people and impoverishing them to the very limit. Mao's brutism, heartlessly intended for the destruction of mankind and diametrically opposed to the interest of science, is in absolute contravention to the peace-loving nature of the Chinese people."[46] According to Chiang, Mao was using science to oppress the Chinese people and to threaten the rest of the world.

> As we all know, the Chinese Communists have beggared the Chinese people with extortionary levies, and have pirated technical knowledge of science to expand their aggressions and threaten humanity with tests of atomic weapons . . . Their knowledge of science is an accomplishment of cruelty, and their progress is like a deformed person limping along on unequal legs. It is not, in reality, scientific knowledge per se; rather is it an anti-climax of science. Theirs is an inhuman, criminal science; while the science that we seek to develop aims at serving the paramount goals of

> national freedom and the people's welfare. We must stress the peaceful use of atomic energy to blaze a trail leading to scientific rehabilitation of our nation. Finally we must solemnly ask scientists and technicians in Communist areas to refuse to take any part in Mao Tse-tung's sinister works of science, and to sabotage nuclear installations intended for vicious aggressive purposes. Let all of us strive together to remove the obstacles to our unfinished Revolution and national recovery. This is the way to assure the bright scientific future of our youths as they work for the national good.[47]

From Chiang's perspective, Mao's was emphatically not a good use of science. The ROC under Chiang's leadership, however, was a benign and peaceful advocate of good science that promoted national development and well-being and threatened no one.

Science, though never well defined in Chiang's lexicon, had as early as the 1930s become one of the bedrock values upon which he hoped the Chinese nation would be built. Most important, a scientific approach to life for Chiang represented a modern approach to life: "The development of science depends upon four elements: 'strict honesty, accumulation of established truths, energetic application, and long-enduring persistence.' Only in this way can we utilize our knowledge and wisdom for the good of the country. The level of our scientific development for peaceful purposes is steadily rising, and our youths' determined efforts to reconstruct the nation by means of science are gaining momentum and efficacy."[48] Science was not something to be studied but a method of living.

As China's Cultural Revolution got under way in 1966, Chiang's references to the value of promoting science took on yet another meaning. Unlike Mao, Chiang saw himself as promoting a good kind of science that would, among other things, protect and defend Chinese culture. As he noted, "Today young people on the mainland are pledging themselves to resist Mao Tse-tung; their unshakable resolve is rooted in traditional Chinese national dedication to morality, democracy, and science."[49] Science thus stood in opposition to Mao and Maoism. As he promoted the 1966 Cultural Renaissance Movement, a direct response to the Cultural Revolution in China, Chiang simultaneously urged students "to help safeguard China's 5,000-year-old culture" and called "for emphasis on science" as they did so.[50]

In August 1967 Chiang still saw science as a contested space between the PRC and the ROC. In a speech to the Committee to Promote the Chinese Cultural Renaissance, he observed that "the Republic of China is developing science for peaceful purposes and for the advancement of Chinese culture, while the Chinese Communists are using science to destroy Chinese culture and world peace."[51] C. K. Yen echoed these sentiments in a 1968 speech to the Conference on Sino-American Science Cooperation: "Since the Chinese Government moved its seat to Taiwan, it has tried hard to make the island a model province of China. While the Peiping bogus regime is milking the people to the last drop in its mad race to build a nuclear arsenal, we in the Republic of China are turning to science for help in our economic buildup and social development so that the fruits of scientific work may be enjoyed by all."[52] The ROC aimed, therefore, not only to preserve Chinese culture but to advance it—and what better way to do so than to embrace scientific modernization?

W. Tozer, in a 1970 analysis of the Cultural Renaissance Movement, argued that the movement itself represented a new commitment to wholehearted modernization and portrayed Chiang as a convert to the new dogma of science, a dogma to which he had merely been paying lip service before.[53] Chiang's late 1960s references to science, however, suggest that his conversion (if, indeed, it was one) was a pragmatic one, spurred as much as anything by a desire to keep the PRC from gaining any edge. Nonetheless, on a purely practical level, the Cultural Revolution had created an opportunity for Chiang and the KMT by making mainland China temporarily unrecoverable and turning ROC politicians' attention toward the development of Taiwan. As Chiang said to participants in the Hornig Mission, the government was taking advantage of the moment to focus on Taiwan and to build a series of new institutions, including the Committee for Science Development.[54] The rhetorical shift of the political leadership and the institutional developments pushed by KMT planners create the overwhelming impression that the ROC in the late 1960s was committing itself firmly to building Taiwan's economy on a foundation of high-level science and technology even if the language the political leaders used to advocate S&T remained vague.

As we have seen, not all parts of the ROC government were talking about science and technology in precisely the same way in the late 1960s. The KMT political leadership took a rather vague and highly politicized rhetorical approach, whereas state planners were more concrete and focused on the relationship between S&T and industrial development. But it is also apparent that in a variety of ways and for a diverse set of reasons S&T had been identified as a key to modernization by both groups, and state sponsorship of science was being described and truly understood as a marker of modernity. As absurd as Chiang Kai-shek's rantings about science and modernity may seem when juxtaposed against the more economically logical and pragmatic comments of K. T. Li and Wu Dayou about the value of S&T to economic development, they come from the same place. Both the political leadership and state planners became acutely aware of the role that could be played by S&T in development in 1965 and after, and the institutional and rhetorical shifts that we see in the period between 1965 and 1969 are all evidence of this. From that point on, the importance of S&T in general and of state planning of S&T in particular were never questioned by the ROC leadership, and the quantity of resources the ROC government committed to S&T constantly grew.

The mid- to late 1960s was the right moment for this shift for a variety of reasons. Domestically, Taiwan's industrial development was on the verge of becoming more sophisticated, and Taiwan's economic planners were well aware that this could not happen in the absence of an adequate supply of well-trained S&T manpower. Taiwan's economy had also reached a point where it could begin to sustain a certain amount of investment in S&T, and so the state was in a better position to support S&T initiatives. Moreover, as a new post-aid showcase of successful development, Taiwan undoubtedly felt pressure to demonstrate that it could continue to modernize its economy on its own. At the same time, Taiwan was clearly looking for a new, post-aid model of interaction with the United States, and scientific cooperation was one vehicle through which Taiwan could continue to reap concrete benefits from its relationship with the United States. Regionally, with respect to China, Taiwan was responding to the pressure created by China's acquisition of nuclear weapons and attempting to display itself as both a political and economic alternative to the radical, anticapitalist Maoism of the 1966–1969 period in the PRC.

The PRC's acquisition of nuclear weapons, the cessation of U.S. aid, and Taiwan's own economic breakthrough, all of which happened at roughly the same time, served as catalysts for a significant shift in the state's approach to promotion of S&T. As had been the case in the 1940s, crisis, or at least a sense of impending crisis, led the state to change. Beginning in the late 1960s, the ROC began to redefine itself in rhetorical terms as a modern, peace-loving nation that at the same time protected and preserved what was good about Chinese culture. An important facet of this self-definition was the idea that the state, unlike the Maoist state, was promoting peaceful economic development that would be built on a foundation of high-level S&T. The S&T institutional developments of the late 1960s demonstrate that this was not merely a rhetorical stance. The KMT state was actively trying to build institutions and plans to enable it to effectively harness S&T for its own economic (and presumably military) benefit. As we shall see in Chapters 4 and 5, more institutional changes were needed, but the transition of the late 1960s was an important starting point.

Without the sense of crisis, ROC political leaders might well have continued along the same path they were on. They might not have chosen to see the importance of S&T to economic development or the need for state investment in S&T to further economic development. Crisis primed the pump, but even so Taiwan's economic planners still felt they needed to employ American advisers to help them make the case for greater state investment in S&T. As we have seen, K. T. Li and Wu Dayou carefully orchestrated the Hornig Mission in the hope that at their final meeting with Chiang Kai-shek members of the mission would advocate for the right things. In fact, the Hornig Mission took the ball and ran further with it than Li and Wu probably imagined they would, and this proved to be helpful in the coming years. Not only was the Hornig Mission important in its own time, but—as we shall see in Chapter 5—it later served as an important model for further S&T institutional reform in the late 1970s.

— 4 —

Coordinating Policy: Manpower Planning and Education

Between 1965 and 1969 a new set of institutions and patterns of interaction between these and existing institutions were developed in the ROC that laid the fundamental institutional framework for the emergence of a coordinated science policy. The web that would link the various institutions was planning, which, as Hornig Mission participants had noted, needed to be strategic and detailed. Between the mid-1960s and the mid-1970s, ROC science development plans did, indeed, become more comprehensive, more specific, and thus more effective than earlier plans related to scientific development had been. We can see evidence of this by looking, in the first instance, at manpower planning, an area that the ROC's Council for International Economic Cooperation and Development (CIECD) took an interest in beginning in 1964, and, in the second instance, at the science development plan that the Committee for Science Development began to implement in 1969.

At the very least, the mere existence of these plans indicates that the state was becoming increasingly committed to science development and especially to development of the kind of scientific and technical manpower that could serve industrial needs. The fact that after 1969 manpower development and science plans were all part of the larger structure of state economic planning also shows that at the planning level, at any rate, there was much greater coordination between various parts of the government than there had previously been. However, a second obstacle continued to plague state planners, and that was the inability of planners to build an integrated relationship between the educational system and the non-state-owned industrial sector. Science education, a key component of both manpower and science development planning, did become more focused and increasingly relevant to economic development after 1969, but even so, observers still criticized education, and especially higher education, for failing to train students to meet the real demands of the job market as late as the early 1980s. The state's failures with respect to S&T education planning, therefore, had little or nothing to do with the state's ability to control or interact with the industrial sector and everything to do with the state's inability to control and guide higher education, which was clearly the domain of the state.

Planning

As we have seen, the construction of new institutions (the Committee for Science Development and the NSC) was one fundamental component of the evolution of the ROC's commitment to promotion of S&T, but for these new centralized coordinating institutions to be of much use, they had to be able to construct and successfully implement plans of relevance to economic development. The need for science planning had been recognized by at least some members of China's political and scientific leadership as early as 1927 when Academia Sinica's *Pingyihui* was first designed, again in the 1940s, and yet again in the late 1950s, but until the late 1960s the necessary infrastructure and general will had never been in position to make plans involving education and research succeed. Other sorts of plans, however, had been successfully implemented on Taiwan prior to the late 1960s.

The ROC began to design large-scale economic development plans fairly soon after its resettlement on Taiwan, this time with considerably greater success than it had had on the mainland, perhaps in part because ROC economic planners in the 1950s and early 1960s were accountable to the United States, the source of most of the resources with which they implemented their plans. Beginning in 1953, the ROC state on Taiwan constructed a series of four-year plans for economic development. Although the first plan, according to Robert Wade, "was little more than a collection of projects already underway," the second plan, from 1958 to 1961, actually "gave targets for the overall rates of growth of national income and investment, and for the share of investment going to the major sectors . . . [and] specified the fiscal and monetary policies which were to improve the investment climate."[1] By the time of the third and fourth plans in the 1960s, Taiwan's economic planners were beginning to emphasize the development of heavy industry, and by the mid-1970s the orientation was toward higher-tech industrial development.[2] Taiwan's economic plans were increasingly responsive to the shifting global economy, forward looking, and targeted at specific development aims.

As Taiwan's economic plans became more complex and sophisticated, their success depended increasingly on the success of various sub- or component plans, such as plans to improve the quality of the labor force and plans to promote the injection of more science and technology into society and economy. The need for these component plans was becoming increasingly apparent to Taiwan's economic planners by the mid-1960s, and it is certainly not coincidental that one of the biggest points made by most, if not all, of the foreign advisers invited to Taiwan in the mid-1960s was that the ROC needed to make broadly coordinated plans that nonetheless had a high level of specificity with respect to goals and that paid attention to the details of implementation.[3] Taiwan's earliest manpower plans and earliest comprehensive S&T plans were both undertaken beginning in the late 1960s.

Manpower Planning

By the early 1960s the authors of ROC economic development plans, especially K. T. Li, were becoming increasingly aware that economic development required appropriately trained manpower. By 1961, therefore, Li was emphasizing the need for the ROC to construct manpower development plans that would respond to and serve the economic development plans. It took some time, however, to sort out precisely what manpower should mean. In a 1961 address, Li, himself, acknowledged the difficulty of defining scientific manpower. On the one hand, he emphasized the importance of S&T professionals to economic development: "with the intensification of industrial competition in the post-war years, scientists, engineers and other professional personnel capable of bringing about changes and improvements in technology have become the most wanted of all human resources." For planning purposes, however, developing countries needed to recognize that highly specialized researchers would be less in demand than broadly trained talent. "We are," he observed, "instead of carrying on basic scientific research or contributing to fundamental scientific knowledge, all devoting ourselves to adaptation of the knowledge and technology of the industrially advanced countries. In so doing, we need trained talent to erect more new factories and plants, to fill the newly created managerial and supervisory posts, and to select and train operatives and foremen through systematic procedures."[4] Manpower development in the context of the ROC, therefore, should mean both training elite scientists and training a large group of skilled and semiskilled workers and managers.

Implicit in Li's observations is that the educational system must respond to the manpower needs of the nation and that this could only happen with proper planning. Following this line of argument, Li proposed a scheme of formulating economic development plans, projecting the manpower requirements of the plans, and shaping the educational system to ensure that it filled these needs. To do this well, however, might mean not doing universal education well, and Li acknowledged that a balance would have to be struck. It also required that the education authorities be able to come up with the necessary teaching talent to make it work; however, Li did not seem in 1961 to anticipate that this might be a difficulty for Taiwan.[5]

Though Li was talking about the need to construct manpower plans in the early 1960s, there was no big push along those lines until the mid-1960s when the NCSD, at the urging of Joseph Platt, and Premier C. K. Yen, responding to a Stanford Research Institute (SRI) report on education and development commissioned by the Ministry of Education at the urging of U.S. advisers, both set up separate manpower development initiatives. These two initiatives, however, were based on different understandings of what manpower was.[6] The academicians and members of the Ministry of Education emphasized training of elite scientists, and the CIECD's Manpower Development Committee (MDC), established by C. K. Yen, was concerned with both training of elites and development of a broad base of skilled workers. At the outset, then, competing definitions of manpower were at play, and there was no common understanding among academic and economic planners of just what it meant to develop manpower in Taiwan.

The NCSD's manpower plan was inspired by a desire to solve the elite brain drain problem, a difficulty that Platt and other advisers had been urging Taiwan to deal with since at least the early 1960s. In January 1965, as part of its overall four-year plan, the NCSD proposed a four-year "Scientific Manpower Development Program" that described itself as "a proposal to establish a four-year program for strengthening the development of the scientific manpower which is urgently needed for social and economic development in the Republic of China."[7] The program's objectives were "to build up highly qualified scientific and technological manpower by establishing efficient and well-equipped research centers; . . . to reduce the exodus of talented youth and scientists from the country; . . . [and] . . . to provide the country with a steady supply of competent scientists and highly trained technological manpower."[8] The cornerstone of the program was to be the creation of five new research institutes in the sciences that would concentrate the best human and other resources in the island on research projects and, more important, train graduate students.

As noted in Chapter 2, one of the principal U.S. advisers to the NCSD was Joseph B. Platt, who presented a paper in March 1965 at a conference on international development titled "Emigration of Scholars and the Development of Taiwan: Chinese-American Cooperation." In it he described Taiwan's high-level scientific manpower problem and addressed both the manpower survey and the five research centers (both mentioned in Chapter 2) as answers to that problem. The brain drain, he argued, had serious implications, and the need to establish these centers was critical.[9]

Repeating a common refrain among Taiwan's academicians, Platt argued that conditions in Taiwan were so bad for elite scientific researchers and educators that the failure of students abroad to return to Taiwan after finishing their studies was completely understandable.

> The best of the graduates, academically, are granted scholarships for study abroad, either by the Government or by foreign graduate schools. Currently, about 2,000 per year are leaving for graduate study abroad. Furthermore, most stay there. The number who return to Taiwan after completing their graduate studies abroad is uncertain, but it is around 5 percent. The net outcome of the training, then, of the ablest of the young people on Taiwan is to provide scientific and technical manpower for other countries, primarily the United States. This loss of talent presents a critical problem. One can understand the reasons for the failure to return. The young man with a Ph.D. joining the faculty of a university in Taiwan receives a salary of from US $50 to 100 per month, including all the fringe benefits. He can command about five times that salary in Hong Kong or Singapore or ten times that salary in the United States. Furthermore, in the United States he has equipment and colleagues and consequently can stay in contact with the most recent developments in his chosen field of study. In China, however, if he is to get a salary in the upper range I mentioned, he will hold at least two jobs and teach perhaps 18 hours a week.[10]

To resolve this problem, according to Platt, "what the Government of the Republic of China hopes to do is to create a sufficiently attractive situation for the ablest of its scientifically inclined young people, so that there will be a valid professional career for them on the island. As Dr. Li Chi [head of

Academia Sinica's Institute of History and Philology] puts it, 'At the moment, the only real choice they have, if they wish to practice their profession, is to leave Taiwan. We would like some of these people to help us build the Chinese economy in Taiwan.'"[11] This could be accomplished, Platt suggested, by using the manpower survey as a basis for planning educational priorities and creating the five research centers. By putting resources into higher education, in particular, the ROC government would embark on a path that was likely to facilitate development. Platt's words echoed the sentiments of the authors of the SRI report, Charles Kidd, and others. "This loss of the cream of the talent in the sciences presents a critical problem for the effort to develop the Chinese economy. In the first place, these people are needed to maintain the educational system itself . . . In the educational pyramid, each person at a particular level of training is responsible for the education and continuing growth of several people at the next lower level. Some part of the normal university production at the doctoral level is needed, at present, just to maintain, and hopefully to raise, the general standard of education. Secondly, there is an immediate industrial demand for trained people, who are very hard to find."[12] Platt clearly saw the centers as having multiple functions. They would train elite scientists, who could conduct research in both academic and industrial capacities, but they would also have a trickle-down effect on the quality of scientific education at all levels.

Both the NCSD and Platt had high hopes for the role that the five research centers would play in resolving Taiwan's manpower crisis. The centers would both provide a stimulating research environment to which overseas Chinese scientists might be induced to return and function as a domestic training ground for additional highly skilled scientists who would be able to contribute to higher education and research in the ROC. Moreover, the centers would (and did) serve as a good vehicle for attracting foreign aid and government funds to the research sciences, and this would improve the position of those few research scientists who were already working in the ROC.

Wang Shijie, then head of both Academia Sinica and the NCSD, made clear use of Platt's arguments in a memo to the Ford Foundation titled "On Proposed Visiting Professorships to Help Stop Brain Drain in Taiwan." The memo opens with a section titled "A Critical Problem" and argues that "the large-scale outflow of trained personnel and promising young scientists and scholars in response to higher incentives and better research environment in economically advanced countries has become a common problem of all developing nations. In the case of Taiwan, the so-called 'brain drain' has reached alarming proportions. We are losing about 2,000 college graduates, roughly one sixth of our annual crop, to the United States every year at a time when our scientific, technological and economic development has reached a point where the demand for personnel with advanced training is escalating."[13] The answer to this problem was the construction of the five research centers, which the NCSD did, in fact, establish in 1965 with the expectation that they would provide places in which academic researchers could work and where young researchers could be trained, thereby serving the dual purpose of stemming the brain drain and training new scientific and technical manpower to serve the developing economy. The research centers received little in the way of government funding, however, and were forced to make frequent applications to the U.S. government, UNESCO, and especially foreign funding agencies such as the Ford Foundation.

The NCSD's manpower development project thus concentrated on stemming the brain drain of the highly educated and training elite scientists. By contrast, the newly established MDC, which had been placed under the development-oriented CIECD, focused its efforts (or at least claimed to) on developing the broad base of skilled S&T manpower that would be needed to sustain more technologically demanding industrial development. The SRI report, which had stimulated the creation of the MDC in the first place, urged the ROC to construct a comprehensive plan for human resource development that would facilitate economic development after finding that "the economy in general is not absorbing students as fast as they are graduating" and that "to date there has been little planned coordination of education with the manpower requirements of the economy." The report also found that in spite of the ROC's professed emphasis on science education, "course content and recognition for student achievement most relevant to the skills and talents needed for economic development have too low a priority in comparison with traditional emphases in education."[14]

To alleviate the ROC's manpower problems, the SRI report recommended three general strategies: integration of education planning with development planning; improvement of the status of skilled and technical workers; and improvement of "the quality and economic relevance of education."[15] The new MDC, one member of which was the omnipresent K. T. Li, was created in response to these criticisms. Its main function through the late 1960s was to compile statistics and perform research that would form a basis for assessing manpower needs. Strategies for meeting these needs would then be worked into the ROC's economic development plans.

By 1969 the ROC's economic development plans (compiled by the CIECD) were all incorporating sections on manpower development. The CIECD's "Fifth Four-Year Plan for Economic Development of Taiwan, 1969–1972" included a twenty-three-page chapter on manpower development in which a "manpower development program" was described in considerable detail. The "manpower development program" had both long-term (ten-year) and medium-term (four-year) goals. Among the long-term goals were "promotion of the development of managerial skills, technological innovation and labor productivity"; improvement of educational facilities; improvement of the occupational structure; establishment of labor standards; increasing employment opportunities; and easing population pressure.[16] Short-term goals included implementing nine years of compulsory education; expanding technical and vocational education facilities; implementing a science development program; improving higher education; promoting cooperation between vocational schools and industry; setting up an employment agency; and a variety of improvements in labor and wage standards.[17]

The program also projected concrete numbers of additional teachers that would be needed for all subjects and laid out a strategy for retraining existing teachers. The largest number of new instructors would be needed to teach Chinese (as improving literacy remained a fundamental goal of ROC educators), but mathematics, natural sciences, and English were projected as the next three fastest-growing fields of study.[18] The program further proposed a substantial increase in the number of vocational schools and junior colleges and included specific enrollment projections for all levels of school.[19]

In a section devoted specifically to science education, the program identified four areas of emphasis, including improvement of science education at all levels, promotion of basic and applied research, training various levels of scientists and technicians needed for economic growth, and training people in management. To accomplish these goals at the primary and secondary levels, teachers would be retrained, curricula would be revised, classrooms and laboratories would be revamped, and textbooks would be revised. At the university level, facilities would be improved, more faculty would be recruited, new textbooks would be written or translated, and new departments "deemed necessary to economic growth" would be opened. In the sciences, as in vocational and technical education, the program projected substantial increases in the numbers of graduates during the period of the plan. Whereas in 1968, 2 Ph.D.'s, 247 M.S.'s, and 6,206 B.S.'s were awarded, the program projected that in 1972 there would be 35 Ph.D.'s, 760 M.S.'s, and 10,570 B.S.'s.[20]

This 1969 Manpower Development Program was considerably broader in scope and more comprehensive, even while maintaining a similar set of basic goals, than the NCSD's 1965 "Scientific Manpower Development Program," which was constructed around the self-serving argument that the construction of five new research centers would be the answer to Taiwan's scientific manpower crisis. The CIECD and the Committee for Science Development, which worked together to produce the 1969 Manpower Development Program, were more motivated by larger economic development concerns than was the NCSD, which was in large part simply attempting to jump-start graduate study in the sciences. If only as an indication that economic planners were beginning to take S&T education and training seriously as they thought about economic development, the 1969 Manpower Development Program appeared quite promising.

Three years later, at the 1972 Sino-American Conference on Manpower Development in Taiwan hosted by Academia Sinica, however, it appeared that not all of the goals of the 1969 Manpower Development Program had been met and that the attempt to meet them had, in some cases, led to the emergence of new problems. Wang Shijie, still president of Academia Sinica, pointed to both unresolved and new problems in his opening remarks to the conference. In particular, he noted a "lack of planning in manpower training" and pointed out that the jobs that were available were often not the sorts of positions that college graduates and graduates of vocational schools had been trained for. "Educational expenditures have been a heavy drain on our limited resources," he observed, "and "wasteful investment in education is a luxury we can ill afford. To avoid the pitfall, we must have our educational and training programs tailored to meet actual needs."[21] It was not enough just to throw relatively scarce resources at scientific and technical education and hope that the right kinds of manpower would be trained. Coordination of education and real industrial needs was not proving to be an easy task. The remarks of C. K. Yen, also present at the 1972 conference, confirm the impression that manpower planning would be an ongoing dilemma for the ROC. He observed, "Manpower development alone is not sufficient to ensure effective utilization of human resources. In the final analysis, the real challenge is how to place the right man on the right job."[22]

The MDC had been saying the right things but was not managing to make them happen. At least part of the problem was that Taiwan's manpower planners were still struggling to define scientific and technical manpower. A report prepared for the 1972 Manpower Conference shows that the MDC had not really made the shift to thinking about technicians trained in vocational schools as scientific and technical manpower. Rather, scientific and technical manpower was still being thought of very much in the terms that the NCSD had used in 1964—as graduates of universities and graduate schools in agriculture, physical sciences, engineering, and medicine.[23] At the same time, however, the 1972 report does show that manpower planners had become much more specific about the aims of vocational training and did see vocational training as an appropriate way to provide both semiskilled and skilled workers for areas of expected industrial development such as electronics and precision instrument making.[24] Workers trained in vocational schools, though not identified as S&T manpower, were seen as important cogs in the industrial machine. This failure to define scientific and technical manpower in a broad way, limiting it to those with elite (and almost by definition less immediately applicable) training, points to a serious flaw in the state's entire approach to the development of scientific and technical education as a component of an overall science policy.

Science Development Planning

As we have seen in Chapter 2, efforts had been made to construct science development plans in Taiwan as early as 1958 when Hu Shi proposed the Long Range Science Development Plan to the Legislative Yuan. The plan focused mostly on the development of science education and scientific research, however, and made little reference to the economic implications of development along those lines. In Chapter 3, we saw that both K. T. Li and Wu Dayou, largely on the advice of foreign advisers such as the participants of the Hornig Mission, were encouraging the state to identify science as an integral and important component of economic development and to construct realistic and meaningful science policy that would serve national development needs. By 1969 the MDC certainly understood the importance of scientific planning and made direct reference to the need to implement a science development plan in its Manpower Development Program.

In fact, in 1968 K. T. Li and the CIECD (of which the MDC was a part) commissioned Dr. Ray H. Boundy, an accomplished chemical engineer with Dow Chemical, to evaluate the state of S&T in the ROC and to make recommendations regarding future development of S&T in Taiwan. Boundy, echoing previous U.S. S&T advisers, observed that "the intelligent management of technology is a cooperative endeavor . . . with the Government taking the responsibility for establishing the broad objectives, goals and plans. Then each industry and school establishing its own program under the framework of the broad objectives, goals and plans."[25] Boundy's report paid special attention to the role of education in promoting the right kinds of manpower, the need to stem the brain drain, ways in which the state might promote R&D, the encouragement of particular industries, and ways in which Taiwan might exploit its natural resources.

Wu Dayou, head of the new Committee for Science Development, was already thinking along the same lines. In a 1968 book titled *China's Scientific Development,* Wu argued that "no matter whether we want to make Taiwan into a model province or are making it into a base from which to recover the mainland, we must be sure to first bring order to society, elevate the standard of living, and increase the economic base." The key to all of these things, in Wu's view, was science, and by 1968, Wu felt, the government was beginning to move in the right direction by constructing comprehensive science development plans.[26] Wu, in fact, was considerably heartened by the creation of the Committee for Science Development, although he understood that the task of constructing a coherent national plan was not to be taken lightly. He observed that the establishment of the new committee

> is an event of deep significance and great importance. For the first time the government has come to realize that the development of science is not a matter of establishing a few research institutes, but needs a policy based on a comprehensive view of the conditions and needs in the social and economic development of the country. For the first time we have the opportunity to look beyond the immediate confines of the individual's position or profession, and to think in terms of the broad spectrum of problems confronting the country. Our guiding principle is therefore that of formulating a broad and basic science development plan in coordination with the development of education, industry, agriculture, etc. This guiding principle cannot be over-emphasized since in China there has always been a big schism between the academic and the industrial.[27]

Wu was eager to construct a science development plan that would be overarching, forward looking, and actually meaningful.

The biggest step in this direction came in 1969 when the Committee for Science Development promulgated a three-stage Twelve-Year Science Development Program. The program, which was to be administered by the NSC, was developed in coordination with the Ministries of Education, Defense, Transportation, and Finance and other institutions such as the NSC and the Atomic Energy Commission. As ROC premier C. K. Yen observed in a speech to the legislature, this program demonstrated that "high administrative priority is assigned to the development of science. We know that the promotion of our national strength depends on scientific research and progress. This is a long-range task that requires coordination of our efforts."[28] Yen went on to observe that "this program is drafted in the light of the overall national interest and will improve and expand science education and research at both the basic and applied levels. Objectives include the training of more scientists; research in pure science, industrial and applied science, nuclear science, medicine, public health, social science and the humanities; and encouragement of agricultural, communications, and national defense science."[29] The structure of the new Twelve-Year Science Development Program acknowledged the interconnectedness between the various levels of education and overall economic development. It also promoted a fairly specific set of scientific development goals, in contrast to earlier state references to science, which had been quite vague.

The three target areas of the new plan were science education, science research, and science as it related to development. The plan identified manpower development as a particular point of emphasis, and to that end it sought to improve every aspect of science education, from curricula and textbooks to pedagogy and infrastructure. In terms of science research, the program sought to improve areas of both basic and applied research. It particularly emphasized the need for research on industrial techniques and new product development with an eye to assisting Taiwan's industrial development. In addition to industry, the plan also targeted agriculture, transportation, national defense, atomic energy, medicine, and public health as areas in need of more research and development.[30] In this important respect, therefore, the program differed substantially from all that had preceded it. It clearly emphasized the role that science could play in virtually every aspect of Taiwan's social and economic development and did so with much greater specificity than any previous effort along these lines. With this plan alone the Committee for Science Development had already achieved a greater degree of success with respect to coordination of education, industry, and the state than any of the ROC's earlier planning organs had managed, with the possible exception of the 1940s Science and Technology Planning Committee, in that it was demonstrating much greater vision than its predecessors had. As C. K. Yen observed, the plan would emphasize "coordination between science and technology and national construction."[31] The plan made it unmistakably clear that the state, as represented by the Committee for Science Development in the first instance, and the various ministries through which it expected to implement the plan, in the second instance, was now recognizing that science and scientific experts were fundamental to the economic development process.

There is little question but that the support of the political leadership would be absolutely critical to make any plan work in the ROC of the 1960s. Although it had briefly flirted with constitutional democracy in the mid-1940s on the mainland, the KMT declared martial law in Taiwan in response to local political protest in 1947 and did not repeal it until 1987. Power was thus firmly in the hands of the executive branch. The executive branch, however, was quite expansive, and within the cabinet, which was presided over by the president and premier, were all of the ministries and ministerial-level organizations. The Ministries of Education, Defense, and Economic Affairs and the National Security Council were all under the authority of the Executive Yuan, or cabinet. The legislature, which had financial oversight responsibilities, was populated by KMT members and would rarely question any expenditure that the executive branch wished to make. Given this structure and the lack of voices either inside or outside of government to challenge the authority of the party-state, it ought to have been relatively easy, once a plan had the support of the president and the premier, for it to be implemented. The ministers of state, working together within the Executive Yuan and with the sanction of their political bosses, could have coordinated a coherent plan that would have been funded by the rubber-stamp legislature that did the bidding of the political leadership. The Committee for Science Development, however, was a mere subcommittee of the National Security Council, and it was headed by Wu Dayou, a physicist with little political experience, rather than by a "proper" minister of state. Even though it appears that simply because of its placement within the structure of the state the Committee for Science Development would have wielded much more authority than the NSC or its predecessor, the

NCSD, the case of science education (as we shall see later in this chapter) suggests that it did not have as much authority as it expected to have and perhaps not as much as the political leadership thought it would have.

As Wang Shijie's 1972 comments on the failure of the Manpower Development Plan show, merely recognizing the link between science and the economy, though a crucial first step, was not adequate. For either manpower or science development plans to be truly successful would require a genuine coordination between educators, planners, and industrialists. This coordination was something that Hornig Mission participants had discussed in 1967 and that the Hornig Mission itself had demonstrated was possible. Planning alone was not adequate, and the two things that were needed most in order to make the plan work were resources and time. As ROC manpower and S&T planners well knew, any good coordinated policy to promote a scientific development process would require a constant supply of appropriately trained manpower, which meant making education serve the concrete needs of the state. In this case, the needs of the state were also the needs of the industrial economy.

Education in the 1960s and 1970s: A Case Study

In the mid-1980s Alice Amsden wrote of education in Taiwan: "That Taiwan has assimilated foreign technology as effectively as it has in no small part harks to its highly educated population. It was thought to be the most educated in all of Asia, with the exception of Japan, when the Japanese occupation of Taiwan ended after World War II. High investments in education continued thereafter, increasingly in the technical fields. By the early 1970s, Taiwan had more engineers per 1,000 persons engaged in manufacturing than all other developing countries for which data are available, with the exception of Singapore. Since then, investments in education have soared in tandem with the rate of growth of output."[32] Amsden's narrative rightly credits the Japanese with educating a broad base of Taiwan's population, but it glosses over the KMT's first two decades on Taiwan, suggesting, if not outright stating, that even in those early days there was substantial emphasis on scientific and technical education and that ROC education policy had always given special attention to the relationship between education and industrial development. Amsden is not the only social scientist to have conveyed this impression. Moreover, if one were to look at nothing more than development plans such as those already mentioned, one might well reach similar conclusions, at least for the period beginning in 1969.

There is no question that the very act of drawing up such plans in itself demonstrates that at least most of the executive branch had achieved a considerable degree of awareness of the importance of education policy to overall economic development and the special value of scientific and technical education within that framework. However, a balanced evaluation of the state's efforts to guide Taiwan toward a more high-tech sort of economic development must evaluate the real successes and failures of the plans as well as the plans themselves. As Amsden correctly observes, Taiwan made rapid strides in education of engineers and other sorts of technicians; but did it actually achieve all that it set out to in its various manpower development and scientific development plans of the late 1960s, and were all of the educational initiatives producing the kinds of manpower that Taiwan needed? A closer look at the ROC education system in the 1960s and 1970s will help us to answer these questions.

In fact, it took until the late 1950s for the ROC on Taiwan to begin to emphasize science education at all, something it had done in an earlier era on the mainland but had ceased to do after the move to Taiwan, and the reason for this is almost certainly because it lacked the funds. The impetus for the ROC's sudden interest in promoting science education in 1957 was a new availability of UNESCO and later U.S. funds for this purpose. In the late 1950s both the U.S. government and UNESCO began to take an interest in promoting science education. In 1957 UNESCO adviser James J. Thompson initiated a plan for the publication of new science textbooks in Taiwan based on the American model of science education for grades one through nine.[33] Beginning in 1959 the U.S. government started to help out with funding, devoting money to a five-year program to develop science education. The program provided a total of U.S.$1,609,300 and NT$169,686,500 for teacher and researcher training, curriculum revision, laboratory construction and equipment, and support for research publications for secondary- and university-level educational institutions. The project was divided into two phases: instructional, which focused primarily on secondary schools; and research, which focused mostly on universities. Funds for the research program were divided among seven universities, Academia Sinica, and a few smaller research institutes. For the most part these funds were used for construction of buildings, bringing in visiting scholars, and funding overseas training of existing personnel. Instructional funds were used for in-service training of science and math teachers, curriculum and textbook revision, and construction of laboratories and to send teachers abroad for further training.[34]

The ROC did little to match the funds coming from the U.S. government. Nonetheless, science and technology remained a point of educational emphasis (at least in terms of rhetoric and planning) from then on, as we have seen in the manpower and scientific development plans described earlier. This is also evident in publications such as the 1974 *Fourth Education Yearbook,* which devoted an entire sixty-five-page chapter to science education *(kexue jiaoyu),* a huge increase over the very short section on the same subject in the 1957 *Third Education Yearbook.*

Real commitment to science education in the ROC was lacking in the early 1960s, however. As K. T. Li observed in a 1961 speech, educational expenditure in developed nations is generally quite high. Even Puerto Rico, he noted, spent about 29 percent of its annual budget on education. The ROC, on the other hand, spent only 12.7 percent of its budget on education in 1961. "It is true," Li noted, "that outlays for social development are not directly instrumental in creating wealth. And, with regard to expenditures on education, the value to be derived is intangible and long in coming." However, given the ROC's pace of development, he went on to say, "it is not too early to start educating the children of today if they are to offer their service as trained manpower ten or twenty years later."[35] K. T. Li, the ROC's premier economic planner, was explicitly acknowledging the importance of education to development as early as 1961, but he was not yet, at that time, in a position to be guiding education policy.

Li's second criticism of Taiwan's educational system was for its failure to promote science education. "The most effective way to raise the quality of science teaching in our schools," he observed, "is to raise the quality of our science teachers." This could be accomplished, Li argued, with retraining seminars or courses every three to five years so teachers could keep up with the latest developments, curriculum improvement, improvement of teaching facilities, and development of a special educational track for students with a gift for the sciences.[36]

The next year USAID echoed Li's criticisms in a status report on the science education program that was very critical of the ROC's achievements: "Until there is a dedicated realization by the Ministry of Education that education must be related to the country's development there is little of permanent value that can be accomplished." The report went on to say that "as one progresses from elementary education in Taiwan, it becomes more apparent that there is less emphasis on helping the citizens and more on education for the sake of education."[37] Clearly USAID was not convinced that the Ministry of Education had truly assimilated the education for development approach of both UNESCO and USAID.

Moreover, the U.S.-sponsored science education program had not been especially successful, and this, too, indicated that the Ministry of Education was failing to recognize the potential value of scientific and technical education to overall development. A survey conducted by the Ministry of Education and USAID of the science education program suggested that the new facilities and equipment had not necessarily yielded any improvements in science education, especially in junior high schools: 30 percent of high schools were rated as below average, 31 percent were average, and 41 percent were above average; 57 percent of junior highs were rated as below average, 31 percent as average, and only 12 percent as above average. It was also found that teachers sent abroad for training were not being utilized as fully as they could be: they were going back to teaching but not leading any in-country training workshops to spread their new knowledge.[38] Nonetheless, the numbers showed that there had been a steady increase in college graduates in the sciences during the 1950s and early 1960s (Table 4.1).

Aside from the rising numbers of graduates in the sciences, many of whom then went abroad for further training or to find employment because the employment and educational opportunities to be found in Taiwan were inadequate, there is little evidence to point to the success of these early efforts at promoting education to serve development and, in particular, scientific and technical education to serve industrial development. Scientific studies continued to be theoretical and basic rather than applied. Teachers at the primary and secondary levels continued to be inadequately trained and unaware of the greater economic or social implications of their mission. And university-level instructors were on the whole too motivated by the desire to get their own labs up and running to give much thought to the overall implications of their approach to training students. Moreover, the Ministry of Education was still grappling in the 1960s with what it undoubtedly saw as the more fundamental problems of promoting literacy and oral communication in Mandarin Chinese, not the native language of most residents of Taiwan, and also promoting the KMT's agenda of sinification of Taiwanese through the school system, all of which took considerable time and resources. The U.S.-sponsored science education program had

Table 4.1 College and university students graduated in the sciences in Taiwan, 1946–1965

	Natural science	Engineering	Medicine	Agriculture
1946	0	26	89	17
1947	10	26	213	44
1948	6	99	135	11
1949	126	243	144	110
1950	87	278	157	199
1951	77	290	0	253
1952	55	407	100	250
1953	107	540	71	303
1954	117	744	18	320
1955	147	789	105	315
1956	146	1,003	127	504
1957	138	1,014	138	541
1958	281	1,204	138	714
1959	388	1,267	232	606
1960	520	1,454	341	624
1961	581	1,309	325	594
1962	642	1,506	402	807
1963	802	1,551	539	849
1964	951	1,738	699	939
1965	1,157	2,338	852	987
Total	6,338	17,826	4,825	8,987

Source: Committee for Science Development, "Science Education and Research," 1967, As-Li, B490–43, p. 10.

been a freebie, and as such the Ministry of Education had willingly accepted the money and attempted to implement the program, but science education was not, in the early 1960s, at the top of that ministry's list of priorities. Further, education in general was not at the top of the state's priority list.

In 1965 the CIECD, trying to prod the Ministry of Education into action, hired a German expert on vocational education, J. A. Wissing, to evaluate the state of vocational education and industrial needs in Taiwan. Wissing argued that the ROC would improve its training of both craftsmen and highly skilled technicians if it were to transform its junior high system to one based on the German model. He proposed the creation of two streams at the junior high level. The first, accommodating about 30 percent of students, would place greater emphasis on science and would prepare students to continue on to academic senior high schools or to be more highly skilled technicians. The second would provide a general education adequate to enable students to progress on to vocational high schools.[39]

Also in 1965, the minister of education, as noted in Chapter 3, announced that in order for education to better serve the needs of the economy the ROC would be moving from six to nine years of compulsory education and improving its vocational education programs. Improvement of vocational education, which took place between late 1965 and 1967, however, did not follow Wissing's suggestions. Rather, it came in the form of vocational curriculum revision and the addition of new five-year vocational schools in which students could enroll as an alternative to regular junior high schools.[40] The regular junior high school curriculum underwent no revision during this period and was thus not reconstructed to follow the German model.

More than anything, 1965 appears, therefore, to have been a rhetorical turning point for the Ministry of Education, much as it was for the ROC's political leadership. In spite of the change in rhetoric, however, the ministry's actual approach to science education did not undergo any significant transformation at that time even though Taiwan's economic planners were clearly trying to push it in that direction. It took until the late 1960s for the Ministry of Education to be actively drawn into the planning and development sphere through the medium of the Committee for Science Development, of which the minister of education was a member. Under the leadership of the Committee for Science Development, improvement of scientific and technical education became the centerpiece of both the 1969 Manpower Development Program and Twelve-Year Science Development Program. But did the now greater complicity of the Ministry of Education in S&T planning indicate that the 1969 plans would work any better than the 1959 science education program had worked? A look at higher education suggests that the 1969 plans were excessively optimistic and not always effectively implemented.

In general, in the early 1970s, according to John Allen Chen who wrote a 1971 doctoral dissertation on higher education in Taiwan, higher education continued to be plagued by many of the same problems that had been identified by critics a decade earlier. Faculty and staff still had low salaries and poor research facilities, and many still had to take on outside jobs. Moreover, universities continued to suffer from shortages of qualified faculty. In addition, the Ministry of Education was not providing adequate funding. Perhaps the most damning of Chen's conclusions, however, was that there was a general lack of cooperation and planning between the ROC's various institutions of higher learning and a failure on the part of the Ministry of Education to take a leading role in the planning and coordination process.[41]

In spite of this inauspicious start of the new science plan, however, higher education in the sciences did experience a period of rapid development in the 1970s and 1980s in terms of numbers of graduates and quantity of funding. In fact, statistics on ROC funding for higher education confirm the impression that by the late 1960s the ROC state was, indeed, beginning to focus more of its attention on education in general and higher education in particular. The percentage of total government expenditures devoted to education increased gradually through the 1960s, although it remained low. Whereas the state devoted 11.6 percent of its total budget to education in 1955–1956, in 1965–1966 it was up to 17.8 percent, and in 1970–1971 it had risen to 20.5 percent, the highest until at least the mid-1980s (1975–1976 was 18.2 percent).[42] Of these amounts, the expenditure on higher education amounted to the following percentages: in 1960, 13.7 percent of the education budget went to higher education; in 1970, the percentage had risen to 27.3 percent.[43] Moreover, by 1972 the Ministry of Education and the National Science Council were offering grants to 60 percent of all M.A. and Ph.D. students at national universities.[44]

Since the mid-1970s there has been a huge (though not totally constant) increase in spending on higher education. In 1976–1977 the government was spending NT$27,530 per university student per year. By 1996–1997, spending had risen to NT$213,401 per university student per year. If we take into account the fact that the numbers of students were steadily rising during this twenty-year period (from just over 300,000 in 1976–1977 to around 720,000 in 1996–1997), then this represents a massive increase in total spending on higher education (from roughly NT$8 billion to NT$153 billion over a twenty-year period).[45] As would be expected, given the constant improvement in resources for higher education, there was also a massive increase in the number of students enrolled in institutions of higher education over the same time period. Whereas in 1952–1953 there were just over 10,000 undergraduates and only 13 graduate students in Taiwan, by 1998–1999 there were over 800,000 undergraduates and nearly 54,000 graduate students.[46]

Over time there has also been a shift in the major fields of specialization among university and graduate students. Whereas in 1952–1953—and, indeed, until the mid-1960s—humanities remained about even with social sciences and were surpassed only by engineering as the most popular field of study, in the mid-1960s the social sciences took off as the most popular area of study until about 1975, when engineering began to catch up and, by 1978, surpass the social sciences in terms of attracting students. Humanities, in the meantime, fell way back in comparative numbers. In 1983–1984 the most popular fields of study were as follows: (1) engineering, (2) business, (3) humanities, (4) medicine, (5) social and behavioral science, (6) education, and (7) math and computer sciences. By 1998–1999, although the top seven fields remained the same, their order of popularity had shifted: (1) engineering, (2) business, (3) medicine, (4) math and computer sciences, (5) humanities, (6) education, and (7) social and behavioral science. Thus we can see that over the course of the 1980s and 1990s there was a substantial increase in the number of students in math and computer sciences (in 1983–1984 there were 11,340, and in 1998–1999 there were 62,264).[47]

Moreover, although the projections of the 1969 Manpower Development Program turned out to have been excessively optimistic, Taiwan did have considerable success in increasing the numbers of students enrolling in its graduate programs in the sciences over the course of the 1970s. By 1978, only 8 Ph.D.'s had been granted in the sciences (of a total of 42 Ph.D.'s granted in Taiwan), but there were 187 students enrolled in doctoral programs in the sciences (out of a total of 469 doctoral candidates in all fields). Masters programs had also experienced a significant increase in enrollment. By 1978, 845 M.A.'s had been granted in the sciences, and 2,297 more students were enrolled in scientific masters programs.[48]

Increases in spending on higher education and increases in enrollment did not necessarily mean that all of the goals of the 1969 plans were being achieved, however, and the rising number of graduates indicates nothing about either the quality of education or its relevance to economic development. In fact, the quality of Taiwan's graduate education in the 1970s was not high, and this low quality was blamed, at least in part, on "the lack of qualified teaching staff and facilities."[49] Even as late as 1980 Taiwan's higher education was still criticized for its failure to produce graduates who could meet the needs of society. Part of the problem was that graduate education was not entirely successful. Rapid expansion of graduate schools over the course of the 1970s had produced more graduates, but how good were the programs from which they had come?[50] As one author wrote: "Due to the rapid expansion of graduate education in recent years, quality of this level, especially in science and engineering majors, has not been improved along with the great increase of capacity. In order to meet the increasing need for higher level professionals in the future, graduate schools must expand instruction in mechanical engineering, chemical engineering and civil engineering. But at the same time, great efforts should be made to improve the quality of education as well. Thus, the establishment of new graduate schools should be strictly scrutinized."[51] In spite of a dramatic increase in the output of scientific experts in Taiwan over the course of the 1970s, higher education in the sciences continued to be plagued by many of the same problems from which it had suffered in the 1960s.

There is also some evidence to suggest that until the mid-1980s, at any rate, the increase in B.A.'s, M.A.'s, and Ph.D.'s in the sciences was not particularly meaningful to Taiwan's industrial development. According to Wu Yuan-li, until at least 1985, vocational schools were apparently more relevant to the business and industrial world than universities.[52] Part of the problem, as noted by C. M. Hou and G. San, is that the economy most needed skilled technicians rather than academically trained scientists. Taiwan's students, however, were motivated by a desire for the kind of status that comes with academic diplomas. To address this problem the state was compelled to create technical colleges beginning in the mid-1970s that would essentially continue the vocational track while offering B.A.'s.[53]

Yet another important obstacle, according to one contemporary American observer and critic, was a failure on the part of institutions of higher education to give thought to their purpose. Thomas L. Martin Jr., in a report on higher education in Taiwan produced for K. T. Li in the spring of 1980, called on all "government supported institutions of higher education [to] have clearly defined statements of purpose—of objectives—that support one or more of the objectives of the Republic of China."[54] He further observed that he had found no evidence of any such mission statements at any institution other than the Taiwan Institute of Technology. Echoing earlier Western critics of the ROC education system, he went on to point out that the examination system and the centralized control of curricula by the Ministry of Education both served as obstacles to the shaping of education to meet specific national needs because they homogenized education. Education, he observed, needs to be diversified to meet diverse national needs.[55]

A second problem, according to Martin, was the failure of graduate programs in the sciences to train students for anything other than high-level academic research. Taiwan's masters in engineering programs, for example, encouraged students to engage in overly substantial research projects for their M.A. theses. This meant that students were becoming better prepared to go into research and pursue further graduate study than to go into industry.[56]

Science education improved over the course of the 1970s in that there was more of it. More students enrolled in scientific fields of study, and more programs in the sciences were set up, but the growth in the number of graduates in the sciences still did not necessarily mean that the right kinds of S&T manpower were being produced. If we can trust the evaluations of the various critics of Taiwan's education system that have been cited here, it appears that science education was not serving the needs of the economy much (if any) better in 1980 than it had in the 1960s. Scientific manpower was being trained, but was it the right kind of scientific manpower?

The fundamental problem may have been in the plans themselves. Perhaps the plans were not adequately specific or not well enough aligned with the needs of the industrial sector. Alternatively, the problem may have been that economic planners still did not have very good control over, or rapport with, all branches of the state, including the Ministry of Education and the public academic sector in general. Yet another possibility is that economic planners still did not have a detailed enough understanding of the real needs of industry or, at any rate, were not able to make the Ministry of Education shape its curricula in a way that responded effectively to those needs. No matter the cause, economic planners were unable to make the educational realm develop in a direction that suited the particular needs of the economy, and Amsden's glowing evaluation of the state's efforts with respect to S&T education seems inappropriate for the 1970s and perhaps for parts of the 1980s as well.

The case of science education raises doubts about the effectiveness, at least during the 1970s, of the ROC's developmental state. If planning alone were enough to make a state developmental, then the ROC would certainly qualify. This brief survey of science education suggests, however, that the plans only worked partway and that the state lacked the necessary control of, or perhaps cooperation with, the academic sector (most of which was under the leadership of the Ministry of Education), to make the kinds of development it was hoping for happen, at least in the short run. Also absent was a connection between the educational sector and the industrial sector, a link that state planners were unable to forge during the 1960s or early 1970s.

By 1969 the state had committed itself in every respect to the promotion of scientific development. The right rhetoric was being employed by people positioned throughout the government, comprehensive and fairly well thought out plans were being laid, coordinating institutions were in place to implement the plans, and the money was gradually beginning to fall into place to support them. It took another decade for all of this to have much meaning, however.

Plans and institutions were not enough to produce the sort of effect that ROC technocrats such as K. T. Li and Wu Dayou and their foreign advisers were hoping for. Even an injection of funding, such as that received by the Ministry of Education in the 1970s, was not enough to make the whole thing work. There were two problems that had yet to be overcome. First, the plans themselves, though considerably more comprehensive than any that had preceded them, were still not complete in that they failed to consider the actual needs of the industrial sector and to plan accordingly. Second, not all parts of the state were on the same page, and the political leadership, though apparently committed to a scientific modernization of the ROC, did not choose to use its authority to forcefully push all relevant ministries and institutions to follow the lead of the Committee for Science Development. Part of the problem was that the Committee for Science Development, though staffed by highly placed technocrats and ministers, was still just a subcommittee under the National Security Council. As such, it was not positioned to exert much authority over the various ministries it would need to control to effectively implement the plans. Moreover, the head of the committee, Wu Dayou, though well respected, was nonetheless a scientist rather than a minister of state. It may be that he did not wield the necessary authority to make the plans work.

As the case of science education shows, the plans did not all work like clockwork. The fact that the state's scientific manpower development plans were not wholly effective throws into question whether the ROC in the 1970s and perhaps even into the 1980s was truly developmental.

— 5 —

The Final Step: The State Comes Together

Taiwan had experienced an important turning point with respect to science and technology policy in the late 1960s, but—as we have seen in Chapter 4—the ROC's new S&T policy was neither sophisticated nor detailed enough to play much of a role in the kind of economic transformation that planners had been hoping for. Throughout the 1970s, members of government, academia, and industry continued to complain that the relationship between the three groups had yet to develop to the desired point. Between 1978 and 1982, however, Taiwan underwent a second important turning point in the evolution of S&T policy, during which time state technocrats were empowered by the political leadership to act not only as planners but also as leaders (with all the authority that word suggests) for coordinating the relationship between government, academia, and industry. From that point on, the state increasingly expanded its role in sponsoring S&T R&D that could help Taiwan's mostly small- to medium-sized industries compete in the international market.

In fact, the argument for state promotion of R&D for industrial development had been made at least as early as 1968, when R. H. Boundy had persuasively suggested in his study of S&T in the ROC that the state should lead the way in promoting industrial R&D. "There seems [*sic*] to be no satisfactory alternates," he wrote, "to the Government taking the initiative and carrying most of the cost of industrial applied research for the next several years."[1] Boundy's report, however, indicates that state planners in Taiwan already had some sense of the need for state-sponsored R&D. He refers extensively to plans that were already under discussion by the CIECD to construct a science park at Hsinchu and to develop the Union Industrial Research Laboratory (UIRL), a small, state-sponsored institute that had been conducting small-scale industrial research since the early 1960s, into a large-scale R&D center. Although these plans may have been in the minds of state planners in 1968, there was no immediate movement on them. The UIRL was not given a greater role until it was subsumed under the Industrial Technology Research Institute (ITRI) in 1973, however, and implementation of the Hsinchu Science Park did not begin until 1979.

Serious state sponsorship of R&D began with the construction of ITRI in 1973. The mere existence of ITRI did not, however, immediately solve the problem of coordinating state, academia, and industry. It took until the late 1970s for the construction of two new institutions, the Science and Technology Advisory Group (STAG) and the Hsinchu Science Park, that would finally manage to accomplish this essential coordinating function, the first through better planning and the second through implementation.

Yet again, external circumstances (another moment of crisis) seem to have been an important catalyst for the creation of new institutions and increased enthusiasm on the part of political leaders to commit resources to the promotion of S&T. When these external pushes converged with a necessary level of economic development in the late 1970s, S&T policy was again substantially reformed, much as it had been in both the Sino-Japanese War period and the late 1960s. Two events of the 1970s helped to propel Taiwan to take a greater interest in sponsorship of R&D. First, the oil crisis of the mid-1970s forced Taiwan's economic planners to look for ways to promote a new sort of economic development that would not depend heavily on oil consumption. Taiwan had scarce energy resources, and by the late 1970s, the "rapidly rising price of oil and the uncertainty of its continued adequate availability" was leading K. T. Li to promote "industries and technologies which are less energy-intensive."[2] The move toward high-tech industry was an obvious answer to this problem.

Second, the state's most concerted push to support S&T for industrial purposes began at precisely the moment that the ROC underwent a serious diplomatic crisis. Over the course of the 1970s the ROC was derecognized, first, by the United Nations and, subsequently, by other states, including, in 1978, the United States. Taiwan, which had been both supported and defended by the United States for most of the postwar era, therefore, suddenly found itself without a patron and, perhaps more important, with no diplomatic recourse to defend its interests. In the absence of conventional diplomatic ties with the major nations of the world, and without representation in nongovernmental organizations such as the United Nations, Taiwan was suddenly compelled to find alternative diplomatic strategies. At the same time, domestic economic, political, and social stability became even more important to the state in this new international environment. Under these circumstances, the political leadership became even more committed to an aggressive strategy for promoting economic growth and for further expanding Taiwan's export economy. Domestically, continued economic growth would help maintain stability, especially as an increasingly vocal political opposition grew that called for an end to KMT rule and a declaration of Taiwan independence. Internationally, by more fully integrating Taiwan's economy into the global economy, the ROC could maintain, at least economically, its relationships with former political allies and keep itself and its political interests in their minds. Economic development in the late 1970s meant moving toward high technology, and to do this would require that Taiwan continue to send students to learn and work abroad and to invite experts and multinational companies to Taiwan to exchange ideas and transfer technology. S&T development could therefore also play an important informal diplomatic function for Taiwan. Exchange of knowledge and technology, and improvement of Taiwan's development profile, could only help it to maintain ties with other nations and market itself as a place worth having a relationship with.

At the same time as the oil crisis and the derecognition crisis were pushing Taiwan from the outside, Taiwan's domestic industrial economy was finally reaching a stage at which a move toward high-tech development seemed to be the next logical step. As K. T. Li noted in a 1977 speech, "There is a new awakening in my country that science and technology must be fully integrated into national policies." Taiwan's industry, he argued, "must be converted from a labour-intensive to a technology- and capital-intensive one."[3] Influential American economist and advocate of modernization theory W. W. Rostow, writing to Li in 1980, argued that at that very moment Taiwan was in the middle of what he called "the drive to technological maturity," a process that required that the entire economy function in a coordinated way. "At the completion of that phase," Rostow said, "an economy (and society) has developed the capacity to apply efficiently all the then existing technologies." In Taiwan's case, Rostow observed, "the completion of the Drive to Technological Maturity requires the development of a capacity to go beyond steel, heavy engineering, chemicals and light electronics to the absorption efficiently into the economy of advanced computer technology, lasers, genetic engineering, advanced communications, and perhaps other unfolding fields of technology rooted in new dimensions of basic sciences."[4] In other words, Taiwan's economy in the late 1970s and early 1980s appeared to both Taiwan's economic planners and foreign economists to be poised for a move from heavy to lighter, higher-technology industry that would depend for its development on new scientific knowledge. A state that was willing to invest in R&D and to share the results of its efforts with the industrial sector would be well positioned to guide private enterprise in particular directions.

Also during the 1970s the ROC underwent a domestic political transition with the death of Chiang Kai-shek, the assumption of the presidency by his son Chiang Ching-kuo, the increasing "Taiwanization" of the KMT, and the gradual technocratization of the political leadership of the KMT government. The KMT entered its second generation of rule over Taiwan at virtually the same moment as the ROC faced the derecognition crisis, and this crisis undoubtedly shaped the priorities of the new political leadership. Strengthening Taiwan became the first priority, and dealing with how to reunite China was put on the back burner. Under these circumstances, it is not surprising that Chiang Ching-kuo would have created a special office in 1976 for K. T. Li in which he could direct Taiwan's S&T development or that he would have appointed the skilled technocrat Y. S. Sun to the premiership in 1978. This combination of circumstances, Taiwan's changing domestic economic and political circumstances and the external crises that Taiwan faced in the late 1970s, was all it took to push the state to a new level of commitment to S&T development.

Throughout the 1980s and 1990s the ROC government pursued several important strategies to promote technological progress, including developing R&D in both the public and private sectors, pursuing a "government policy of promoting internationalization which encourages enterprises to develop international networking," and reversing the brain drain by attracting large numbers of scholars to return to work in Taiwan.[5] These strategies were designed and implemented by a new set of institutions that were put into place in the late 1970s and 1980s and that largely replaced the Committee for Science Development as the principal constructor of science policy in Taiwan.

ITRI and the Beginnings of State-Sponsored Industrial R&D

The ROC on Taiwan's first concerted efforts to sponsor R&D specifically intended for the use of the industrial sector came under the auspices of a new

R&D institution established by the Ministry of Economic Affairs in 1973. The Industrial Technology Research Institute was the first and most significant in a series of new government-sponsored research institutions that Taiwan constructed in the 1970s, 1980s, and 1990s.[6] These new institutions were specifically designed to provide R&D services for Taiwan's industrial sector. As Sun Chen and others have noted, it was necessary for the government to step in to promote this kind of R&D since "Taiwan's small and medium-size business firms, which dominate its manufacturing sector, do not enjoy sufficient economies of scale to justify extensive spending on R&D."[7] A major facet of Taiwan's late 1970s economic policies was the encouragement of small- and medium-sized industries to participate in the export economy. Without the kinds of R&D undertaken by ITRI, it is unlikely that they would have been able to play the important export role they did play.[8]

ITRI was set up by Minister of Economic Affairs Y. S. Sun, who was later appointed premier, as an umbrella organization to direct a set of preexisting small-scale research organizations including UIRL, the Mining Research and Service Organization, the Metal Industries Research Laboratories, the Precision Machine Tools Center, and the Electronics Industry Research Center.[9] Though initially sponsored entirely by the state, over time ITRI increasingly benefited from the joint sponsorship of government and the private sector. Its primary functions were, and have continued to be, development and dissemination of technologies to local enterprises, often at the request of the enterprises, and promotion of cooperative ventures between foreign and locally owned industries and Taiwan's universities. It not only developed its own R&D programs; it also conducted seminars and training programs and engaged in some subcontracting through which companies learned how to perform certain tasks and could "upgrade their technical capabilities."[10] In addition, ITRI conducted market studies with an eye to promoting certain types of industrial development.[11] In other words, ITRI has been, from the beginning, very self-consciously market and industry oriented, and its principal concern has been to provide services to Taiwan's industrial sector.

ITRI rapidly began to play a role in promotion of high-tech industrial development, sending, for example, a group of thirty-eight scientists to the United States for short-term semiconductor training in the mid-1970s, who then returned to perform research in ITRI's Electronics Research and Service Organization (ERSO), which was dedicated to research in information technology.[12] However, even as late as 1980 ITRI was not all that it might have been and still suffered, according to a performance evaluation of the 1979 S&T Development Program, from limited staffing and funding.[13] Nonetheless, ITRI did grow substantially through the 1970s and 1980s and, as will be discussed in the concluding chapter, came to play a very important role in Taiwan's shift toward export-oriented high-tech development. The establishment of ITRI, much more than the promulgation of the Twelve-Year Science Development Program, demonstrated that the state was beginning to take concrete action by the mid-1970s toward forging meaningful ties between state, academia, and industry. The state was at last beginning to walk the walk as well as talk the talk.

ITRI has been touted by both the ROC government and foreign scholars seeking to explain Taiwan's economic miracle as having been a key to Taiwan's rapid industrial development in the 1980s and 1990s. Perhaps as important was the role played by Y. S. Sun, the original creator of ITRI, in supporting greater linkages between the state-sponsored R&D sector and the industrial sector. Sun, an electrical engineer, had been among a group of young technicians sent by the NRC to the United States in the 1940s for further training. In Taiwan he worked for and eventually became head of Taiwan Power. In 1973 he was appointed minister of economic affairs by Chiang Ching-kuo, who was then vice-premier and in charge of economic policies. It was in this role that Sun established ITRI and developed the understanding of the need for better connectedness between Taiwan's research and industrial communities that would serve Taiwan so well after his appointment to the premiership in 1978.[14]

The Committee on Applied Technologies

State economic planners created a further opportunity for increased state investment in S&T with the new Six-Year Plan of 1976, which, according to Robert Wade, "gave an even more prominent role to the state" than had earlier economic plans, in addition to calling for further development of heavy and chemical industries and increased spending on education and vocational education in particular.[15] The Six-Year Plan also called for improvements in industrial infrastructure and especially in R&D in applied technology.

By way of demonstrating the state's resolve to pay greater attention to applied technology, in late November 1976 at its 1,503rd session the Executive

Yuan created the Committee on Applied Technologies *(yingyong jixu yanjiu fazhan xiaozu)* as a ministerial-level committee, with K. T. Li as its head. The new committee effectively replaced the Committee for Science Development as the new planning and coordinating organ of the state. Chiang Ching-kuo, who had by then succeeded his father as president, explained the need for the committee by arguing that the new Six-Year Plan required good coordination of the numerous institutions and groups involved in applied science research and development. "Because of the scattered functions and responsibilities and the lack of coordination," he said, "neither the scope of work nor its progress has produced the desired results with little hope of reaching the targets set in the Six-Year Plan."[16] The Committee on Applied Technologies consisted of representatives from the Ministry of Economic Affairs, the Ministries of Communications, Education, and National Defense, the Nongfuhui, the NSC, and the Taiwan Provincial Government and would be led by K. T. Li.

Like Y. S. Sun, K. T. Li's career paralleled the span of KMT interest in science and technology. Li began to study physics at Southeast University in Nanjing in 1926, went to Cambridge University for graduate training in 1934, and returned to China in 1937 to do war-related machine and physics work, and eventually joined the iron and steel committee of the NRC. After the war, Li worked first for the Central Ship-building Corporation in Shanghai and, beginning in 1948, for the Taiwan Ship-building Corporation, of which he became general manager in 1951. In 1953 Li was recruited by Taiwan's leading economic technocrat, K. Y. Yin, to join the Industrial Development Commission of the Economic Stabilization Board. From that point on, he was near or at the center of the ROC's economic planning technocracy and, as we have seen in earlier chapters, was the ROC's principal architect of economic development strategy through the 1960s.[17] Like Y. S. Sun, Li had a strong and well-established background in both economic planning and S&T. Li was thus a good choice for the position.

By constructing this new committee, making it subordinate to no one other than the president and premier, and placing Li at its helm, the political leadership was sending an important message to the state and the nation. They were simultaneously according a much higher level of importance than before to S&T development and ensuring that all sectors of the state would respond to the directives of the new committee in a way that, as we have seen in the case of science education, they did not to the Committee for Science Development. Li was already well established as the

ROC's principal economic planner. Though he had in 1976 left the post of minister of finance after a policy disagreement with Chiang Ching-kuo, he had since been appointed minister without portfolio and continued to garner the respect of most of those around him.[18] When he became head of the Committee for Applied Technologies, his power was extended well beyond its previous scope. He was now in a position to direct virtually everything having to do with economic development, including S&T, an area on which he had long held opinions but over which he had thenceforth had comparatively little control. Largely because of his record as an economic planner, but also because he had a close relationship with Premier Y. S. Sun, Li had considerably more clout and authority than Wu Dayou had ever had.[19] By placing Li, rather than Wu or another academic scientist, at the head of this new institution, the KMT's political leaders were also making the link between economic development and S&T much more explicit than ever before.

The committee was established to smooth the way for implementation of the new Six-Year Plan. It was responsible for developing policy for R&D in applied technologies and pushing forward the details of the economic plan, coordinating the execution of R&D plans, pushing and supporting private enterprise to strengthen its R&D work, and encouraging overseas experts to participate in domestic R&D programs.[20] In other words, it was expected to coordinate the interests and needs of government, academia, and industry in the area of S&T R&D. Whereas the creation of ITRI had signaled a new interest in state-sponsored R&D in the early to mid-1970s, the establishment of the new Committee on Applied Technologies demonstrated that the state (the executive branch) intended to increase its role in oversight and encouragement of S&T R&D that would serve the economic development aims of the state in both the public and private arenas. The executive branch was thus applying its weight and authority to the improvement and expansion of Taiwan's S&T capacity.

The new committee was clearly intended to centralize all government R&D activities. All of the committee members were ministers, viceministers, or heads of nonministerial groups such as the NSC, JCRR, and the Farmer's Association *(nongfuhui)*. None of the committee members were from the private sector. Records of the committee's first meeting indicate that it was concerned with rationalizing and making more efficient efforts at implementing national economic plans, fostering better communications across economic sectors, and rationalizing communications with international expert advisers. A representative of each ministry or group reported on the particular concerns of that ministry or group with respect to the development or utilization of S&T R&D, and at the end of the first meeting, K. T. Li indicated that, in accordance with the stated goals of the Six-Year Plan, the new committee would make its priority the full utilization of existing human and material resources and the construction of R&D policy to support the implementation of the economic plan.[21] The establishment of the new committee proved to be the first step toward construction of an entirely new set of institutions for directing science policy in the ROC. The second step was less formal and perhaps less deliberately preconceived by ROC planners but equally important in the process.

The Texas Instruments Visit and the 1978 Turning Point

In the winter of 1978 the Ministry of Economic Affairs invited the board of directors of Texas Instruments (TI) to Taiwan with the express purpose of luring TI into investing further in Taiwan by expanding production and setting up R&D units in the still-unimplemented Hsinchu Science Park (which will be discussed in greater detail later in this chapter and in the concluding chapter).[22] Through this process, Taiwan would benefit not only from expanded foreign investment but also from technology transfer and improvement of its high-tech economic profile. At the same time, the TI visit provided an opportunity for a group of elite American scientists, technicians, and businessmen with expertise in the computer industry to evaluate and make recommendations for Taiwan's future development; the structure of the visit, which was very much like that of the Hornig Mission, certainly facilitated this process.[23] Four members of TI's board of directors arrived in early May 1978 for a series of site visits and meetings with ROC officials.

On the afternoon of May 3, the TI board members met with a large group of ROC officials from the Ministry of Economic Affairs, the Ministry of Education, the Industrial Development Bureau, the Council for Economic Planning and Development, the Industrial Development and Investment Center, ITRI, and the NSC, at which point they were asked to comment on the industrial and technological development of Taiwan. Among the many suggestions made by Patrick Haggerty, chairman of the board of TI, was that the ROC needed to create some sort of advisory council made up of members of industry, academia, and government. The function of such a group would be to build more effective links between academia and R&D institutes, on the one hand, and industry, on the other.[24] Haggerty and the TI group had identified exactly the same problem that observers from the 1960s and early 1970s had noted. Government, education, and industry had still not found a way to work together effectively.

Upon their return to the United States, Haggerty and the TI team produced a report that reiterated and refined the points they had made while in Taiwan. The written report was considerably more detailed and specific in its suggestions for strategies to unite academic and government S&T research capacity with industrial needs. They again recommended "the formation of an advisory council whose sole function is to enhance this coupling."[25] The group, they said, should include members of industry and of the major academic institutions, the NSC, ITRI, and other similar institutions, but should be kept to the smallest possible size, ideally around fifteen or sixteen members. Its chairman should be an industrialist with a deep commitment to high-tech industrial development. The industrial representatives on the council should be appointed by the president of the ROC and should be drawn from innovative, young Taiwanese industries, well-established technology-based Taiwanese industries, multinational corporations, and possibly also trade associations. The council should meet monthly for an entire day, and it should also conduct annual multiday seminars to evaluate the research programs and facilities of major educational institutions and R&D facilities. It should take as a particular mission the identification and support of small, new, innovative industries, and it should be given the financial resources to sponsor R&D programs related to industrial needs. It should also support efforts to develop markets for Taiwan's high-tech products.[26]

The TI visit was but one of a series of events that took place throughout 1978 and 1979 that showed not only that the state was finally trying to take a truly leading role in guiding Taiwan's S&T development but also that the entire state leadership was now listening carefully to the outside advisers that it brought in. At roughly the same time as he was beginning to organize the TI visit, K. T. Li, acting in his position as chair of the Committee on Applied Technologies, called a national conference on science and technology, which was held in January 1978 and attended by 170 government officials, academics, and entrepreneurs.[27] The conference yielded a new Science and Technology Development Program, launched in May 1979. Also in 1979, according to Frederick Seitz, the president of Rockefeller University who was later recruited into STAG, Haggerty kept pushing for the creation of an advisory council and was further motivated in this by the U.S. decision to derecognize Taiwan. "Immediately after President Carter's Decision," Seitz wrote in his memoir, "Haggerty came to me with the suggestion that we form an advisory committee of a dozen or so members from the United States, to continue to provide whatever advisory help we could, and to make it clear that many individuals in our country supported the Republic of China."[28] In November and December of 1979 plans were drawn up for a new Science and Technology Advisory Group.

The 1979 Science and Technology Development Program

By 1979 it was clear to ROC planners that the 1969 Twelve-Year Scientific Development Plan was out of date and that a new S&T plan needed to be constructed. The new S&T development plan was promulgated in May of that year by the Executive Yuan's Committee on Applied Technologies. It was the product of the January 1978 state-sponsored national conference on science and technology, followed by months of consultation between numerous government ministries and groups, which had drafted and re-drafted the plan.[29] The new plan was, as Robert Wade has noted, "amongst the handful of top priorities of the government's whole development strategy."[30] The 1979 Science and Technology Development Program aimed "to effect an across-the-board development of science and technology in order to fully develop the national potential, accelerate national reconstruction, improve living standards, and reduce reliance on external help." It proposed to accomplish these goals by improving science education and research and interaction between universities and industry, monitoring both public and private sector R&D, importing new technologies, strengthening contact with overseas Chinese researchers, establishing a science-based industrial park, and promoting international technical cooperation.[31] The plan placed special emphasis on high-technology development, particularly in the area of information technology.[32]

The 1979 plan was proactive rather than reactive, as the 1969 Twelve-Year Scientific Development Plan had been, and was built on a sophisticated understanding of the role that the state could play in fostering scientific development. In those respects, it was considerably more state centered than its predecessor. Of course, science education and basic research remained at the center of the new plan, but the additional elements of the plan (emphasis on technology transfer, promotion of international technical cooperation, and increased state involvement in R&D oversight, for example) all pointed to a major shift in the way the state was approaching science policy. Whereas the 1969 plan had indicated in rather vague terms that links between academia and industry should be strengthened, it had not laid out a clear strategy for achieving this. The 1979 plan, on the other hand, did, and it located the state very squarely at the center of the process.

The plan placed specific tasks in the hands of specific government ministries or agencies. The Ministry of Education, for example, was called upon to revise rules governing faculty employment to make it easier for people with industrial but limited academic experience to take teaching jobs and for academics to take on part-time industrial R&D work. The Ministries of Economic Affairs and Communications were also urged to follow concrete strategies for encouraging links between academia and industry, such as targeting specific scholars and encouraging them to conduct research for the chemical and technology-intensive industries. The state also undertook to encourage the creation of S&T societies that might attract people from all sectors.[33]

The plan placed considerable emphasis on the role that the state could play in promoting R&D. The Ministries of Economic Affairs and Communications would sponsor projects aimed at upgrading industry, especially in the areas of electronics, machinery, chemicals, agriculture, food processing, and energy. Large public enterprises would build or expand their own R&D departments, which would then conduct, among other things, projects assigned by the government. The responsibilities of existing government R&D institutes, such as ITRI, the Telecommunications Research Laboratories, and the R&D units of state-owned enterprises such as Taiwan Power and Taiwan Sugar were refined and clarified. In particular, a number of ways in which such institutions could assist private enterprise were spelled out. The state also undertook to reform the patent system so as to protect the products of local R&D efforts.[34]

Yet another important facet of the 1979 S&T Development Program was the emphasis it placed on promotion of international technical cooperation, technology transfer, and strengthening contact with overseas Chinese.[35] All three of these approaches to developing S&T would have the simultaneous effect of using S&T to build closer relationships with other nations. These closer relationships could lead to economic benefit for Taiwan through sharing of technology and knowledge, creation of investment channels, and opening of markets. They could also serve the purpose of promoting Taiwan internationally as a modern, scientific place that would make a good business partner and an important economic ally.

The 1979 S&T Development Program, therefore, took ROC science planning much further on several important points than it had previously gone. First, it placed the state in a much more central and guiding position than it had ever previously occupied, and rather than simply designating a particular organ (like the NCSD or the Committee for Science Development) as official coordinator of science policy, it acknowledged that all relevant ministries and bureaus of government needed to play very specific roles to make the policy work. It also went much further than any previous plan to clarify precisely how each part of government could contribute to the success of the overall plan.[36] Second, it paid detailed attention to the role that the state could play in promoting R&D, something that had been discussed only in vague terms in earlier plans. And third, it openly acknowledged the importance of maintaining international ties to successful S&T development. The ROC state had always been cognizant that the ROC's own S&T development would be dependent on ties with foreign states and foreign companies, but it had not before made the forging of such ties an explicit target of an S&T development plan.

The Science and Technology Advisory Group

Even as the new plan was being promulgated, however, K. T. Li was still searching for an appropriate way to establish better ties between government, academia, and industry. On December 11, 1979, he hosted a meeting of S&T academics from a wide variety of technical schools and universities that he intended as the first in a series of three meetings to discuss the question. The second meeting would be of industrialists, and the third would be a combined meeting.[37] This meeting must have been more oriented toward marketing to academics the idea that better ties were essential than toward information gathering, since although Li solicited suggestions, he already had a plan for how to overcome the problem.

His plan was to create a new Science and Technology Advisory Group (STAG) that very closely resembled the council that Haggerty had imagined. The proposal to create STAG was made in late 1979, and the group met for the first time in 1980. It was created in direct response to Haggerty's suggestion of "coupling of university and government science and technology base to industry by the formation of an advisory council," and its shape, composition, and scope were discussed in correspondence between Haggerty and Li throughout 1979.[38] According to a May 1980 status report on the implementation of Haggerty's suggestions, "The Executive Yuan has set up a 'Science and Technology Advisory Group,' and foreign experts have been invited to serve as its members and also an 'Industrial R&D Working Group' with domestic scholars and entrepreneurs to serve as its advisors."[39] The latter appears to refer to the group of scholars and representatives of industry that K. T. Li had gathered together in December 1979.

Not surprisingly, STAG closely resembled the body that Haggerty had proposed. It was to have between five and fifteen members, who would be appointed directly by the premier and who would serve terms of two or three years. It would be composed of both local and overseas experts who would make suggestions on national R&D policy, evaluate implementation of S&T development programs, and facilitate cooperation between government, academia, and industry.[40] Though STAG would become a continuous body under the Executive Yuan, its board would typically meet only once a year.[41]

The fact that, as Robert Wade has noted, STAG was composed almost entirely of foreign or foreign-born Chinese advisers suggests that one of its important aims was to further develop ties with the international scientific and technical community along the lines already discussed with respect to the 1979 S&T Development Program.[42] Particularly telling in this respect is the fact that the second meeting of STAG, in August 1980, was held in Chicago. Between 1980 and 1992 STAG had a total of twenty-one foreign advisers, most of them American, though there were also advisers from France, Germany, Italy, and Japan.[43] These advisers helped to maintain back-door diplomatic channels, they facilitated some technology transfer, and their prestige gave weight to the decisions of STAG.

At STAG's first meeting in January 1980, the principal questions under discussion were how to manage science policy to achieve economic goals, how to reorient education at all levels to better meet the needs of industry, how to promote better interaction between industry and universities, and how to encourage R&D investment in the private sector.[44] STAG, therefore, was being enlisted to provide answers to the questions that the TI group had raised and that had guided the 1979 S&T Development Program.

Perhaps the most important single feature of STAG was that it regularized and institutionalized the relationship between the ROC government and the American academic and industrial elite whom K. T. Li and others had cultivated over the years. The list of participants in a STAG meeting says quite a bit about just how the state expected to use STAG. The board members at the third meeting of STAG, which took place in both April and May of 1981, were drawn from two groups. First were ROC government ministers and other elite civil servants and academics with an interest in science and technology. These included Premier Y. S. Sun; K. T. Li; Walter Fei, also minister without portfolio and formerly minister of communications (1960–1969) and minister of finance (1976–1978); C. H. Yen, member of the NSC, minister of education (1965–1969), and president of both Qinghua University and the Chungshan Institute of Science and Technology in the 1970s; Qian Siliang, chemist and president of Academia Sinica; and Y. S. Tsiang, member of the NSC and the NCSD and minister of education (1972–1977). Second were American advisers drawn from academia, public service, and industry. These included Frederick Seitz, chair of the USA Committee for Scientific and Scholarly Cooperation with the ROC and president of both Rockefeller University and the National Academy of Sciences; Carl Gerstacker, director of Dow Chemicals; Ivan Bennett, physician and president of New York University; Thomas Martin, president of the Illinois Institute of Technology; Sterling Wortman, plant geneticist connected to the Rockefeller Foundation and a member of the White House Advisory Committee on S&T; Chauncey Starr, physicist and vice-chairman of the Electric Power Research Institute; and Simon Ramo, in aviation and space technology and chair of the President's S&T Task Force under both Gerald Ford and Ronald Reagan.[45] In addition to the board, composed in 1981 of the fourteen men listed above, a much larger group of ministers, members of government committees, university presidents, heads of research institutes, and the chairmen of ten private and state-owned enterprises such as President Enterprises, Far Eastern Textile, Yue Loong Motor, China Steel, and Taiwan Power were also included in the STAG meetings. Membership of the board and participants in STAG meetings were not completely constant over time, however, and some shifting of personnel occurred nearly every time STAG met.

Unlike earlier S&T planning organs, STAG had the full support of the political leadership. Letters of invitation to join STAG came from the office of Premier Sun, for example, who was clearly kept abreast of the entire planning process. Moreover, there is evidence to suggest that Sun, who was himself an electrical engineer and deeply committed to high-tech development in the ROC, understood better than his predecessors the significant role that could be played by S&T in development. At the opening of the first STAG meeting in 1980, Sun noted that Taiwan was looking for ways to make "science and technology to truly benefit society." He went on to declare that "our government is determined to remove all constraints which hinder the successful achievement of this objective."[46]

In many respects, STAG's meetings followed the model that had been established by earlier missions of U.S. advisers to the ROC such as the 1965 Hornig Mission and the 1978 TI visit. As not all of the members of the STAG board could travel to Taiwan at the same time, the spring 1981 meeting, for example, took place at two separate times, with technical manpower and education, energy, and agriculture as the topics of discussion for one group, and basic sciences, public health and the environment, chemical industry, and high-tech electronics as the topics for the other. ROC members of the board were all high-ranking members of the technocratic and party elite who had been involved to one degree or another in virtually every science development initiative that the ROC on Taiwan had pushed. The foreign participants, likewise, were well-established professionals with solid academic or industrial reputations and experience in building institutions and advising governments. The agenda was set by the local participants, but they then set the foreign advisers to the task of evaluating ROC successes and failures and recommending strategies for future development. To this end, the foreign advisers were each given rigorous schedules of meetings and facilities tours relating to their specific areas of expertise, followed by two final meetings, first with STAG as a whole and then with the Executive Yuan. At the final meeting or shortly thereafter, the foreign board members presented the board with written reports on their findings, and these written reports served as the basis for future action by STAG.[47]

The written reports were farmed out to the appropriate government ministries or organs, and responses were drafted. In the months following the 1981 STAG meeting, for example, a series of reports were compiled into a "Status Report on Recommendations of the First Science and Technology Advisory Board Meetings." This status report included collections of relevant data and progress reports on implementation of specific measures recommended by STAG's foreign advisers.[48]

STAG's agenda, though originally based in large part on the 1979 S&T Development Program, was thus increasingly shaped by the specific reactions that STAG's foreign board members had to the ROC's efforts to implement that program. In its first year or two, acting both in the spirit and on the recommendations of the S&T Development Program, STAG sought to promote rationalization of the S&T development process while still encouraging active participation on the part of numerous government agencies. To this end, STAG oversaw several important efforts. In September 1980 the NSC proposed, and the Executive Yuan agreed, that all R&D projects would be first evaluated and revised by the NSC and then approved by the Executive Yuan, to which the final report of results would also be submitted.[49] This system was intended to eliminate duplication of projects and to promote a more rational system of approval and funding of projects. Under this system, all projects would be evaluated "from an overall national point of view."[50] Further rationalization came with the creation of offices of S&T in all government organs that would answer to STAG as well as their own organs. In addition, several data collection projects were implemented. At the urging of STAG, the NSC undertook to perform annual surveys of manpower resources and R&D expenditures so as to provide the Executive Yuan and other government agencies with data to help with planning.[51] It also set up a Scientific and Technical Information System that would have databases on S&T projects, research facilities, manpower, and research funding, all of which would assist with the management of S&T projects.[52]

A central focus of STAG from its inception was coordination of R&D for industrial use. Some solutions were implemented under the S&T Development Plan. R&D expenses were made tax exempt, and ITRI was made more relevant to private industrial development in microprocessors, microcomputers, red-mudded plastics, and fiber spinning technology.[53] STAG pursued the question by having the National Science Council conduct a survey of where R&D was being conducted. According to the survey, 32.82 percent was being done in colleges and universities, 32.02 percent in business enterprise, 28.12 percent in government institutions (17.96 percent of that in public research institutes), and 7.04 percent in nonprofit institutions. Not entirely satisfied with the limited scope of the survey, the NSC sent four of the people who conducted it to the National Science Foundation in Washington and the Bureau of Science and Technology in Japan to help "build a more reasonable working model" for how to evaluate Taiwan's R&D situation.[54] In a related move, STAG also solicited a survey of the average size of industries in Taiwan that found that the average size of industry in Taiwan was too small to sustain the expense of R&D.[55] These data helped to form the basis upon which S&T policy continued to develop in the 1980s.

By late 1981 STAG's agenda was shifting toward promotion of recommendations by its foreign advisers rather than implementation of the specifics of the 1979 S&T Development Program (though the two were not necessarily mutually exclusive). The section "Summary on the Progress of the Recommendations on Education" from the "Status Report on Recommendations of the First Science and Technology Board Meetings" indicates that some of American adviser Thomas Martin's suggestions for making higher education more relevant and accountable were put into effect (as was discussed in Chapter 3). So, for example, universities were asked to draft mission statements and five-year plans and to provide education that served their stated institutional objectives. Curricula were to be revised, and foreign S&T advisers were asked to recommend improvements to S&T departments. On the other hand, Martin's implicit suggestion that the examination system be altered or abolished was rejected. Likewise, some efforts were being made by 1981 toward responding to Ivan Bennett's recommendations for addressing environmental pollution, drug safety, food hygiene, and health care for the elderly and rural residents. And Bennett's hepatitis B program is frequently touted as STAG's most important and successful program in its early period. In addition, Wortman's recommendations for improving agricultural research and education and the various recommendations of the other foreign STAG participants were all taken seriously. STAG was thus heavily guided by foreign advice.

As noted earlier, rationalization of the development process was also a key point of emphasis for STAG. As part of its efforts in that direction, STAG undertook an evaluation of the 1979 S&T Development Program in March 1981 in which it listed the concrete actions taken thus far toward implementation of each of twenty-three recommendations made by the S&T Development Program and then offered a brief evaluation and suggestions for further action. Education had remained a key concern of both the creators of the 1979 S&T Development Program and STAG, and among these recommendations three pertained to education, two of which were reiterations of recommendations that had been made repeatedly since 1958. The first of these was to "Set Up a Special Task Force to Review and Improve Science Education in Secondary Schools," a recommendation that was addressed by the Ministry of Education, which set up a science education advisory committee in 1979 with Wu Dayou as chairman. By 1981 this committee had undertaken yet another curriculum reform in natural sciences and mathematics in junior and senior high schools and vocational schools, focusing especially on the drafting of new textbooks, some of which had been drafted by the time of the report. A second recommendation, also addressed by the Ministry of Education, was for "Improvement of Technological and Vocational Education," the main objective of which was to "cultivate intermediate and lower-echelon technical personnel for national reconstruction projects." The Ministry of Education yet again sought to achieve this goal by improving teaching quality and facilities and by attempting to make the curriculum relevant to industrial development.[56]

Times had changed since 1958, and so had the sorts of scientific and technical skills that would be relevant to Taiwan's industrial economy; so it was, perhaps, inevitable that the Ministry of Education would have overseen a seemingly endlessly repetitive series of science education reform efforts that focused on curriculum review, teacher training, upgrading of facilities, and assessment of the relevance of science education to the economy. The fact that these processes were being undertaken yet again in response to the recommendations of the 1979 S&T Development Program should not necessarily be read as an indictment of earlier efforts to revamp science education. In fact, the third recommendation to "Plan on the Improvement of Computer Application Education," also overseen by the Ministry of Education, had as its objective "Improve computer application education, and cultivate the students' capability in computer application to accelerate the nation's science and technological development."[57] Surely the very fact that the Ministry of Education was now able to focus on applied computer education indicates that its earlier science education reform efforts had yielded some upgrades in science education.

The performance evaluation also addressed the state's efforts to develop state-sponsored R&D. One of the recommendations of the S&T Development Program was that "ITRI should work with other governmental and private research institutions to establish a corporation for the promotion of efficient transfer of technologies from domestic as well as foreign institutions." For this purpose, ITRI created an Industrial Technology Transfer Company, which in turn created its own United Microelectronics Corporation, both of which aimed to encourage technology transfer. The following recommendation was that ITRI "should increase its effort in the research and development of applied technology" by acquiring technology, developing new technologies and products, and providing assistance to local companies. ITRI not only developed its own R&D programs; it also conducted seminars and training programs and engaged in some subcontracting through which companies learned skills and were able to "upgrade their technical capabilities." Interestingly, there is a complaint of limited staffing and funding for ITRI in the report.[58] Even in the early 1980s, ROC science organs were still not as well funded as they needed to be.

Another important R&D-related initiative in the 1979 S&T Development Program, implementation of which was overseen by both STAG and the NSC, was the establishment of a science-based industrial park in Hsinchu. The project's objectives were "to promote the development of advanced technology industries, to cultivate scientific and technological manpower . . . [and] to encourage intensive research and development of industrial technologies."[59] The park was located in Hsinchu rather than Taipei because of the high concentration of S&T intellectual resources in Hsinchu, which already housed ITRI as well as Qinghua and Jiaotong universities, two of Taiwan's most scientifically oriented institutions of higher education. And, as noted in Chapter 4, the idea for the Hsinchu park had already been floating around for at least ten years.

The Hsinchu park was envisioned as a sort of state-designed S&T melting pot that would utilize Taiwan's indigenous state-sponsored S&T resources in combination with returning scholars and entrepreneurs and the know-how imported by foreign companies. It was intended to serve as a recruiting instrument in the battle to reverse the brain drain and encourage educated Taiwanese to return to Taiwan. Over the course of the 1980s and 1990s, it went a considerable distance toward achieving that goal. Nearly half of the companies that located there were founded by returning scholars. At the same time, it was intended as a space in which industry, state, and academia could intersect in a way that had not always happened in the past, and again, it achieved some success along those lines. ITRI technicians performed R&D for Hsinchu companies, and over the years, many ITRI technicians moved to these companies, thus transferring skills and training from the public to the private sector and establishing networks between public and private.[60] Various industries at the park have also had extensive relations with academicians at the two nearby universities, which house many of Taiwan's best departments in the sciences and engineering.

Most important, the Hsinchu Science Park was part of the ROC's early 1980s strategy for encouraging the development of non-state-sponsored R&D. By offering industries a complex in which they could be near each other, share facilities, and take advantage of the proximity of the ROC's most important state-owned industrial research facility (ITRI), the ROC hoped to stimulate more active interest in R&D on the part of local industry. At the same time, ROC S&T policymakers were very much hoping that Hsinchu would attract foreign-owned enterprises and thus become a locus for technology transfer.[61] By March 1981 the NSC had already contracted with an American company to advertise the science park in the United States so as to attract potential clients. It was also beginning to target specific enterprises in the United States, Japan, and Europe in the hope of luring them to set up shop at the new science park. This was all being done "in view of meeting the needs of domestic industrial development"[62]—in other words, to facilitate industrial cooperation and technology transfer, both of which were crucial to Taiwan's drive toward technological maturity.

The Hsinchu park was focused entirely on high-tech industry and actively recruited enterprises producing electronics, communications products, optical instruments, and precision machinery. To this end, in addition to basic facilities, the park offered special incentives such as duty-free import of raw materials and high-tech machinery, other tax incentives, and modern communications facilities.[63] The park offered high-tech local capabilities as a lure to potential clients such as computerized databases on "parts, components and processing technologies of domestic industries." Construction of such databases, though well under way by March 1981, was nonetheless hampered by a paucity of computer professionals.[64] The science park was, in its early stages, on the cutting edge of Taiwan's industrial development. It aimed to promote high-tech development but depended to a certain extent on the existence of what was still a very small indigenous high-tech sector to get off the ground.

Hsinchu got off to a relatively quick start, attracting fifteen industries in its first year of operation, but it took years to meet the expectations of its creators, failing, in particular, to attract the number of foreign-owned enterprises that they had been hoping for. Nonetheless, it continued to grow through the 1980s and 1990s, and by 1997 there were 68,000 people employed there.[65]

In 1982 the Executive Yuan sponsored a Second National Science and Technology Conference at which the 1979 S&T Development Program was refined. As in the past, most of the participants in the conference were from government and academia.[66] The revised program identified eight target areas of S&T (energy, materials, information technology, product automation, biotechnology, electro-optics, hepatitis control, and food technology) and placed renewed emphasis on basic scientific research. According to

K. T. Li, it also laid plans for "a 'co-operative division of labour,' within which the Executive Yuan would lay down basic policy and ministries and agencies would be responsible for planning and implementation."[67] In addition, as a result of the conclusions reached at the Second National Science and Technology Conference, state R&D expenditures in 1982 were raised from 0.6 percent to 1 percent of Taiwan's GNP.[68] The Committee on Applied Technologies was given the job of "promoting the programme by co-ordinating the activities of the various agencies concerned."[69] Through the 1980s and 1990s the Executive Yuan continued to sponsor National Science and Technology Conferences that yielded revised plans for the development of science and technology. These plans continued to be evaluated by STAG, overseen by the Committee on Applied Technologies, and implemented by ITRI and other state-run agencies.

Although the state continued to invest in R&D with an eye to assisting indigenous industries, it was also the case that it increasingly tried to encourage the private sector to take over some of this burden. Beginning in 1983 the government "introduced a number of incentives to encourage industrial research and innovation in the interest of industrial improvement." The state began to provide financing for enterprises that planned to develop in strategic areas, it granted tax credits for R&D expenses in certain strategic areas, and it offered grants to encourage new product development.[70] The state thus used its financial powers and resources to help manage or direct economic development in its target areas. In a general sense, this was a strategy that the state had already been employing since the 1950s; however, this was the first point at which private industrial R&D had been a focus of state support.

The basic institutional patterns of science policy that were established in the late 1970s and early 1980s continued to operate through the remainder of the twentieth century. Government support for R&D grew steadily, and numbers of graduates in S&T-related fields continued to grow and were absorbed into the economy with increasing success. Development priorities shifted periodically as they had in 1982 with the revision of the S&T Development Program to meet the needs of the rapidly growing and changing domestic and global economy.

Whereas the political leadership in the 1960s had taken no initiative with respect to constructing a science policy, and had taken only baby steps in that direction from 1967 on, by 1978 it had permitted a redefinition of the state's role and had become aggressively proactive and managerial. This shift was due, at least in part, to a change in the face of the political leadership. By 1978 an alliance had formed between state planners and politicians, most notably K. T. Li and Premier Y. S. Sun, who worked closely to create effective, rational structures to guide S&T development. Motivated, in the first instance, by the desire to continue to stimulate rapid economic growth in a world where economic development was increasingly tied to possession of scientific and technical knowledge, ROC economic planners wholeheartedly embraced their new role as S&T planners in the late 1970s, identifying S&T R&D, in particular, as their most important point of emphasis for future development. Their efforts to direct the economy away from energy-intensive industries and toward more high-tech, low-energy-usage industries were influenced by the rising cost of energy in the 1970s. The strategies these planners implemented for promoting S&T development were also unquestionably influenced by the ROC's need to find new ways of institutionalizing and maintaining contacts with foreign states and foreign experts in the wake of the series of derecognitions of the ROC that took place through the 1970s.

As the ROC began to move toward a more intensive and proactive support of S&T development, it created a new set of institutions that worked together with some existing institutions (the NSC, ITRI, ministries, and academic institutions) to manage S&T development both inside and outside of the state. The new institutions were more streamlined and more clearly located at the center of government. The Committee for Science Development, which had been a mere subcommittee of the National Security Council, was effectively replaced by the Executive Yuan's Committee on Applied Technology. The new committee sponsored national S&T conferences and oversaw the construction and implementation of the 1979 S&T Development Program and subsequent S&T plans as well as the creation of STAG and the Hsinchu Science Park. The Committee on Applied Technology played what was essentially a managerial role, bringing together high-level government officials from all relevant ministries and groups with foreign advisers and local entrepreneurs (through STAG) and academic researchers (through the S&T conferences). Its position as a cabinet-level committee endowed it with more authority than its predecessors, and the fact that K. T. Li was at its helm reinforced this authority. It thus managed the relationship between government, industry, and academia in a way that neither the

NCSD nor the Committee for Science Development had previously been able to do.

The main focus of all of these new institutions was the promotion of S&T R&D and technology transfer that would have concrete and immediate industrial utility. Beginning with sponsorship of ITRI, the state increasingly invested in the establishment of R&D institutions and encouraged ties between these institutions and industry. These institutions pursued research projects deemed by the Committee on Applied Technology and STAG to be of concrete value to industry and thus enabled Taiwan's many small- and medium-sized enterprises to compete in a global environment. STAG and the Hsinchu Science Park both played important roles in bringing foreign know-how and advice to Taiwan. Both institutions facilitated technology transfer, exchange of ideas, and connections with skilled scientists and technicians. By centralizing and bringing order to these processes and by committing significantly more resources to R&D and the construction of R&D institutions, the ROC greatly expanded upon 1960s recommendations by development agencies and truly established itself, in the realm of S&T development, as a developmental state.

Conclusion: Is Taiwan's Past China's Future?

This study has three important implications for our understanding of developmental states and how they come into being. First, states with developmental tendencies are not necessarily equally developmental at all times. Second, for states to function developmentally requires a coordination of interests between technocrats/state planners and political leaders. Third, the state may not always actually be the principal agent of development. Because a developmental state must respond to the interests of the private sector, outside actors, sometimes invited, sometimes not, are likely to influence state policy.

The case of state-sponsored science policy in the ROC shows quite clearly that not all parts of the ROC state were equally development minded at all times. The phrase *developmental state* has been used to describe ROC actions as early as the 1930s on the mainland and for the period beginning, at the latest, in the mid-1960s on Taiwan. However, to suggest that the ROC was consistently or evenly developmental before the 1980s is problematic. As we can see in the case of S&T policy, different groups within the broad state structure had different developmental agendas at different times.

For the state to function in a coordinatedly developmental manner required that the interests of these various groups converge. This tended to happen, in the case of S&T policy, at moments of crisis that threatened the political and economic stability of the nation. The Sino-Japanese War, the period immediately following the PRC announcement that it had acquired nuclear weapons, and the period after which the United States derecognized the ROC were all what we might call "propitious" moments that propelled ROC political leaders to take up the calls more regularly made by technocrats and external advisers for advancement in S&T as a solution to social and economic problems. The motivations of political leaders may not have been identical to those of the technocrats, but what was important was the convergence of interests and goals of the two groups. As we have seen, however, these moments of convergence were temporary, although the period since 1978 has been such an extended moment that it may constitute a permanent reorientation rather than a lengthy propitious moment.

In many ways, the notion of the propitious moment is rather common sense. And yet it is an idea that has not been fully developed in developmental state literature. Stephan Haggard proposed in 1990 that "critical historical junctures" could shift "the balance of power among sectors in predictable ways and provide . . . incentives to institutional innovation"; more recently, Wu Yongping has argued that political factors are at least as important as economic concerns in shaping the state's economic development policies.[1] Neither author has really framed this as a question of how it is that a state that is not developmental becomes developmental, however. What conditions are required for this transformation to occur? This study goes some way toward answering this question and concludes that developmental states become developmental, at least in part, by accident. A necessary accident, however, is that the political leaders adopt the developmental perspective and throw their support to the technocratic elite.

The technocracy, however, was not always the main guide of state policy, and even at moments when it sought to guide policy, it often brought in outside advisers to make its case more compellingly. This feature of the developmental state is not so apparent for the mainland period, though this may be because I have not yet found the right sources. In the ROC's Taiwan period, however, there is no doubt but that outside advisers, mostly foreign experts and Chinese/Taiwanese academics, not only sought to guide state policy but also succeeded in doing so. Hardly any ideas for new institutions or new points of policy emphasis from the late 1950s on were generated from within the state. Instead, they came from outside advisers.

Even when technocratic elites did have an internally generated agenda to push, however, they sought outside advisers to help them make the point. The Hornig Mission, the TI Mission, and STAG all illustrate this point. The ROC political leadership, which controlled the purse strings and ultimately approved any major institutional or policy changes, needed to be convinced that the vision of state planners was worthy of investment, and the best strategy that the technocrats had to convince them was to bring in experts (preferably foreign experts) to help them make the case.

The case of ROC science policy further demonstrates that relatively poor states made up of groups with disparate agendas can still unite sufficiently to function as developmental states, at least temporarily. More permanent, unified developmental tendencies, however, depend on the construction of stable, flexible, and embedded institutions such as STAG and ITRI and the willingness of the political leadership to throw its authority behind them.

The Outcome

K. T. Li suggested that the reason for Taiwan's slow start in science and technology was the ROC government's pragmatic, "problem-oriented approach to policy formulation." Problems were dealt with only in the order in which they appeared, and it was not until the late 1970s that "the need for Taiwan to upgrade the technological sophistication of its industrial structure became obvious."[2] While it may be true that the need for technological development did not become apparent to the political leadership until the late 1970s, there is no doubt that Li himself, other technocrats, Taiwan's various foreign advisers, academics, and entrepreneurs could all see this need from at least the mid-1960s and in some cases even earlier. The turning point in the late 1970s came when the political leadership changed and the new political leaders, some of whom were themselves technocrats, understood the merits of S&T development.

By 1982 the ROC had in place the basic institutions and policies that would guide science and technology development for the rest of the century. Just as important as the institutions themselves was the fact that they had the full support of the ROC political leadership. With the backing of Chiang Ching-kuo, Premier Y. S. Sun, Lee Teng-hui, and others, STAG, in particular, wielded the political and economic authority to bring all necessary sectors of the state into line with policy and to incentivize industry to participate in state-guided development projects. Bolstered by the marriage of political authority and technocracy that took place in the late 1970s when the engineer Y. S. Sun was appointed premier, these institutions were able to function with increasing effectiveness over the course of the last two decades of the twentieth century.

Taiwan's increasingly precarious international position was surely one reason for the new support that K. T. Li and the technocratic elite gained in the late 1970s. STAG resulted from Li's efforts to institutionalize and rationalize international networks and relationships that he had been cultivating since the 1960s. By organizing these relationships into an institutional framework, Li rationalized the process through which Taiwan acquired foreign advice. This process of institutionalization was quite self-conscious and was something that the ROC had already embarked on with respect to overseas Chinese prior to the creation of STAG.[3] These efforts were particularly important in the context of the late 1970s, a period during which Taiwan became fully aware that it would require technological advice and technology transfer in order to reach the next stage of development but during which its last significant diplomatic tie, with the United States, was cut. In the early to mid-1980s, in fact, the Committee on Applied Technologies began to implement a sort of S&T diplomacy with Europe as well, through the construction of a Sino-European Science and Technology Cooperation Working Group modeled on the Sino-American Science Cooperation Committee and by inviting a French scientist to join STAG. In addition, the ROC added science divisions to some of its various pseudo-consulates such as the Association of East Asian Relations in Japan and several branches of the Coordinating Council for North American Affairs in the United States.[4]

Although the diplomatic dimension of STAG was important, its most important function was to plan for and promote Taiwan's S&T development. STAG drew together technocrats from throughout the state, foreign advisers, and industrialists to develop policy, and it continued to operate according to the original pattern, meeting semiannually, through the 1980s and 1990s.[5] STAG defined goals and shaped policy, pushing, in particular, for continued development in high technology and the encouragement of R&D in the private sector as major goals for the period from the 1980s to 2000.[6]

STAG oversaw the promulgation of a series of S&T Development Programs, the establishment of the Hsinchu Science Park, the development of Academia Sinica's first and second five-year plans, the convening of a series of national S&T conferences, and the promulgation of a training and recruitment S&T Personnel Program in 1983. In addition to these various plans and events, STAG oversaw the construction in the 1980s and 1990s of a large number of new research institutes in the sciences, engineering, and information technology, many of which were divisions of ITRI and others of which were located at Academia Sinica and Taiwan's elite universities.[7] STAG constructed these academic research institutes to push for greater cooperation between academia and industry.[8] The two most important institutions in terms of facilitating STAG's plans have been the Hsinchu Science Park and ITRI.

Although it got off to a slow start in the 1980s, the Hsinchu Science Park has become important enough to the Taiwan economy that the experiment is now being emulated elsewhere in Taiwan. By 1993 Hsinchu's total sales accounted for 2 percent of Taiwan's GNP, and by 2000, Hsinchu was the third largest exporter of information technology in the world.[9] Two of the major reasons for Hsinchu's success are the role of ITRI and the focus on development of particular industries. Most of Hsinchu's success has been in the IT industry, and most of the R&D being undertaken in the park has been in integrated circuits, computers and peripherals, opto-electronics, and telecommunications, with much greater investment going into integrated circuits than anything else.[10] Computers and peripherals, and telecommunications, however, have been the most productive industries for Hsinchu, netting more sales than other areas.[11] Hsinchu became a center for IT industrial development in large part by offering strategically focused R&D grants to its residents.[12] These grants, in combination with the close relationship between Hsinchu resident companies and ITRI, have pushed Hsinchu's companies to the forefront. According to Otto Lin, about half of the companies located at Hsinchu in the late 1990s were in technical relationships of one sort or another with ITRI, and a number of the Hsinchu companies actually spun out of ITRI projects.[13]

Since the mid-1990s Taiwan has constructed several similar parks based on the Hsinchu model in Tainan and Luchu in the south and Taichung in the central part of western Taiwan. The intention is to construct a technology corridor stretching the length of western Taiwan. Smaller science parks dedicated to developing particular technologies have also been established in the vicinity of existing research centers. Near Academia Sinica in Nankang, for example, the government and the private sector worked together to create the Nankang Software Park, which offers similar sorts of incentives to investors as Hsinchu.

Although every effort has been made to construct the new parks near existing research centers, not all of Taiwan's research centers have had the same success as ITRI. ITRI started off in 1973 with about 450 employees and a focus on information technology.[14] Through the 1980s and into the 1990s it was Taiwan's most important research and development center, carrying out roughly one-fourth of the ROC's nondefense R&D projects between 1983 and 1994.[15] By 1999 ITRI was employing 6,000 people and was "engaged in innovative research in almost all major areas of industrial technology."[16] Its annual budget had grown to more than U.S.$500 million, and it had developed relationships with over 20,000 companies.[17] By the mid-1980s ITRI was spinning off research teams, some of which formed new businesses and others of which became new research centers.[18]

In the 1970s and early 1980s, the costs to the ROC state of S&T development were tremendous. The ROC had to finance tax breaks to incoming multinationals and local start-ups; offer incentives, partly through infrastructural development, to lure skilled scientists and technicians from abroad; train new manpower at home; construct research facilities; and support R&D.[19] Though, as we saw in Chapter 4, not all of these investments yielded immediate results, they did start to pay off in the late 1980s. According to government statistics, in the years between 1987 and 1997, Taiwan made significant progress in the realm of R&D (a set of statistics that the ROC had not compiled prior to 1987).

During this time the state committed substantial resources to R&D.[20] In terms of GDP, the level of scientific and technical R&D compares well to that of other highly developed countries. By 1996 Taiwan had achieved a level of R&D spending in terms of percentage of GDP that was comparable to that of the United Kingdom (just under 2 percent).[21] By 2002 it had reached 2.3 percent of GDP, a percentage generally comparable to those of Western European states but lower than Japan (2.94 percent in 1999 and 3.09 percent in 2001) and the United States (2.65 percent in 1999 and 2.82 percent in 2002).[22]

The state was not the only source of funds for scientific and technical R&D in Taiwan, however, and over the course of the 1990s, with the encouragement of the state, the private sector gradually overtook the state as the main source of R&D funding. In 1989, STAG established targets for future R&D spending, one of which was to improve the ratio of government-to-private R&D spending. In 1986 the ratio had been 51:49. The hope was that by 1995 it would have shifted to 40:60.[23] Although the targets set for 1995 were overly optimistic, by 2001 the private sector was finally investing 63 percent of total R&D spending, as opposed to the government, which was providing 37 percent. The lion's share of this private sector investment was made by industries in their own R&D programs. By 2002 it was still the case that state-led R&D institutes, universities, and colleges were receiving the vast majority of their funding from the state and were getting very little from private sources.[24] However, the division of R&D labor suggests that the public sector has continued to provide services to the private sector. In general, the division of R&D labor between industry and the public sector in 2002 was such that all basic research was being conducted in the public sector, as was the majority of applied research. Moreover, though most experimental development was conducted in the private sector, it remained the case that public S&T research institutes were devoting over one-third of their resources to experimental development as well. Experimental development, rather than either basic or applied research, was the major recipient of all R&D funding throughout the 1990s and beyond, and the share of funding it received grew steadily.[25] Not surprisingly, much more of both public and private R&D money has been funneled into the information and electronics industries than any other industrial sectors.[26]

The huge increases in R&D spending coupled with shifts in educational planning led also to a doubling of R&D manpower in the ten years from 1987 to 1997.[27] As was shown in the analysis of Taiwan's education statistics in Chapter 4, there was a large increase in the numbers of both undergraduate and graduate students in engineering, computer science, and mathematics during that decade, indicating that the Ministry of Education was succeeding in its goals of increasing the percentage of the workforce with scientific and technical skills. By the late 1990s and early twenty-first century the percentage of the population engaged in scientific and technical professions was high, and it continues to grow. According to the *Statistical Yearbook of the Republic of China, 2003,* in 1999, 231,000 people of a total population of just under 22 million and a labor force of 9.6 million were working in scientific and technical professions. By 2002 that number had risen to 285,000 of a total population of 22.4 million and a labor force of just under 10 million.[28] These numbers do not include members of the workforce engaged in educational services (477,000 in 1999 and 487,000 in 2002), of whom a significant proportion are involved in scientific and technical education. Of these scientific and technical professionals, about 122,000 were engaged in research and development in 2001. Nearly two-thirds of those researchers were employed in industry.[29] In terms of percentage of the population, Taiwan's numbers of researchers are thus comparable to other developed nations.[30]

ROC statistics also suggest that the relationship between industry, R&D institutes, and the educational system, by the 1990s, was finally mutually reinforcing. The number of researchers with university degrees or higher as a percentage of the total number of researchers in Taiwan rose steadily over the course of the 1990s, as did the number of researchers with a university degree or higher as a percentage of the total population and workforce.[31] Not only have more people been trained in major fields of R&D, but they have also increasingly been absorbed into the industrial workforce. In addition, although the private sector is only a minor source of R&D funding for educational institutions and public S&T institutes, the fact that the private sector contributes at all indicates at least a limited effort at coordinating educational agendas and private sector R&D interests. It appears, therefore, that by the 1990s scientific and technical education in Taiwan had become relevant to industry, something that had not been the case even as late as the 1980s.

A second important facet of Taiwan's manpower development program, brain drain reversal, has also become much more effective since the early 1980s, perhaps owing to reasons that were not explicitly part of the manpower program, such as Taiwan's democratization and its steadily rising standard of living. Since the 1980s increasing numbers of locals trained in foreign companies have returned to Taiwan, bringing with them technology and skills learned abroad. According to Heather Smith, "The ratio of returnees from abroad to students abroad increased from 15.6 per cent during 1971–1981 to 21.6 per cent during 1982–93. In particular, returnees with science and engineering degrees totaled 6172 in 1993, almost 5.6 times of the number returning in 1982."[32] As the economy has developed, more jobs have been created to absorb foreign-trained students, and these students are even more eager than their predecessors to return to a Taiwan where they can have a high standard of living and real opportunities for advancement in industry.

By 1997, when the National Science Council published the first "White Paper on Science and Technology" for the ROC, most of the ideas that scientists, foreign advisers, and technocrats had worked so hard to bring to the attention of Taiwan's political leadership in the 1960s and 1970s were taken for granted, and the tone of the white paper was clear and authoritative. "Technology is considered to be the most important factor in raising industrial competitiveness," it states. "The key to success in today's commercial world is to continuously invest in R&D and introduce new products and technologies faster than one's competitors. In addition, since knowledge of science and technology is crucial to the formulation of policies meeting the needs of a diversified society, scientific and technological information is especially vital as a decision-making tool."[33]

Taiwan has clearly moved into a new stage of S&T development, and the white paper made this patently clear as it presented a plan for the reconstruction of Taiwan as a science and technology island. It envisioned a Taiwan that, by 2010, would have established itself as a major regional research center and a major manufacturer of high-tech products and that had developed a network of science parks and science cities throughout the island.[34] The numerous new science and technology parks that have sprung up over the past few years make it abundantly clear that this process is well under way, although the increasing outward flow of technology manufacturing from Taiwan to China throws Taiwan's high-tech manufacturing future into question, and Taiwan's government may need to rethink this plan.

The Democratic Progressive Party (DPP), which gained control of the executive branch in 2000, has followed up on these ideas with considerable enthusiasm, focusing on the reconstruction of Taiwan as a knowledge-based economy and as a green silicon island. As one of Taiwan's diplomatic magazines reported in 2001, "The ROC government has already implemented a 'Plan to Develop a Knowledge-based Economy in Taiwan.' This plan will establish a mechanism for stimulating innovation and venture capital. It will lay the foundation for a high-bandwidth Internet environment and strengthen the application of information technology, thereby raising Taiwan's overall industrial competitiveness."[35] Taiwan has clearly identified information technology as its principal industrial focus, and the government continues to support the development of this industry and to tie its economic future to it.

Taiwan's Developmental State Today

Both the Ministry of Economic Affairs (STAG, in particular) and the National Science Council have continued to be the major shapers of S&T policy into the twenty-first century and have continued to get the largest budgets (excluding defense) for S&T development.[36] Even so, since the elections of 2000, the future of Taiwan's developmental state has been in question. To a certain extent, this sort of shift is expected in that it has long been the goal of STAG, for example, to see a transfer of responsibility for S&T development—R&D in particular—from the public to the private sector. Recent changes go farther than that, however. The coalition of government and technocracy appears to have fallen apart as democratization has led to political change at the top. The DPP government, in power since 2000, lacks the coercive authority that the KMT still had even after the lifting of martial law. The DPP has taken an explicitly antitechnocratic approach to staffing ministerial-level positions so that unlike the KMT government of the 1980s and 1990s, the DPP cabinet is no longer filled with Ph.D.'s or at least does not have as many. Moreover, the DPP has alienated and caused the retirements of many of the technocrats who rose through the ranks under the KMT. Although the question of whether or not democratization must inevitably be fatal to the developmental state is not one that this study will take up, it seems safe to say that Taiwan must now find new strategies for guiding economic development that are more compatible with democracy.[37]

Even if Taiwan's developmental state is in decline, however, China's is just hitting its stride. As the Chinese state searches for new strategies to promote industrial development, Taiwan's experience seems particularly relevant both as a model and as a part of a long-term process that began in mainland China and that is now being taken up again by Chinese leaders. Taiwan's experience thus serves as a bridge from early- to late-twentieth-century China. In spite of the fact that the Taiwan model came into existence in large part owing to a series of particular political crises, Taiwan's experience nonetheless serves as a model of how a Leninist party-state can merge political authority and the modernizing impulses of its technocrats to build institutions and coordinate educational and economic plans to promote economic modernization and development.

The story of ROC science policy tells us a good deal about the evolution of Taiwan's developmental state but also gives us some insight into twentieth-century Chinese perspectives on development, the role of the state in promoting development, and the value of science and technology to modernization. Twentieth-century Chinese modernizers have tended to be firm believers in planned economic development and in the significance of science and technology to the modernization process. Chinese political leaders, however, have not always been convinced and have not always been willing or able to support S&T development. The moments in which the aims of modernizers and political leaders have converged have been comparatively rare. Taiwan from 1978 until 2000 experienced one such extended moment. The PRC in the post-Mao era is also pursuing a model of scientific development that is very similar to that of the ROC's KMT.

China's Past

One of the earliest acts of the newly established PRC was to create a Chinese Academy of Sciences that subsumed the former institutes of Academia Sinica and the Beijing National Academy of Sciences. With this act,

China's scientific community was reorganized into a set of highly centralized soviet-style research institutions.[38] At the same time, it became apparent that the state intended to take a proactive role in pushing for scientific and technical development. Nonetheless, and owing in large part to a tension within the highest leadership circles between soviet-style modernizers and Maoists, for about a twenty-year period from the mid-1950s to the Deng Xiaoping era, China had an uneasy relationship with science and technology.

The state made big propaganda pushes in the 1950s to popularize science and technology and to promote general application of the scientific method by all of its citizens for the simplest activities.[39] In terms of economic policy, the PRC promulgated a Twelve-Year Plan for Scientific Development in 1957 that called for scientific development to meet national needs in areas such as economic development of mining and industry, agriculture, atomic energy, transportation, and health and simultaneously proposed that over 10,000 "advanced scientists" be trained by 1967.[40] A new institution, the Scientific Planning Commission, which would later become the Ministry of Science and Technology (MOST), was created to oversee implementation of the plan. This program led to some of the PRC's most notable scientific successes, such as mastery of the atomic and hydrogen bombs and the construction of space rockets. However, not long after the promulgation of the plan, as part of the new Great Leap Forward mass movement, Mao called for recognition of redness, that is, commitment to the revolution, over expertise, and because most Chinese were expected to have absorbed the scientific method, skilled scientists and technicians were rarely invited to participate in industrial and agricultural planning and implementation. Except in the case of certain fields, such as nuclear physics, scientists and technocrats were out, and revolutionaries were in.[41] Although scientists regained some of their former prestige in the early 1960s, following the failed Great Leap Forward, by 1966 they were again shunted aside, their professional organizations were disbanded, their journals were no longer published, and their conferences ceased to take place.[42]

Beginning with the Four Modernizations in 1977 and 1978, however, the winds shifted once more, and science and technology again became important developmental targets for the Chinese state. The push for planned and strategic scientific and technical development came, in particular, from China's new political leaders in the wake of Mao's death and the demise of the Gang of Four. In 1977 Hua Guofeng called for S&T development, and the following year China's first National Science Conference was held at which both Hua Guofeng and Deng Xiaoping spoke on the significance of S&T to national economic development before a group of about 6,000 scientists, technicians, and bureaucrats.[43] Since that time, the PRC has steadily taken on a developmental role that is quite similar to that of KMT-controlled China and Taiwan with one important difference. The driving force behind China's S&T development has been the political leadership rather than economic planners, scientists, or outside advisers.

By the late 1980s, China had what Tony Saich has described as "a comprehensive S&T system that would be the envy of most developing countries."[44] This system was built on a foundation of centralized, state-sponsored research institutions and was increasingly staffed by foreign-trained Ph.D.'s.[45] It was guided by a series of centralized plans that considered the relevance of S&T to general economic development and to the development of particular sectors of the economy. To a certain extent, Taiwan has served as a model for this process.

Learning from the Taiwan Experience

Though it would be overstating the case to suggest that Taiwan has served as China's only development model in the post-Mao era, there is no question but that Chinese intellectuals and the Chinese government have sought to learn from the Taiwan experience since at least 1986, when Nankai University established an Institute of Taiwan Economics. This institute, located at Wu Dayou's alma mater, was among the earliest of several institutes at China's universities dedicated to the study of Taiwan. It emphasized research on Taiwan's economy, cross-straits trade relations, and comparison of economies across the straits and was set up to train graduate students in these areas of study.[46] In other words, its purview was to research and learn from Taiwan's development experience as well as to learn more about Taiwan, which, after all, the PRC considers to be a part of China.

By the early 1990s, architects of Taiwan's S&T development process such as Wu Dayou and K. T. Li were themselves having increasing contact with the PRC. Li had been interacting with Chinese S&T leaders since at least as early as 1990, when Zhu Lilan, then vice-minister of science and technology for the PRC, praised his work in promoting Taiwan's development while introducing him as a keynote speaker at the Pacific Economic Cooperation Conference in Seoul.[47] In 1992, Wu, then president of Academia Sinica, visited China and subsequently invited twelve PRC scientists to visit Taiwan in an effort to encourage intellectual exchange.[48]

By the mid-1990s the Chinese had honed in on K. T. Li as a leading figure in Taiwan's economic development, and high-level Chinese leaders were seeking his advice. In 1993, at the suggestion of Stanford economist Lawrence Lau (Liu Zunyi), China's vice-minister of finance, Lou Jiwei, invited K. T. Li to attend a World Bank–sponsored conference in Dalian on China's economic reforms. Following the conference, at which the eighty-three-year-old Li presented a paper on "Taiwan's economic development successes and problems," Li met with both Jiang Zemin and Zhu Rongji in Beijing. During these meetings, Li discussed a variety of topics, such as elevating salaries of civil servants to cut down on corruption, implementation of a fair tax system, and cross-straits S&T cooperation. Li went on from Beijing to his hometown of Nanjing, where his alma mater Dongnan University (Southeast University) inaugurated a reading room in his name, as well as a new Institute of Taiwan Economics in its School of Economics and Management.[49]

Following this trip Li remained in touch with some of the people he had met and continued to correspond with them on topics related to Chinese economic reform. Lou Jiwei, for example, has written that Li sent him some of his own writings on the construction of a national treasury in Taiwan that had a considerable influence on Lou's own efforts to help the Chinese Ministry of Finance construct such a national treasury in China.[50] Likewise, Zhu Lilan, by that time China's minister of science and technology, met with Li on a 1998 visit to Taiwan to attend, in her capacity as Peking University Professor, a seminar on industrial technology and electronics.[51] At the same time, numerous volumes of Li's works have been published in simplified character editions in China.[52]

While the focus of much of the PRC's interest in K. T. Li and his policies was on his approach to finance, it seems clear that mainland planners interested in S&T development were also investigating the Taiwan model, and the character of China's recent S&T development suggests that they found in that model elements worthy of emulation. Central to China's developmentalism are many of the features that this volume has discussed in the cases of both Taiwan and KMT-controlled China.

Technocracy

In the Taiwan case, it took quite some time for the political leadership and the technocracy to merge. In the 1950s and 1960s, these were two clearly distinct groups that worked together on matters of importance to the technocrats. Moreover, Taiwan's technocracy included both economic planners who were appointed to their positions by the state and academicians who worked in state-sponsored research institutions but who did not, by and large, regard themselves as bureaucrats or servants of the state. The leading S&T technocrats of the 1960s and 1970s were all deeply committed to the KMT regime. In addition, they were all of the same broad generation, a generation shaped by a commitment to May Fourth scientism and a belief that science and technology were necessary tools of modernization. Nonetheless, the academicians among this group often had interests that were separate from those of the state, and it took a consistent and long-term campaign from foreign advisers to convince them to begin to push for coherent state policies to promote S&T development. In the early 1960s academicians and foreign advisers were the loudest voices calling for development of S&T and were joined by economic technocrats only in the mid-1960s. The political leadership, on the other hand, only occasionally noted that there might be some reason to support S&T development and was very slow to put its full weight behind such a strategy. It was not until the political leadership itself became more technocratic that S&T development strategies really began to work in Taiwan. The downside of this slow process of coming together of technocracy and political leadership may have been that S&T development came at a slower pace than might otherwise have been the case. The upside, however, is that the advocates of S&T development in Taiwan (academics and technocrats) were forced to build coalitions with each other and with foreign advisers to develop workable strategies to promote S&T development in the absence, through much of the 1960s and 1970s, of very much political support. As the political leadership became increasingly technocratized, beginning in the late 1970s, then, it continued to promote S&T development along lines that technocrats and academics had already come up with and embraced, in particular, outside advice.

Since the beginning of the Deng Xiaoping era the PRC's political leadership has taken a much keener interest in promoting S&T than Chiang Kai-shek's government ever did. As a result, the PRC has taken a more top-down approach to promoting scientific and technical development. This process began with the first National Science Conference in March 1978 (held, coincidentally, just two months after K. T. Li held his) and continued when Deng set the ball rolling for a series of development-minded engineers to succeed him in the top leadership positions, thus guaranteeing that S&T development would continue to be a pressing concern for China's political leadership.

In the post-Mao era, leaders at both the provincial and central levels have increasingly been selected, at least in part, for their educational attainment and their managerial and technocratic skills. As Lyman Miller has argued, "Deng differed profoundly from Mao, seeking not a socially transformative state but rather a regulatory state that could guide rapid modernization to build China's wealth and power."[53] This meant, at least in part, the regularization of processes to promote highly educated and managerially skilled people into positions of power, even at the highest level. Since the Deng era the Politburo has become increasingly technocractized so that by 2002, twenty-two of the twenty-five members of the Politburo had university educations, eighteen of those in engineering or other sciences. None of the members of the 1982 Politburo had university-level educations.[54]

A similar process has been under way at the provincial level as well. As Cheng Li has shown, whereas in 1982, 20 percent of provincial leaders were college graduates, by 2003, 98 percent of them had gone to college, and nearly 20 percent of those held Ph.D.'s. Engineers constituted the single largest group among those technocrats appointed to provincial leadership positions in the 1980s and 1990s, but more recently the educational backgrounds of the leadership have diversified, so that the number of leaders with degrees in economics and management now surpasses the number with engineering backgrounds.[55]

This emphasis on technocracy shows, perhaps more than anything else, that during the past two decades the CCP at all levels has fully adopted the belief of earlier KMT planners that economic development could be planned through scientific management and that it was the job of the government to plan and oversee development. The first prerequisite for this process is to staff government with skilled planners and managers. CCP leaders are thus returning to a pattern that was established in the first half of the twentieth century and that served the KMT well on Taiwan from the 1970s on.

Planning

Like the KMT, the CCP has long emphasized centralized planning of S&T development (and most other things as well). More recently, however, plans have focused on investment in R&D, construction of science and technology parks, and improvement of science education. By the mid-1990s, the PRC government was beginning to push comprehensive S&T development plans linked to five-year economic plans in much the same way that the KMT had done in the 1970s and 1980s.[56] In May 1995 the Chinese government held a national science and technology conference attended by CCP leaders and 6,000 delegates at which it was decided to accelerate China's S&T progress.[57] Shortly before the conference the CCP Central Committee and State Council had agreed upon a "Decision of the Central Committee of the Chinese Communist Party and the State Council on the Acceleration of Progress in Science and Technology," which outlined China's S&T goals. Among these goals were the plan to increase Chinese R&D spending (both public and private) to 1.5 percent of GDP by 2000 and the plan to simultaneously decentralize research in the applied sciences. At the conference, Jiang Zemin followed up on these ideas by suggesting that although the government should continue to support basic research, applied research should increasingly be undertaken by the private sector or in cooperative ventures. He further argued that China needed to work harder to improve its capacity to innovate and undertake its own R&D projects.[58]

At the same time, the "Decision" implicitly emphasized a continuing, central role for the state by arguing the need for both short-term and long-range plans with an emphasis on "limited objectives . . . [and] well defined priorities."[59] The "Decision" urged the state to focus, in particular, on popularizing science and technology among the masses, emphasizing science and technology in education, funding basic research, and creating an institutional and social environment that would allow for greater academic freedom and thus encourage innovation.[60]

Both the public and private sectors consistently worked to achieve the goals outlined in the 1995 "Decision," but by 2003 the time was ripe for the construction of yet another S&T plan. Between 2003 and the spring of 2006 the PRC government worked to construct a new overarching fifteen-year plan for science and technology. There is no question but that the political leadership was interested in this plan, as its construction was overseen by Premier Wen Jiabao, himself an engineer. Wen chaired a ministerial committee that oversaw a collection of twenty working groups made up of around 2,000 scientists and officials charged with designing the plan. The resulting plan was unveiled at the 2006 National Conference on Science and Technology and became a part of the eleventh five-year plan that was promulgated in March 2006. It focused on developing the areas of high-tech, energy, life sciences, and environment through increasing investment in R&D, offering tax breaks to companies performing their own R&D, and setting up policies to protect the intellectual property of Chinese researchers.

Education and Manpower

As in the case of Taiwan, science education has been a concern in China since the 1950s, and China has historically been more active in promoting mass science education than the KMT was. Like Taiwan in the 1950s and 1960s, China's efforts to promote S&T education were not linked in concrete ways to economic development planning until the mid-1980s. However, again like Taiwan, the educational policies promulgated by the CCP's Central Committee in 1985, calling for the training of economically and developmentally relevant manpower, did not yield immediate results. Instead, there was a disjuncture between top-down policy and the actual capacity of schools at all levels to respond to the policy.[61] Since the mid-1980s, observers have noted problems in China's S&T education such as a lack of qualified teachers, particularly at the university level; low remuneration for most, though not all, teachers; examinations that stress memorization over innovation; inadequate government financing of the nine-year compulsory education system in many rural areas; and the difficulty in developing good curricula and textbooks.[62] The PRC government has developed strategies to more fully engage higher education in China's overall scientific development process, however. According to statistics compiled by MOST, in 2005, 10.2 percent of China's R&D was being performed by institutions of higher education.[63] Through the creation of university-based science parks, MOST has attempted to promote increases in this output and to put university-level researchers to work on applied research that can assist industrial growth and development.

In addition, the CCP has supported various mass education strategies for both children and adults that are highly reminiscent of those employed by the KMT in the 1930s and 1940s and the CCP in the 1950s and 1960s. For example, Xinhua News Agency made a point of publicizing Hu Jintao's visit to the China Science and Technology Museum on International Children's Day of 2004.[64] Along similar lines, in November 2004, the China Association for Science and Technology co-sponsored a two-week-long Beijing International Scientific Film Festival showcasing films about advancements in the sciences.[65] On a more general level, the 2006 S&T development plan proposes increases in state funding for popularization of science, and both national and provincial government organs have increasingly used the Web to disseminate S&T educational resources for use in classrooms or elsewhere. Even so, S&T manpower remains a concern for the Chinese government, and one can find endless references in Chinese newspapers and Web sites to the need for talented manpower in particular sectors. This awareness parallels the experience of Taiwan from the 1960s through the 1980s.

Rhetoric of Scientism

As in the case of the KMT, CCP policy and rhetoric have increasingly reflected a kind of scientism, a belief in the utility of science to strengthen the nation. In the late 1970s the phrase "science and technology" began to appear with increasing frequency in official statements. By the time of the national science and technology conference in 1995, a new phrase, *kejiao xingguo,* "revitalizing the nation through science, technology, and education," was gaining popularity.[66] Scientific and technical education was becoming the key to China's economic development, and the government not only had adopted the rhetoric but was also working hard to popularize the idea.

Nonetheless, even as the rhetoric has become nearly ubiquitous, it still sometimes seems to be little more than rhetoric. For example, in 2001 Xu Guanghua, the minister of science and technology, said in a speech to the World Economic Forum, "We always believe that an energetic national economy will be one with S&T and economic impetus unceasingly pouring into newly emerged industries."[67] Sounding very much like political, rather than technocratic, KMT advocates of scientism in the 1930s and 1960s, Xu further observed,

> One salient feature of S&T in contemporary social development has been the integration of S&T and culture and the combination of scientific spirit and scientific rationale. A people lacking scientific culture is bound to be constrained in terms of livelihood and aspiration. The competition among

> nations has been largely embodied by the possession of, or extent of the possession of the power of S&T and culture. On the basis of Chinese civilization heritages we shall accept the guidance by scientific rationale, inherit the true spirit of science, facilitate the integration of scientific and humanistic spirits, and loyally safeguard the border of science.[68]

Science and a scientific spirit should thus infuse the Chinese people.

Beginning during the SARS battle in the fall of 2003, Hu Jintao promoted the "scientific development concept" *(kexue fazhanguan)*, which, among other things, "combines efforts to bring into play the role of science and technology with efforts to bring into play the advantages of human resources."[69] Among the problems that Hu has sought to address with this scientific development concept are those related to regional economic disparity, rural development, ecology, and the development of science and technology.[70] By 2006 the idea behind the term seemed to be that through scientific development would be brought about "an all-round progress of economy, society, and humanity."[71] Moreover, at least one observer suggested that Hu was positioning the concept as his own personal ideological contribution to the development approach initiated by Deng Xiaoping and Jiang Zemin.[72] Scientism has thus been fully embraced by China's political leadership.

Emphasis on R&D

One area in which the Chinese government has rapidly surpassed Taiwan is in the construction of technology parks designed, at least in part, along the lines of the Hsinchu model. These parks have followed two broad patterns. The earliest parks, some of which were constructed at roughly the same time as Hsinchu, were set up by universities in an effort to promote coordination of research between universities and enterprises. By 2006, fifty such parks had come into being, most in the period since 2000, and MOST announced that it planned to construct thirty more by 2010.[73] More recently, China has set up hundreds of technology parks located in industrial regions. Both the national and local governments actively support the construction of such parks and facilitate the process at the front end by "moving people around . . . to make way for developers," on the one hand, and fast-tracking bureaucratic processes for the residents of the parks, on the other hand.[74] These parks serve primarily as a vehicle for attracting foreign direct investment to support economic development in general and R&D in particular, and they have had considerable success in this area. In the spring of 2005, for example, eight multinational corporations, including major companies such as Philips, Cisco, and Honda, all announced that they would be investing millions of dollars to establish new research centers in Shanghai.[75] China appears to have had even more success than Taiwan in attracting foreign R&D investment to construct research centers in Chinese technology parks.

The downside of these technology parks, however, has been the insistence by multinational corporations that they should hold the patents for the results of R&D conducted with their funding. So although the parks have helped attract foreign businesses to China and boost the Chinese economy, they have, by and large, fostered a research environment that does not serve Chinese national interests. Few, if any, of the parks have been built around R&D institutions such as ITRI, and it may be that China should look more closely at that particular aspect of the Hsinchu model.

By 2006 the PRC government was clearly aware of its failure to promote the sort of R&D results that can help keep the economy booming. The 2006 S&T plan reflects this concern and emphasizes R&D and innovation above all. The plan called for China's spending on R&D to jump from 1.23 percent of GDP in 2004 to 2.5 percent of GDP by 2020. It identified sixteen key technologies into which the bulk of this R&D spending would be funneled and made innovation in these technologies the principal aim of the increase in R&D spending.[76] Innovation became the new catchphrase of the Chinese government in 2006, and both Hu Jintao and Wen Jiabao routinely spoke of the need for more innovation and, in particular, for the importance of increasing the number of patents held by Chinese-owned firms and Chinese people as it continues on the path of high-tech economic development.[77]

The Marriage of Political Authority and Technocracy

Both the structure of China's main S&T planning organ, the State Leading Group for Science, Technology, and Education, and the tale of the creation and promulgation of the 2006 S&T plan suggest that China has not found the same balance between political authority and technocracy that Taiwan was able to develop over the course of the 1970s, and this may be a problem. In 1996, the State Leading Group for Science, Technology, and Education was charged with overseeing the implementation of the "Decision" that had been promulgated at the 1995 National Conference on Science and Technology. This group was headed by then-Premier Zhu Rongji, and its membership consisted of the heads of the various ministries and other bureaucratic institutions responsible for various dimensions of S&T development, including the ministers of education, finance, and agriculture, as well as the head of MOST, the president of the Chinese Academy of Sciences, and others. Absent from the group were industrialists, entrepreneurs, and government outsiders, although experts from outside the government are sometimes brought in to report on topics under discussion.[78] The very structure of the group suggests that the PRC has chosen to take an insular and hierarchical approach to S&T development and that it has not elected, at least thus far, to use STAG as a model.

Between 2003 and 2006 the State Leading Group began to develop a new S&T development plan (briefly described earlier). In the early stages of the planning process, however, not all Chinese scientists at home or abroad liked the direction that the plan appeared to be taking. In the fall of 2004, the journal *Nature* published a Chinese supplement made up of articles by elite Chinese scientists, most of whom were located overseas, that critiqued China's existing S&T programs, institutions, and R&D funding system. They commented on the problem of promoting innovation in a bureaucratic and hierarchical culture, the difficulty of promoting good research in the absence of a system of blind peer review in place for grants or publications, the problematic structure of MOST, and the inherent inflexibility of large-scale planning projects.[79] Rather than listening to the critique, MOST looked for help from the General Administration of Press and Publication, the organ responsible for censoring the press, which subsequently banned further distribution of the *Nature* supplement and warned "Chinese editors not to play into the hands of foreign forces."[80] In other words, the fact that many of the critics were located abroad and working in systems other than the Chinese system made MOST suspicious rather than welcoming of their suggestions.

By early 2006 the approach that the political leaders of the PRC were taking to guiding China's S&T development became even clearer. At the opening of the Fourth National Conference on Science and Technology on January 9, 2006, China's president Hu Jintao said that one of the main tasks for the conference was to "make clear the development tasks and deploy the implementation of the country's middle-and-long-term program for science and technology development from 2006 to 2020."[81] Precisely who would make this clear was left vague, but Hu's statement leaves one with an overwhelming sense that the S&T plan was going to be imposed from the top and that China's researchers were expected to fall into step with the plan.

This story suggests two ways in which the PRC has not yet perfected its efforts to implement a Taiwan-style system of S&T development, if indeed it is attempting to do so, and two lessons that the PRC might learn from the Taiwan experience. First, while it is true that Taiwan's success in promoting S&T industrial development came in large part from its ability to marry political authority and technocratic expertise, Taiwan's political leaders were never the ones actually devising the S&T development plans or even designing the institutions, and this remained the case even after the political leadership became technocratized. The PRC, however, is still trying to find a balance in its marriage of political authority and technocracy, and thus far it appears that the political leadership is more activist in its attempts to guide the planners and scientists than Taiwan's political leadership ever was. Second, although under martial law Taiwan's political leaders were quite willing to silence certain types of criticism, they never used their authority to quiet technocratic or scientific voices that sought to critique but also to improve Taiwan's system. In fact, leading technocrats and advocates of S&T development, with the approval of, but little financial assistance from, the political leadership, created spaces such as the NCSD, national science conferences, and STAG, in which scientists and especially foreign advisers were invited to offer sometimes hard-hitting critiques. They would then respond to the comments they received as they constructed new policy and institutions. Although there is ample evidence that the PRC has sought advice from outsiders, it appears that MOST and the political leadership only want to hear criticism that fits into their existing plans and are not interested in criticism that challenges these plans. In other words, although the Chinese national government as well as Chinese local governments routinely invite overseas Chinese and foreign advisers to consult on particular projects, and there are any number of formal relationships and agreements between the Chinese and other states on science and technology, there does not yet seem to be a mechanism such as STAG in place for an open exchange of ideas, some of which might challenge the designs of the political leadership.

If the PRC is truly interested in following the Taiwan model, then it will need to overhaul the State Leading Group to include more scientists and entrepreneurs, some from abroad, perhaps, who can offer constructive criticism from a perspective that is not that of the state. Moreover, the political leadership must be willing to listen and respond to this criticism. Taiwan's political leaders prior to the late 1970s were mostly fairly ignorant of the potential importance of science and technology to the state and were often seen by modernizers as obstacles to development. It may be that the PRC's political leaders, by contrast, are both too interested in S&T development and too certain that they know the right path. In Taiwan, economic planners were almost certainly more conscientious and thorough in their efforts to solicit and make use of outside advice precisely because they had to convince the political leadership of the value of S&T. Even after they had a willing audience in the political leadership, Taiwan's technocrats continued to follow the patterns they had established earlier and continued to solicit and respond to foreign expert advice. Perhaps the technocratization of the PRC's political leadership is itself an obstacle rather than a help to the S&T development of China.

Whether or not Taiwan's approach to science policy has been viewed by the PRC as a model, it is clear that the PRC is following a very similar approach to what we have seen in the ROC.[82] The PRC has expanded its emphasis on science planning and science education while at the same time seeking to coordinate R&D efforts with the private sector. Moreover, as happened in Taiwan beginning in the late 1970s, the PRC's political leadership has become more technocratic and therefore more sensitive to the role to be played by S&T in economic development, although, as noted above, this technocratization of the political leadership may have brought a new set of problems. The rise of the technocracy, the coordination of technocratic and political leadership, the emphasis on planning, R&D, and manpower development are all part of a larger pattern of state-led development that characterized the ROC on the mainland in the 1930s and 1940s and again on Taiwan from the late 1970s on, a pattern that has reemerged in post-Mao China, and this does not seem coincidental. The PRC, which attempted to strike out in its own, unique direction after its founding, is falling back on a set of beliefs—albeit beliefs that come with all sorts of new, high-tech trappings—that have been shared by nearly all Chinese modernizers of the twentieth century. This time, however, the modernizers are also the political leaders, and such was not the case in Taiwan until the late 1970s. Thus far, Chinese modernizers have had the greatest success in Taiwan, where technocrats were able to harness state power while simultaneously listening and responding to the advice of outsiders. Whether the PRC can find a similar balance remains to be seen.

Notes

Note: For archival abbreviations in the notes, see page 195.

Introduction

1. Several authors have undertaken to write histories of Taiwan's industrial development, most of which focus on fiscal policy, the relationship between the state and the market, and the relationship between the state and private enterprise. See, for example, Robert Wade, *Governing the Market: Economic Theory and the Role of Government in East Asian Industrialization* (Princeton: Princeton University Press, 1990); Samuel P. S. Ho, *Economic Development of Taiwan, 1860–1970* (New Haven: Yale University Press, 1978); Wu Yongping, *A Political Explanation of Economic Growth: State Survival, Bureaucratic Politics, and Private Enterprises in the Making of Taiwan's Economy, 1950–1985* (Cambridge: Harvard University Press, 2005); Heather Smith, *Industry Policy in Taiwan and Korea in the 1980s: Winning the Market* (Cheltenham, UK: Edward Elgar, 2000); Cheng Tun-jen and Chu Yun-han, "State-Business Relationship in Taiwan: A Political Economy Perspective," in Peter C. Y. Chow, ed., *Taiwan's Modernization in Global Perspective* (Westport, CT: Praeger, 2002); Thomas B. Gold, *State and Society in the Taiwan Miracle* (Armonk, NY: M. E. Sharpe, 1986); Shirley W. Y. Kuo, "Government Policy in the Taiwanese Development Process: The Past 50 Years," in Erik Thorbecke and Henry Wan, eds., *Taiwan's Development Experience: Lessons on Roles of Government and Market* (Boston: Kluwer Academic Publishers, 1999).
2. All of the literature on Taiwan's S&T development has focused on the period of success as dated by the creation of particular institutions to guide S&T development. Their starting point is typically 1974, 1978, or the early 1980s. These works include Walter Arnold, "Science and Technology Development in Taiwan and South Korea," *Asian Survey* 28 (April 1988); Constance Squires Meaney,

"State Policy and the Development of Taiwan's Semiconductor Industry," in Joel D. Aberbach, David Dollar, and Kenneth L. Sokoloff, eds., *The Role of the State in Taiwan's Development* (Armonk, NY: M. E. Sharpe, 1994); Otto C. C. Lin, "Science and Technology Policy and Its Influence on Economic Development in Taiwan," in Henry S. Rowen, ed., *Behind East Asian Growth: The Political and Social Foundations of Prosperity* (London: Routledge, 1998); Paul K. C. Liu, "Science, Technology and Human Capital Formation," in Gustav Ranis, ed., *Taiwan: From Developing to Mature Economy* (Boulder, CO: Westview Press, 1992); Sun Chen, "Toward a Knowledge-Based Economy: Taiwan's Experience in Developing Science and Technology-Based Industries," *Industry of Free China* (March 1999).

3. René Maheu, "Introduction," in Philip Gillon and Hadassah Gillon, eds., *Science and Education in Developing States* (New York: Praeger, 1971), p. 3.

4. See, for example, Ming-cheng M. Lo, *Doctors within Borders: Profession, Ethnicity, and Modernity in Colonial Taiwan* (Berkeley: University of California Press, 2002); Ka-che Yip, *Health and National Reconstruction in Nationalist China: The Development of Modern Health Services* (Ann Arbor: Association for Asian Studies, 1995); T. H. Shen, *The Sino-American Joint Commission on Rural Reconstruction: Twenty Years of Cooperation for Agricultural Development* (Ithaca: Cornell University Press, 1970); Joseph A. Yager, *Transforming Agriculture in Taiwan: The Experience of the Joint Commission on Rural Reconstruction* (Ithaca: Cornell University Press, 1988).

5. See, for example, Smith, *Industry Policy,* who argues that "there is insufficient evidence to support the view that direct government intervention was important in furthering the industrial development of Taiwan during the 1980s" (p. 179). However, even Smith notes that technology policy probably did have a positive impact on the industrial sector. Other critics of the state-centered narrative of Taiwan's development include Frank S. T. Hsiao and Mei-chu W. Hsiao, "Taiwanese Economic Development and Foreign Trade," *Harvard Studies on Taiwan* 1 (1995); Lawrence J. Lau, "The Role of Government in Economic Development: Some Observations from the Experience of China, Hong Kong, and Taiwan," in Masahiko Aoki, Kim, Hyung-ki and Masahiro Okuno-Fujiwara, eds., *The Role of Government in East Asian Economic Development: Comparative Institutional Analysis* (Oxford: Clarendon Press, 1997); Cheng-tian Kuo, "Private Governance in Taiwan," in Steve Chan, Cal Clark, and Danny Lam, eds., *Beyond the Developmental State: East Asia's Political Economies Reconsidered* (New York: St. Martin's Press, 1998). Some of these works appear motivated by a reluctance to credit an authoritarian KMT with having had any positive impact on Taiwan.

6. See Wang Huei-Huang, *Technology, Economic Security, State, and the Political Economy of Economic Networks* (Lanham, MD: University Press of America,

1998), p. 141. Wang further argues that the KMT state discouraged the development of business networks in parts of the private sector that it did not wish to see develop.

7. Wu, *A Political Explanation.*
8. William C. Kirby, "Engineering China: Birth of the Developmental State, 1928–1937," in Yeh Wen-hsin, ed., *Becoming Chinese: Passages to Modernity and Beyond* (Berkeley: University of California Press, 2000); Morris L. Bian, *The Making of the State Enterprise System in Modern China: The Dynamics of Institutional Change* (Cambridge: Harvard University Press, 2005); David A. Pietz, *Engineering the State: The Huai River and Reconstruction in Nationalist China, 1927–1937* (New York: Routledge, 2002); Margherita Zanasi, "Nationalism, Autarky, and Economic Planning in 1930s China" (Ph.D. diss., Columbia University, 1997).
9. Linda Weiss, "Developmental States in Transition: Adapting, Dismantling, Innovating, Not 'Normalizing,'" The *Pacific Review* 13:1 (2000); Chalmers Johnson, "Political Institutions and Economic Performance: The Government-Business Relationship in Japan, South Korea and Taiwan," in Frederic C. Deyo, ed., *The Political Economy of the New Asian Industrialism* (Ithaca: Cornell University Press, 1987); Stephan Haggard, *Pathways from the Periphery: The Politics of Growth in the Newly Industrializing Countries* (Ithaca: Cornell University Press, 1990); Alice H. Amsden, "The State and Taiwan's Economic Development," in Peter B. Evans, Dietrich Rueschemeyer, and Theda Skocpol, eds., *Bringing the State Back In* (Cambridge: Cambridge University Press, 1985); Chien-kuo Pang, *The State and Economic Transformation: The Taiwan Case* (New York: Garland, 1992); Cheng Tun-jen and Chu Yun-han, "State-Business Relationship in Taiwan"; Meredith Jung-En Woo-Cumings, ed., *The Developmental State* (Ithaca: Cornell University Press, 1999).
10. Johnson and Weiss make the point that the state and private enterprise act in concert by using each other to achieve mutually beneficial ends. While I agree that a developmental state will not function if the private sector does not see some benefit in cooperating—and in fact I argue that the impetus for most of the reform of the S&T infrastructure came from outside the state—I nonetheless believe that the state must be in control of the direction of policy in order for it to be truly developmental. See Chalmers Johnson, "The Development State," in Woo-Cumings, *Developmental State,* p. 60; and Linda Weiss, *The Myth of the Powerless State* (Ithaca: Cornell University Press, 1998), p. 45.
11. Steven Chan, Cal Clark, and Danny Lam, "Looking beyond the Developmental State," in Steven Chan, Cal Clark, and Danny Lam, eds., *Beyond the Developmental State: East Asia's Political Economies Reconsidered* (New York: St. Martin's Press, 1998), p. 2; Johnson, "Political Institutions"; Karl Fields, *Enterprise and the State in Korea and Taiwan* (Ithaca: Cornell University Press, 1995),

p. 23; Cheng Tun-jen, "Transforming Taiwan's Economic Structure in the 20th Century," *China Quarterly* 165 (March 2001): 27.

12. Alice Amsden, basing her argument in part on the work of Edwin Winckler, sees the state as having been constituted of militarists, a group that would include Chiang Kai-shek and the political leadership, and technocrats, a group that came into being in the 1950s solely to facilitate the work of the USAID mission. See Amsden, "The State and Taiwan's Economic Development," p. 83.
13. Haggard, *Pathways from the Periphery;* Wu, *A Political Explanation.*
14. Wu, *A Political Explanation,* p. 11.
15. See, for example, Cheng Tun-jen, "Political Regimes and Development Strategies: South Korea and Taiwan," in Gary Gereffi and Donald L. Wyman, eds., *Manufacturing Miracles: Paths of Industrialization in Latin America and East Asia* (Princeton: Princeton University Press, 1990), pp. 159–160.
16. Haggard, *Pathways from the Periphery,* p. 3.
17. See, for example, Yang Tsui-hua, *Zhongjihui dui kexue de zanzhu* (Patronage of sciences: The China Foundation for the Promotion of Education and Culture) (Nankang: Institute of Modern History, Academia Sinica, 1991); Yang Tsui-hua and Huang Yi-long, eds., *Jindai zhongguo kejishi lunji* (Science and technology in modern China) (Nankang: Institute of Modern History, Academia Sinica, 1991); Daniel W. Kwok, *Scientism in Chinese Thought, 1900–1950* (New York: Biblo and Tannen, 1970); Peter Buck, *American Science and Modern China, 1876–1936* (Cambridge: Cambridge University Press, 1980).

1. Starts and Stops

1. Nathan Rosenberg, "Science and Technology Policy for the Asian NICs: Lessons from Economic History," in Robert E. Evenson and Gustav Ranis, eds., *Science and Technology: Lessons for Development Policy* (Boulder, CO: Westview Press, 1990), pp. 136–137.
2. Immanuel Wallerstein, *Unthinking Social Science: The Limits of Nineteenth Century Paradigms* (Cambridge: Polity Press, 1991), pp. 52–55. Wallerstein himself, of course, takes issue with this narrative of human progress.
3. Charles Gillispie, *Science and Polity in France at the End of the Old Regime* (Princeton: Princeton University Press, 1980).
4. Loren R. Graham, "The Development of Science Policy in the Soviet Union," in T. Dixon Long and Christopher Wright, eds., *Science Policies of Industrial Nations: Case Studies of the United States, Soviet Union, United Kingdom, France, Japan, and Sweden* (New York: Praeger, 1975), p. 15.
5. Stephen Awokoya, "Unesco's Science Education Experience in the Developing Countries," in Philip Gillon and Hadassah Gillon, eds., *Science and Education in Developing States* (New York: Praeger, 1971), p. 73.

6. See, for example, UNESCO, *Science and Technology in Asian Development* (Paris: UNESCO, 1970); Gillon and Gillon, *Science and Education;* UNESCO, *Science, Technology and Development in Asia and the Pacific* (Paris: UNESCO, 1983).
7. René Maheu, "Introduction," in Gillon and Gillon, *Science and Education,* p. 3.
8. Maheu, in ibid., p. 5.
9. See Joanna Waley-Cohen, "China and Western Technology in the Late Eighteenth Century," *American Historical Review* 98:5 (December 1993); Benjamin Elman, *On Their Own Terms: Science in China, 1550–1900* (Cambridge: Harvard University Press, 2005).
10. Mary C. Wright, *The Last Stand of Chinese Conservatism: The T'ung-chih Restoration, 1862–1874* (Stanford: Stanford University Press, 1957), p. 68.
11. Jonathan Porter, *Tseng Kuo-fan's Private Bureaucracy* (Berkeley: Center for Chinese Studies, 1972), pp. 44, 124, 126.
12. Elman, *On Their Own Terms,* pp. 283–319.
13. David Pong, *Shen Pao-chen and China's Modernization in the Nineteenth Century* (Cambridge: Cambridge University Press, 1994), p. 302.
14. Ibid., p. 308.
15. Li Hongzhang and Zeng Guofan, "The Proposal of Tseng and Li in 1871," in Teng Ssu-yu and John K. Fairbank, eds., *China's Response to the West: A Documentary Survey, 1839–1923* (Cambridge: Harvard University Press, 1961), p. 93.
16. Edward A. McCord, *The Power of the Gun: The Emergence of Modern Chinese Warlordism* (Berkeley: University of California Press, 1993), pp. 32–33.
17. Ibid., p. 49.
18. Ruth Hayhoe, "Cultural Tradition and Educational Modernization: Lessons from the Republican Era," in Ruth Hayhoe, ed., *Education and Modernization: The Chinese Experience* (Oxford: Pergamon Press, 1992), p. 51.
19. Marianne Bastid, *Educational Reform in Early Twentieth Century China,* trans. Paul J. Bailey (Ann Arbor: Center for Chinese Studies, University of Michigan, 1988), p. 56.
20. See James Reardon-Anderson, *The Study of Change: Chemistry in China, 1840–1949* (Cambridge: Cambridge University Press, 1991); Charlotte Furth, *Ting Wen-chiang: Science and China's New Culture* (Cambridge: Harvard University Press, 1970); Peter Buck, *American Science and Modern China, 1876–1936* (Cambridge: Cambridge University Press, 1980); John Z. Bowers, ed., *Science and Medicine in Twentieth-Century China: Research and Education* (Ann Arbor: Center for Chinese Studies, University of Michigan, 1988).
21. For details on the timing of and debates over the creation of Academia Sinica, see Chen Shiwei, "Legitimizing the State: Politics and the Founding of Academia Sinica in 1927," *Papers on Chinese History* 6 (Spring 1997): 33.
22. *Academia Sinica with Its Research Institutes* (Nanjing, 1929), p. 1.

23. *Daxue Yuan Gongbao* (University Council report) (Shanghai: Daxue yuan gongbao bianzhuan chu, 1928), pp. 63–65.
24. Ding Wenjiang, "Zhongyang yanjiu yuan de shiming" (Academia Sinica's mission), *Dongfang zazhi* (Eastern Miscellany) 32:2 (January 16, 1935): 5–8.
25. Margherita Zanasi, "Nationalism, Autarky, and Economic Planning in 1930s China" (Ph.D. diss., Columbia University, 1997), p. 7. Zanasi shows that much of the financing for the NEC was solicited by Minister of Finance T. V. Soong from private sources.
26. Ibid.; David A. Pietz, *Engineering the State: The Huai River and Reconstruction in Nationalist China, 1927–1937* (New York: Routledge, 2002); *Zhongguo xiandai shi cidian* (Dictionary of modern Chinese history) (Taipei: Jindai zhongguo chuban she, 1987), 2:398; *Chinese Year Book* (Shanghai: Commercial Press, Ltd., 1936–1937), pp. 363–388; *China Yearbook 1936* (Taipei: China Publishing Company, 1936), pp. 30–36.
27. William C. Kirby, "Technocratic Organization and Technological Development in China: The Nationalist Experience and Legacy, 1928–1953," in Denis Fred Simon and Merle Goldman, eds., *Science and Technology in Post-Mao China* (Cambridge: Harvard University Press, 1989), p. 29.
28. Zanasi, "Nationalism," p. 10.
29. William C. Kirby, "Continuity and Change in Modern China: Economic Planning on the Mainland and on Taiwan, 1943–1958," *Australian Journal of Chinese Affairs* 24 (July 1990): 126–127; Kirby, *Germany and Republican China* (Stanford: Stanford University Press, 1984), p. 92.
30. Nanjing-NBIR 448.
31. Nanjing-NRC 28–253; AS-Jingjibu 18–22–114, "Fazhan guofang kexue ji peiyang jishu renyuan xunlian jishu renyuan jihua dagang" (Outline plan to develop national defense science and cultivate technical personnel and train technical personnel), p. 10.
32. "Daxue ji zhuanke xuexiao zhi zuzhi fa" (Organizational law for universities and vocational schools), in Zhongguo wenhua jianshe xiehui, ed., *Shinian lai de zhongguo* (China's last ten years) (Changsha: Shangwu yinshu guan, 1937), p. 505; John Cleverley, *The Schooling of China: Tradition and Modernity in Chinese Education*, 2nd edition (Sydney: Allen and Unwin, 1991), p. 57.
33. *Higher Education in China* (Joint Office of the Educational and Cultural Organizations of China, 1936), p. 25.
34. Cleverley, *Schooling*, p. 57; *Shinian lai de zhongguo*, p. 522.
35. C. H. Becker, M. Falski, P. Langevin, and R.H. Tawney, *The Reorganization of Education in China* (Paris: League of Nations Institute of Intellectual Cooperation, 1932), p. 150.
36. *Higher Education in China*, p. 27. *Di er ci zhongguo jiaoyu nianjian* (The second China education yearbook) (Nanjing, 1948), 1: 3, also claimed that the

Ministry of Education's efforts to get more people into sciences had been very effective.

37. *Di er ci zhongguo jiaoyu nianjian,* 7: 1412, 1414.
38. Chen Duxiu as quoted in Chow Tse-tsung, *The May Fourth Movement: Intellectual Revolution in Modern China* (Stanford: Stanford University Press, 1960), p. 59.
39. Richard P. Suttmeier, *Research and Revolution: Science Policy and Societal Change in China* (Lexington: Lexington Books, 1974), p. 2.
40. Buck, *American Science and Modern China,* p. 207.
41. Ibid., p. 185.
42. Daniel W. Kwok, *Scientism in Chinese Thought, 1900–1950* (New York: Biblo and Tannen, 1970), p. 3.
43. Chiang Kai-shek, *Xin shenghuo yundong* (The New Life Movement), 5th edition (Nanjing: Zhengzhong shuju, 1935), p. 61.
44. See, for example, Chiang Kai-shek, "Daxue zhi dao" (The way of learning), "Kexue de daoli" (The reason of science), and "Wei xue banshi yu zuoren jiben yaodao" (Essential points for study, work, and being a person), in *Jiang zongtong yanlun lubian* (Collected speeches and writings of Chiang Kai-shek), vol. 16 (Taipei: Zhengzhong shuju, 1956).
45. Chiang Kai-shek, "Kexue de daoli," pp. 86–87.
46. Ibid., pp. 94–104.
47. Chiang Kai-shek, *China's Destiny,* trans. Philip Jaffe (New York: Roy Publishers, 1947), p. 180.
48. AS-Jingjibu 18–22–114.
49. AS-Jingjibu 18–22–114, "Fazhan guofang kexue yundong ji zhubu gongye kexue rencai fangan" (Proposal to develop the National Defense Science Movement and increase industrial science talent), p. 2.
50. Ibid., pp.2–5.
51. Nanjing–Ministry of Education 5–12244, 5–12249, 5–12265.
52. Nanjing–Ministry of Education 5–12280, 5–12282.
53. "Fazhan guofang kexue," pp. 11–14; AS-Jingjibu 18–22–104.
54. "Fazhan guofang kexue," p. 7; Nanjing-NRC 28–1641.
55. Joseph Needham, *Chinese Science* (London: Pilot Press Ltd., 1945).
56. Ren Hongjuan (H. C. Ren), as quoted in Hubert Freyn, *Chinese Education in the War* (Shanghai: Kelly and Walsh, Ltd., 1940), p. 96.
57. Zhu Jiahua, "Quanguo xueshu huiyi zhaoji yiyi" (The significance of calling together a meeting of scholars of the entire nation), in Wang Yijun, ed., *Zhu Jiahua xiansheng yanlunji* (Dissertations of Dr. Zhu Jiahua) (Taipei: Institute of Modern History, Academia Sinica, 1977), p. 5.
58. Zhu Jiahua, "Kexue shijie yu jianguo qiantu" (A scientific world and the future of nation-building), in Wang Yijun, *Zhu Jiahua xiansheng yanlunji,* p. 35.

59. Chinese Ministry of Education, ed., *China Handbook, 1937–1943: A Comprehensive Survey of Major Developments in China in Six Years of War* (New York: Macmillan Company, 1943), p. 406.
60. Ibid., pp. 407–411.
61. Nanjing-NBIR 448–2313.
62. Qian Changzhao, "Qian fuzhuren weiyuan xunci" (Vice Head Qian's lecture), in *Ziyuan weiyuanhui Weng Wenhao, Qian Changzhao yanlun* (Speeches by the NRC's Weng Wenhao and Qian Changzhao), Nanjing-NRC 28(2)–314, p. 13.
63. See, for example, Nanjing-NRC 28(2)–695, for communications between Weng Wenhao and the French ambassador to China, Henri Maux, or Nanjing-NRC 28–1533 for information on requests and receipts of microfilms from the U.S. State Department's Cultural Relations Division.
64. Weng Wenhao to Ambassador Clarence Gauss, July 25, 1944, Nanjing-NBIR 448–544.
65. Letter to Dr. Ku and Co-workers from Wm. Han-chu Lee et al., January 1945, Nanjing-NBIR 448–540.
66. AS-Jingjibu 18–22–104, "Letter from V. Bush to Ku Yu-hsiu." The charter of the U.S. Office of Scientific Research and Development and other information sent by Bush was all translated in its entirety into Chinese, which does not appear to have been a very common practice at the time. This suggests that the committee was quite serious about adapting the U.S. model to the Chinese case. Translations of the documents can be found in Nanjing-NRC 28–1641.
67. Nanjing–Academia Sinica 393–699.
68. *China Handbook, 1937–1945* (New York: Macmillan Company, 1947), p. 343.
69. Wilma Fairbank, "A Study of Chinese Educational Needs and Programs of U.S.-Located Agencies to Meet Them," Report to UNESCO, 1948, pp. 79–82.
70. Ibid., pp. 83–85.
71. Ibid., pp. 114–124.
72. Patricia Tsurumi, *Japanese Colonial Education in Taiwan, 1895–1945* (Cambridge: Harvard University Press, 1977), p. 254.
73. Results of a 1950 NRC survey of scientific talent *(kexue rencai)* in Taiwan suggest that Taiwanese respondents numbered between 20 percent and 25 percent of the total number of respondents. (AS-Jingjibu-NRC 24–06–1). Wang Fansen's biography of Fu Sinian, first president of the new National Taiwan University, also suggests that 88 percent of the staff at the old Taihoku had been Japanese who, of course, departed in 1945. By the beginning of Fu's tenure at NTU, as a result of these departures and the subsequent white terror in 1947, during which many of the remaining faculty were arrested or executed, less than 1 percent of the previous faculty were left. (Wang Fan-sen, *Fu Ssu-nien: A*

Life in Chinese History and Politics [Cambridge: Cambridge University Press, 2000), p. 187].) For a full discussion of the medical profession as it evolved in Taiwan under the Japanese, see Ming-cheng M. Lo, *Doctors within Borders: Profession, Ethnicity, and Modernity in Colonial Taiwan* (Berkeley: University of California Press, 2002).

74. The Science and Technology Planning Committee and the NBIR were not reconstructed on Taiwan.
75. The NRC, however, was disbanded and replaced by CUSA and the Industrial Development Commission in 1952.
76. AS-Jingjibu-NRC 24–06–1.
77. AS-Jingjibu-NRC 24–06–1, 2, and 3.
78. Zhang Jiyun (Chang Chi-yun), "Researches in Chinese Culture during Recent Years," in *China Yearbook 1957–58* (Taipei: China Publishing Company, 1958), p. 404.
79. Chang Peng-yuan, "Sino-American Scholarly Relations as Seen from Taiwan, 1949–1979," in Cecilia S. T. Chang, ed., *U.S.-R.O.C. Relations: From the White Paper to the Taiwan Relations Act* (New York: Institute of Asian Studies, St. John's University, 1984), pp. 42–52.
80. The Institute of History and Philology packed up its materials and sent them along with the National Palace Museum and National Central Library materials in the autumn of 1948 (the first shipment went out in December 1948, the second shipment in January 1949). No other institutes sent materials to Taiwan. The Institute of History and Philology materials included its library, artifacts, and archives (including the Zongli yamen archives) and totaled 1,151 boxes. They were shipped to Jilong and from there were sent to a warehouse in Yangmei in Taoyuan County (other artifacts were sent from there to a sugar warehouse in Taichung). Wu Dayou, *Zhongyang yanjiuyuan shi chugao* (A historical sketch of Academia Sinica) (Nankang: Zhongyang yanjiuyuan zong banshi chu, 1988), p. 63.
81. Ibid., p. 77.
82. Ibid., p. 80.
83. One reason for Academia Sinica's relative powerlessness was that, after its move to Taiwan, not only were its institutes scattered to the winds; it also no longer had a functioning governing body, and it took until 1956 for the Academy to begin to construct a plan on how to proceed. In 1956 the Academy did a registration of all *Yuanshi* (Academy members) and found that only 19 of the original 150 were in "free areas." On April 10, 1959, the *Yuanshi huiyi* voted in 14 new members. See Wu Dayou, *Zhongyang yanjiuyuan*, pp. 217–219.
84. See T. H. Shen, *The Sino-American Joint Commission on Rural Reconstruction: Twenty Years of Cooperation for Agricultural Development* (Ithaca: Cornell University Press, 1970); Joseph A. Yager, *Transforming Agriculture in Taiwan: The*

Experience of the Joint Commission on Rural Reconstruction (Ithaca: Cornell University Press, 1988); K. S. Yum, *Successful Economic Development of the Republic of China in Taiwan* (New York: Vantage Press, 1968).

85. Li Xianwen, who became head of Academia Sinica's new Institute of Botany, illustrates this point. He had been sent to Taiwan by Academia Sinica in 1947 to do research on sugar cane, and in 1949 he was the only highly trained botanist with any prior ties to Academia Sinica on the island. He rapidly became one of the most powerful biologists on the island.
86. As noted above, many of Taiwan's educated elite were jailed or killed during the white terror following the February 28 incident in 1947. Of those who remained, few spoke Mandarin, thus creating a separate problem. Moreover, the KMT, who had been in a protracted war against the Japanese on the mainland, tended to view Japanese-educated Taiwanese with a considerable degree of suspicion.
87. See, for instance, *China Yearbook, 1958–59*, p. 394, on the preparatory office of the Institute of Botany. "The Institute of Botany, still in preparatory stage, is concerned not only with theoretical study but also with the practical application of botanical knowledge." In all prior editions of the *China Yearbook* and *China Handbook* the Institute of Botany advertised itself as doing primarily theoretical research. In fact, USAID documents reveal that even during the early 1960s Chinese scholars failed to see the practical advantages of pursuing applied rather than basic research. See, for example, "Topics Discussed at Dinner Meeting, June 2, 1961," AS-Qian, Box 75, p. 1.
88. Zhu Jiahua, *Guoli zhongyang yanjiu yuan jianshuo* (A brief sketch of Academia Sinica) (Taipei: Academia Sinica, December 23, 1953), p. 19.
89. George St. Louis to Martin Wong (CUSA Secretary-General), May 4, 1955, AS-Zhu, Box 185.
90. Ibid.
91. Yen Chen-hsing, "Dui fazhan woguo yuanzi neng de zhanwang" (My views and hopes in relation to our development of atomic energy), *Yuanzineng weiyuanhui lubao* (Chinese AEC Bulletin) 2:3 (June 1966): 1.
92. "Agreement for Cooperation between the Government of the United States of America and the Government of the Republic of China Concerning Civil Uses of Atomic Energy," July 18, 1955, reprinted in Stephen P. Gibert and William M. Carpenter, eds., *America and Island China: A Documentary History* (Lanham, MD: University Press of America, 1984), pp. 168–172.
93. Bruce Billings, "The Republic of China and America: Seven Decades of Science and Technology Relations," in Sun Tung-hsun and Morris Wei-hsin Tien, eds., *R.O.C. and U.S.A. 1911–1981* (Taipei: American Studies Association of the Republic of China, 1982), p. 27; *China Yearbook 1958–59*, p. 416.
94. *China Yearbook 1958–59*, p. 416.

95. Paul R. Byerly Jr., "End of Tour Report, to AID/W from USAID/Taipei," August 6, 1963, AS-Qian, Box 77, p. 15.
96. Yen Chen-hsing, "Dui fazhan," p. 1.
97. David Albright and Corey Gay, "Taiwan: Nuclear Nightmare Averted," *Bulletin of the Atomic Scientists* 54:1 (January–February 1998): 56, say that "U.S. officials believed that the Chungshan Institute . . . hosted a nuclear weapons program."
98. Albright and Gay, ibid., pp. 55–56, say that Wu Dayou, who was consulted as a government science adviser, was asked to review a Chungshan Institute proposal for nuclear weapons development in 1967. One of his suggestions was that Taiwan's entire nuclear program be put under the guidance of the AEC. This suggestion led to the creation of the INER and the reorganization of the AEC.
99. Joseph A. Yager, ed., *Nonproliferation and U.S. Foreign Policy* (Washington, DC: Brookings Institution, 1980), p. 80.
100. *China Yearbook 1958–59*, p. 417.
101. Billings, "Republic of China and America," p. 27.
102. Albright and Gay, "Taiwan," p. 55.
103. "Memorandum Prepared in the Department of State," December 30, 1958, *FRUS*, 1958–1960, vol. 19, China, pp. 509–510.

2. The First Push

1. Wang Shijie, "Kexue shamo de luhua" (The greening of the scientific desert), written in memory of Professor Liu Dazong, October 20, 1975, AS-Wang, Box 11, p. 1.
2. Robert Wade, *Governing the Market: Economic Theory and the Role of Government in East Asian Industrialization* (Princeton: Princeton University Press, 1990), p. 195.
3. Cheng Tun-jen, "Political Regimes and Development Strategies: South Korea and Taiwan," in Gary Gereffi and Donald L. Wyman, eds., *Manufacturing Miracles: Paths of Industrialization in Latin American and East Asia* (Princeton: Princeton University Press, 1990), pp. 159–160.
4. Wu Yongping, *A Political Explanation of Economic Growth: State Survival, Bureaucratic Politics, and Private Enterprises in the Making of Taiwan's Economy, 1950–1985* (Cambridge: Harvard University Press, 2005), p. 28.
5. Stephan Haggard, *Pathways from the Periphery: The Politics of Growth in the Newly Industrializing Countries* (Ithaca: Cornell University Press, 1990); Alice H. Amsden, "The State and Taiwan's Economic Development," in Peter B. Evans, Dietrich Rueschemeyer, and Theda Skocpol, eds., *Bringing the State Back In* (Cambridge: Cambridge University Press, 1985).

6. Constance Squires Meaney, "State Policy and the Development of Taiwan's Semiconductor Industry," in Joel D. Aberbach, David Dollar, and Kenneth L. Sokoloff, eds., *The Role of the State in Taiwan's Development* (Armonk, NY: M. E. Sharpe, 1994), p. 172.
7. Ibid. See also Paul K. C. Liu, "Science, Technology and Human Capital Formation," in Gustav Ranis, ed., *Taiwan: From Developing to Mature Economy* (Boulder, CO: Westview Press, 1992), pp. 357–393.
8. Walter Arnold, "Science and Technology Development in Taiwan and South Korea," *Asian Survey* 28 (April 1988): 438.
9. Ibid., p. 444.
10. Ibid.
11. Jennie Hay Woo, "Education and Economic Growth in Taiwan: A Case of Successful Planning," *World Development* 19:8 (August 1991): 1032.
12. Ibid., p. 1041.
13. Ibid., p. 1032.
14. Thomas B. Gold, *State and Society in the Taiwan Miracle* (Armonk, NY: M. E. Sharpe, 1986), pp. 72–73.
15. William C. Kirby, "Continuity and Change in Modern China: Economic Planning on the Mainland and on Taiwan, 1943–1958," *Australian Journal of Chinese Affairs* 24 (July 1990): 136.
16. Neil H. Jacoby, *U.S. Aid to Taiwan: A Study of Foreign Aid, Self-Help, and Development* (New York: Praeger, 1966), pp. 60–61.
17. Wade, *Governing the Market,* p. 199; Jacoby, *U.S. Aid,* pp. 60–61.
18. Joseph A. Yager, *Transforming Agriculture in Taiwan: The Experience of the Joint Commission of Rural Reconstruction* (Ithaca: Cornell University Press, 1988), p. 268.
19. Chang Peng-yuan, "Sino-American Scholarly Relations as Seen from Taiwan, 1949–1979," in Cecilia S. T. Chang, ed., *U.S.-R.O.C. Relations: From the White Paper to the Taiwan Relations Act* (New York: Institute of Asian Studies, St. John's University, 1984), pp. 43–47.
20. Ibid., pp. 35–87.
21. See Woo, "Education."
22. According to Lee Bih-hearn, "State and Socio-economic Development in Taiwan, 1950–1989: The Transition from Early Industrialization to Postindustrialism" (Ph.D. diss., Temple University, 1991), p. 76, expenditures by the ROC government on education, science, and culture never surpassed 1 percent of total Central Government expenditures in the first half of the 1950s.
23. Wu Dayou, as quoted in Chang Peng-yuan, "Sino-American," pp. 37–38.
24. Chang Peng-yuan, "Sino-American," p. 38.
25. Jiang Tingfu (Tsiang T'ing-fu), "Diary," September 27, 1957, Widener Library, Harvard University.

26. Ibid., April 3, 1959.
27. Zhu Jiahua, *Guoli zhongyang yanjiu yuan jianshuo* (A brief sketch of Academia Sinica) (Taipei: Academia Sinica, December 23, 1953), pp. 14–15.
28. *Zhongyang yanjiuyuan gaikuang (minguo shiqi nian zhi sishiwu nian)* (Academia Sinica [1928–1956]) (Taipei: Academia Sinica, 1956), p. 16.
29. *China Yearbook 1963–64* (Taipei: China Publishing Company, 1964), p. 505.
30. According to Chang Peng-yuan, "Sino-American," pp. 38–39, Wu Dayou first came up with the idea of some kind of foundation for science in 1956 and proposed it to Zhu Jiahua. Chang also notes that the NCSD came about as a result of conversations between Hu Shi and Mei Yiqi, president of Qinghua University and minister of education.
31. *China Yearbook 1959–60*, pp. 508–509.
32. *China Yearbook 1960–61*, p. 536.
33. According to the constitution of the ROC, Academia Sinica falls under the jurisdiction of the Office of the President of the ROC, and the Ministry of Education is under control of the Executive Yuan.
34. Arnold, "Science and Technology," p. 444.
35. Qian Siliang, "Recent Development of Science Education and Research in Taiwan," address to the Rotary Club of Taipei, February 9, 1961, AS-Qian, Box 157, p. 3.
36. Paul R. Byerly Jr., "End of Tour Report, to AID/W from USAID/Taipei," August 6, 1963, AS-Qian, Box 77, p. 1.
37. Joseph A. Yager, "Telegram from the Embassy in the Republic of China to the Department of State" (Taipei, December 31, 1959), *FRUS*, 1958–1960, vol. 19, China, 1959–1960, p. 644.
38. "Memo on FY 1960 Science Education Grant Project from Y. C. Chu, CIECD to Howard Parsons, Director US AID/C," AS-Li, A120–6.
39. Byerly, "End of Tour Report," p. 1.
40. Nancy Bernkopf Tucker, *Taiwan, Hong Kong, and the United States, 1945–1992: Uncertain Friendships* (New York: Twayne Publishers, 1994), p. 82.
41. Ibid., p. 54.
42. According to its charter, Academia Sinica was supposed to oversee and coordinate the research being done at all state-sponsored institutions. This function had been performed to a limited extent by the Academy's advisory council, the *Pingyihui*, which was created in 1936.
43. Li Xianwen, as quoted in Chang Peng-yuan, "Sino-American," p. 53.
44. George E. Taylor, "Report on the Conference," in *Sino-American Conference on Intellectual Cooperation Report and Proceedings* (Seattle: University of Washington, 1960) p. 7.
45. Jiang Menglin (Chiang Monlin), "JCRR as an Example of Effective Sino-American Cooperation," AS-Qian, Box 171, p. 1. Depending on exactly what

Chiang meant by "local enterprise," this advice may have been in direct opposition to that given by USAID, for example, on the need to use such organizations to stimulate industrial development.

46. Taylor, "Report," p. 8.
47. "Report of the Committee on Natural Sciences," in *Sino-American Conference,* pp. 123–124.
48. Lee C. Teng, "Thoughts on Sino-American Intellectual Cooperation," in *Sino-American Conference,* p. 290.
49. "Report of the Committee on Natural Sciences," p. 125.
50. Wang Shijie, "27 October 1963 Address to the Sino-American Cultural Society in Washington," *FCR* 13:12 (December 1963): 13, AS-Wang, Box 11.
51. National Council for Scientific Development (NCSD), "Promotion of Science and Technology in Taiwan," December 1964, AS-Wang, Box 14, p. 6.
52. Wang Shijie, "Sino-American Science Cooperation," 1965, AS-Wang, Box 11, p. 6. According to Qian Siliang, "A General Report on the National Council on Science Development," AS-Qian, Box 41, p. 2, between 1959 and 1961 the government had provided NT$12.5 million to the NCSD. But beginning in 1961 the government began to set a percentage of profits from specific state enterprises, 3 percent in 1961 and 5 percent in 1963 (the actual NT$ amount for 1963 was NT$33.7 million). If both Wang Shijie and Qian Siliang are correct, then both the percentage and the real NT$ amount of the contribution by the government were less in 1965 than they had been in 1963.
53. Qian Siliang, "New Patterns of Inter-University Cooperation in the Natural and Physical Sciences," AS-Qian, Box 191, p. 3.
54. Qian, "General Report," p. 4. In NCSD, "Promotion of Science and Technology," p. 1, the NCSD provided different statistics on the use of the council's funds: "the Council has received appropriations totaling approximately NT$315 million or an equivalent of US$7.8 million, of which 70 per cent has been spent on construction of buildings and procurement of scientific equipment, books and references, and the remaining 30 per cent, on research grants, subsidies for research professors and other teachers and investigators, fellowships for studying abroad, and grants on scientific publications, and a small sum for administrative purposes."
55. Qian, "General Report," p. 4. See also Qian "New Patterns," p. 3; and Wang, "Address to the Sino-American Cultural Society," p. 12.
56. Qian, "Recent Development," p. 4.
57. Jiang Tingfu, "Diary," September 10, 1962.
58. Qian, "General Report," p. 1.
59. Wang, "Address to the Sino-American Cultural Society," p. 12.
60. Byerly, "End of Tour Report," pp. 8–9.

61. "Report of the Committee on Natural Sciences," p. 125.
62. Tucker, *Taiwan,* p. 82.
63. Wang, "Sino-American Science Cooperation," p. 3.
64. Ibid., p. 4.
65. Joseph B. Platt, "Joseph Platt to Wang Shijie," August 8, 1964, AS-Qian, Box 78.
66. Wang, "Sino-American Science Cooperation," pp. 3–4.
67. NCSD, "Promotion of Science and Technology," pp. 1–3.
68. Ibid., p. 3.
69. Ibid., pp. 3–5.
70. Wang Shijie, "Shuqi kexue yantaohui kaimushi: Wang Shijie yuanzhang baogao" (Summer science seminar opening session: A report by Wang Shijie, president of Academia Sinica), June 29, 1964, AS-Wang, Box 12, pp. 1–5.
71. Wang, "Sino-American Science Cooperation," p. 5.
72. NCSD, "Promotion of Science and Technology," p. 1.
73. Ibid.
74. "Scientific Manpower Development Program," January 1965, AS-Wang, Box 11, p. 1.
75. Ibid.
76. Charles V. Kidd, "The Loss of Scientist from Less to More Developed Countries" (National Institutes of Health, Bethesda, 1961?), AS-Qian, Box 41, p. 1.
77. Ibid., p. 5.
78. NCSD, "Promotion of Science and Technology," p. 2.
79. Ibid.
80. Possibly by C. K. Jen (a physicist at Johns Hopkins University), "The Planning of Science Education and Science Research in the Republic of China: A Preliminary Proposal for Cooperation and Assistance in Providing Advisory Services," 1963, AS-Wang, Box 7, p. 3.
81. Wang, "Address to the Sino-American Cultural Society," p. 10.
82. Wang Shijie, "Kexue zai Taiwan" (Science in Taiwan), December 10, 1966, speech to the Zhonghua nongyehui, AS-Wang, Box 12, pp. 1–11.

3. The State Gets Interested

1. K. T. Li, "Industrial Development and Industrial Research Activities in the Republic of China," April 15, 1964, AS-Qian, Box 41, p. 10.
2. Ibid.
3. Ibid., p. 12.
4. K. T. Li, "Address on 'Development of Human Resources and Its Relation with Science Education,'" address to JCRR, November 7, 1961, AS-Li, A-175, p. 1.
5. Ibid., p. 2.

6. C. K. Yen, "Premier C. K. Yen's Oral Administrative Report to the 1st Meeting of the 37th Session of the Legislative Yuan," *FCR* 16:3 (March 1966): 89.
7. Ibid.
8. "Culture, Science and Education," *FCR* 15:6 (June 1965): 75.
9. "Culture, Science and Education," *FCR* 15:12 (December 1965): 68.
10. C. K. Yen, "Yen yuanzhang yu diyijie kexue huiyi kaimu" (Opening Address to the First Science Meeting), November 2, 1965, AS-Li, B489–1, p. 1.
11. Ibid., pp. 1–4.
12. Ibid., p. 8.
13. "Di yi jie kexue huiyi: Yian shangyao lubian (di yizu)" (First National Science Conference: Record of discussions of proposals of the first session), AS-Li, B-489–3, p. 3.
14. Ibid., p. 4.
15. Ibid., pp. 6–8.
16. "Culture, Science and Education," *FCR* 16:7 (July 1966): 73.
17. "Culture, Science and Education," *FCR* 16:10 (October 1966): 83. This was a much more substantial commitment than anything the NCSD had been able to obtain in previous years. These state-sponsored activities were not the only new initiatives in the sciences in 1966. At the same time, the Chinese Engineers Associations of New York and Taiwan began to organize an ongoing series of technology and engineering lectures (the Modern Engineering Technology Seminar), which has gone on ever since. See Eric Lin, Xu Bingyan, Yang Meiping, and Xue Wenzhen, "Chinese with an American Education and Taiwan's Scientific and Technological Development," *Chinese Studies in History* 36:3 (Spring 2003): 22–37.
18. Committee for Science Development, "Report on the Development of Science and Technology in the Republic of China," 1967, AS-Li, B490–42, p. 1.
19. Wu Dayou, "Science Education and Research," 1967, AS-Li, B490–37, p. 4.
20. *China Yearbook, 1967–68* (Taipei: China Publishing Company, 1968), p. 130.
21. "Guojia anquan huiyi kexue fazhan zhidao weiyuanhui di yi ci huiyi jilu" (Records of the first meeting of the Committee for Science Development), March 29, 1967, AS-Li, B-493, p. 1. Other members included two national policy advisers to the president, Shen Yi and Chen Xueping.
22. Wu Dayou, "Kexue fazhan zhidao weiyuanhui" (Committee for Science Development), AS-Qian, Box 81, p. 1.
23. Wu Dayou, "Duiyu 'guojia changchi fazhan kexue weiyuanhui' wenti zhi jianyi" (Recommendations on the problems of the NCSD), April 10, 1969, AS-Qian, Box 81, pp. 1–3.
24. Donald F. Hornig, "Taipei News Conference Arrival Remarks by Dr. Donald F. Hornig," September 17, 1967, AS-Li, B490–18, p. 1.

25. Committee for Science Development, "Report on the Development of Science and Technology," pp. 2–3.
26. Wu Dayou, "Science Education and Research," p. 3.
27. Committee for Science Development, "Prospects of Industrial Development and Research Needs in the Republic of China," 1967, AS-Li, B490–44, p. 17.
28. K. T. Li, "Welcome Address to Hornig Mission," AS-Li, B490–19, p. 2.
29. "Minutes of Meeting with US S&T Advisory Team." AS-Li, B490–20, p. 1.
30. Hornig, "Taipei News Conference," p. 3.
31. "Minutes of Meeting with US S&T Advisory Team," p. 3.
32. Ibid., p. 2.
33. Ibid.
34. "Summary of Meeting with CKS," AS-Li, B490–23, 3; "Minutes of Meeting with Dr. Hornig and His Colleagues on Science Development in the Republic of China," AS-Li, B490–24, p. 14.
35. "Minutes of Meeting with Dr. Hornig," pp. 4–5.
36. Fisk, as quoted in ibid., p. 8.
37. "Summary of Meeting with CKS," p. 5.
38. Ibid.
39. "Minutes of Meeting with Dr. Hornig," p. 2.
40. "Summary of Meeting with CKS," pp. 1–2.
41. Wu Dayou, "Fazhan woguo kexue de xin jueci" (New plans for developing China's science), New Year's 1967, AS-Li, B488–8, pp. 1–2.
42. Ibid., pp. 3–4.
43. K. T. Li, "Memo to Eugene R. Black on Cooperation in Science and Technology Development in the Republic of China," October 11, 1968, AS-Li, A161–5.
44. "United States–Republic of China Cooperative Science Program, January 23, 1969 through June 30, 1971," AS-Qian, Box 43, p. 1.
45. C. K. Yen, "Address at the Fourth Joint Conference on Sino-American Science Co-operation," August 30, 1968, AS-Qian, Box 42, p. 5.
46. Chiang Kai-shek, "President Chiang Kai-shek's Youth Day Message," *FCR* 15:5 (May 1965): 78.
47. Ibid., p. 79.
48. Chiang Kai-shek, "President Chiang Kai-shek's Youth Day Message," *FCR* 16:5 (May 1966): 88.
49. Ibid.
50. "Culture, Science and Education" *FCR* 16:10 (October 1966): 83.
51. "Culture, Science and Education," *FCR* 17:9 (September 1967): 88.
52. Yen, "Address at the Fourth Joint Conference," p. 3.
53. W. Tozer, "Taiwan's 'Cultural Renaissance': A Preliminary View," *China Quarterly* 43 (July–September 1970): 96.
54. "Summary of Meeting with CKS," p. 4.

4. Coordinating Policy

1. Robert Wade, *Governing the Market: Economic Theory and the Role of Government in East Asian Industrialization* (Princeton: Princeton University Press, 1990), p. 81.
2. Ibid., pp. 87–97.
3. This is a point that is constantly reiterated in reports by Hornig, Platt, Kidd, Boundy, and others.
4. K. T. Li, "Address on 'Development of Human Resources and Its Relation with Science Education,'" address to JCRR, November 7, 1961, AS-Li, A-175, pp. 1–2.
5. Ibid., pp. 4–5.
6. Henry F. McCusker Jr. and Harry J. Robinson, *Report on Education and Development: The Role of Educational Planning in the Economic Development of the Republic of China* (Menlo Park, CA: Stanford Research Institute, October 1962). Paul Byerly, a USAID representative, also wrote in 1963 that the biggest problem for the development of scientific research capabilities in the ROC was the lack of qualified personnel. See Paul R. Byerly Jr., "End of Tour Report, to AID/W from USAID/Taipei," August 6, 1963, AS-Qian, Box 77, p. 9.
7. "Scientific Manpower Development Program," January 1965, AS-Wang, Box 11, p. 1.
8. Ibid., p. 1.
9. Joseph B. Platt, "Emigration of Scholars and the Development of Taiwan: Chinese-American Cooperation," *Development Digest* 4:1 (April 1966): 44.
10. Ibid., p. 43.
11. Ibid., p. 46. Li Ji (Li Chi) was the head of Academia Sinica's Institute of History and Philology and was one of the leading academicians in Taiwan in the 1950s and 1960s. He appears to have been in contact with most academic visitors from abroad, and references to his analyses of the dire situation of Taiwan's academic arena can be found in other sources as well. It is interesting that Platt met with Li Ji, since, as a natural scientist and representative of the American National Academy of Sciences, Platt's mission in Taiwan was clearly to offer solutions to the scientific manpower problem, and Li was typically more concerned with the improvement of Taiwan's social science and humanities infrastructure.
12. Ibid., p. 44.
13. July 19, 1967, memorandum to Ford Foundation titled "On Proposed Visiting Professorships to Help Stop Brain Drain in Taiwan," AS-Wang, Box 17, p. 1.
14. McCusker and Robinson, *Report on Education and Development*, pp. 7–8.
15. Ibid., p. 8.
16. CIECD, "The Republic of China's Fifth Four-Year Plan for Economic Development of Taiwan, 1969–1972" (Taipei: CIECD, 1969), p. 245.
17. Ibid., pp. 245–246.

18. Ibid., p. 249.
19. Ibid., pp. 260–261.
20. Ibid., p. 263.
21. Wang Shijie, "Address by Dr. Wang Shih-chieh at the Opening of Sino-American Conference on Manpower in Taiwan, June 26, 1972," AS-Wang, Box 12, p. 2. Wang's criticism would be repeated by ROC scholars throughout the decade. See, for example, Chang Pei-Chi, "Higher Education and Manpower Planning in Taiwan, the Republic of China," *Industry of Free China* (July 1980).
22. C. K. Yen, "Text of Address by Vice President C. K. Yen to the Sino-American Conference on Manpower in Taiwan at Its Opening Ceremony Held in Taipei, June 26, 1972," AS-Qian, Box 34, p. 5.
23. Manpower Development Committee, "Manpower Development in Republic of China," Executive Yuan, CIECD, June 1972, AS-Qian, Box 34, pp. 20–21.
24. Ibid., pp. 22–23.
25. R. H. Boundy, "Science and Technology in the Republic of China, The Report of a Study," February 20–May 10, 1968, AS-Li, A161–2, p. 4.
26. Wu Dayou, *Woguo de kexue fazhan* (China's scientific development) (Taipei: Xin shidai, 1968), pp. 6–8.
27. Wu Dayou, "Science Development in Taiwan and Sino-American Cooperation," *Industry of Free China* (July 1969): 6.
28. C. K. Yen, "Prime Minister C. K. Yen's Oral Report at the First Meeting of the 43rd Session of the Legislative Yuan," *FCR* 19:3 (March 1969): 73.
29. Ibid., pp. 73–74.
30. *Di sici zhonghua minguo jiaoyu nianjian* (Fourth education yearbook of the ROC) (Taipei: Zhengzhong shuju, 1974), pp. 922–923.
31. C. K. Yen, "Prime Minister Yen Chia-kan's Oral Report on the Administration of the Executive Yuan at the First Meeting of the 44th Session of the Legislative Yuan," *FCR* 19:10 (October 1969): 79.
32. Alice H. Amsden, "The State and Taiwan's Economic Development," in Peter B. Evans, Dietrich Rueschemeyer, and Theda Skocpol, eds., *Bringing the State Back In* (Cambridge: Cambridge University Press, 1985), pp. 96–97.
33. *China Yearbook 1957–58* (Taipei: China Publishing Company, 1958), p. 409.
34. See CIECD, "Accomplishments under Science Education Project as from FY1959–FY1964," AS-Qian, Box 41, p. 1; "Status Report of Science Education," AS-Qian, Box 77, pp. 1–5.
35. Li, "Development of Human Resources," pp. 3–4. Li did observe, however, that the ROC had to contend with a heavy defense burden that most other developing nations did not.
36. Ibid., pp. 8–9.
37. USAID, "Status Report of Science Education," August 6, 1962. AS-Li, A-175, p. 6.
38. Ibid., pp. 4–5.

39. J. A. Wissing, "Industrial Education and Training in Taiwan," *Industry of Free China* 24:5 (November 1965): 14.
40. *China Yearbook 1966–67,* pp. 388–389.
41. John Allen Chen, "Higher Education in the Republic of China (Taiwan)" (Ph.D. diss., University of Southern California, 1971), pp. 113–116.
42. Jennie Hay Woo, "Education and Economic Growth in Taiwan: A Case of Successful Planning," *World Development* 19:8 (August 1991): 1040. Woo's statistics are based on Ministry of Education sources.
43. H. Steve Hsieh, "University Education and Research in Taiwan," in Philip G. Altbach, ed., *Scientific Development and Higher Education: The Case of Newly Industrializing Nations* (New York: Praeger, 1989), p. 197.
44. Patrick J. Kennedy, *Republic of China: A Study of the Educational System of the Republic of China and a Guide to the Academic Placement of Students in Educational Institutions of the United States* (Washington, DC: U.S. Department of State, 1977), p. 61.
45. Council for Economic Planning and Development, *Taiwan Statistical Data Book, 1999* (Taipei: Council for Economic Planning and Development, 1999), pp. 281, 273.
46. Ibid., p. 273.
47. Ibid., pp. 275–277. From 1983 Taiwan's education statistics were compiled differently, so that, for example, business, which had previously been lumped in with the social sciences, was identified as a separate category from what was thereafter called "social and behavioral sciences."
48. Chang Pei-chi, "Higher Education," p. 18. Chang's statistics do not differentiate between the NCSD's research centers and other graduate programs that had come into being in the period leading up to 1978, so it is not possible to determine how many of these Ph.D.'s and M.A.'s were produced at the research centers.
49. Ibid., p. 14.
50. Ibid., pp. 10–14.
51. Ibid., p. 17.
52. Wu Yuan-li, *Becoming an Industrialized Nation: ROC's Development on Taiwan* (New York: Praeger, 1985), p. 80.
53. C. M. Hou and G. San, "National Systems Supporting Technical Advance in Industry—The Case of Taiwan," in R. Nelson, ed., *National Innovation Systems* (Oxford: Oxford University Press, 1993), p. 393.
54. Thomas L. Martin Jr., "Report to the Honorable K. T. Li, Minister without Portfolio, on the Visit to the Republic of China–Taiwan," March 1980, AS-Li, C26–2, p. 8.
55. Ibid., pp. 10–11, 13–14.
56. Thomas L. Martin Jr., "Report on Technical Manpower and Education," May 7, 1981, AS-Li, B-492, p. 3.

5. The Final Step

1. R. H. Boundy, "Science and Technology in the Republic of China, The Report of a Study," February 20–May 10, 1968, AS-Li, A161–2, p. 26.
2. K. T. Li, "Raising the Level of Science and Technology in Taiwan," in K. T. Li, *Economic Transformation of Taiwan, ROC* (London: Shepheard-Walwyn Ltd., 1988), pp. 232–233. As Wu Yongping observes, Taiwan's economic planners faced considerable criticism in the mid- to late 1970s over their early 1970s emphasis on building up heavy industry, and so the move toward high-tech development was at least in part a response to this criticism. At the same time, Wu notes, the state did not abandon all heavy industry because the KMT had vested interests in areas such as petrochemicals. See Wu Yongping, *A Political Explanation of Economic Growth: State Survival, Bureaucratic Politics, and Private Enterprises in the Making of Taiwan's Economy, 1950–1985* (Cambridge: Harvard University Press, 2005), pp. 240–241.
3. K. T. Li, "Strategy for Technological Development," in Li, *Economic Transformation of Taiwan.* p. 224.
4. W. W. Rostow, "Some Reflections on Taiwan: The Next Ten Years," Memo to K. T. Li, June 6, 1980, AS-Li, C4–85, p. 1.
5. Sun Chen, "Toward a Knowledge-Based Economy: Taiwan's Experience in Developing Science- and Technology-Based Industries," *Industry of Free China* (March 1999): 105. See also Otto C. C. Lin, "Science and Technology Policy and Its Influence on Economic Development in Taiwan," in Henry S. Rowen, ed., *Behind East Asian Growth: The Political and Social Foundations of Prosperity* (London: Routledge, 1998); K. T. Li, *The Evolution of Policy behind Taiwan's Development Success* (New Haven: Yale University Press, 1988).
6. By 1989 the Ministry of Economic Affairs was supporting twenty-two industrial research institutes, including ITRI. See H. Steve Hsieh, "University Education and Research in Taiwan," in Philip G. Altbach, ed., *Scientific Development and Higher Education: The Case of Newly Industrializing Nations* (New York: Praeger, 1989), pp. 188–189. See also *Zhonghua minguo yanjiu jigou minglu* (List of research organs in the ROC) (Taipei: zixun zhongxin, 1994). This volume is a directory of all research organizations in the sciences, social sciences, and humanities in Taiwan.
7. Sun, "Toward a Knowledge-Based Economy," p. 97.
8. Wu, *A Political Explanation,* p. 283, observes that between 1981 and 1985 small- and medium-sized enterprises (SMEs) produced over 60 percent of exports.
9. Ibid., p. 265.
10. "Performance Evaluation of Science and Technology Development Program," AS-Qian, Box 36, p. 24.

11. Nagy Hanna, Sandor Boyson, and Shakuntala Gunaratne, eds., *The East Asian Miracle and Information Technology: Strategic Management of Technological Learning* (Washington, DC: World Bank Discussion Paper 326, 1996), p. 126; "Industrial Technology Research Institute," AS-Li, B502–6, p. 2.
12. Sun, "Toward a Knowledge-Based Economy," p. 95. For more on ITRI and ERSO, see Constance Squires Meaney, "State Policy and the Development of Taiwan's Semiconductor Industry," in Joel D. Aberbach, David Dollar, and Kenneth L. Sokoloff, eds., *The Role of the State in Taiwan's Development* (Armonk, NY: M. E. Sharpe, 1994).
13. "Performance Evaluation of Science and Technology Development Program," p. 23.
14. Lutao Sophia Kang Wang, *K. T. Li and the Taiwan Experience* (Hsinchu: National Tsing Hua University Press, 2006), pp. 65, 86; Wu, *A Political Explanation,* pp. 76–79, 196. According to Wang, p. 191, Chiang Ching-kuo knew little about economic affairs and was quite stubborn. Wu (p. 76) is similarly critical of Chiang Ching-kuo's economic leadership skills and says that he shifted his own policy emphasis to economic affairs after 1969, not because he had particular skills in that area but because he already had control over national security, the military, and party affairs and wanted to further cement his control over remaining sectors of the party-state.
15. Robert Wade, *Governing the Market: Economic Theory and the Role of Government in East Asian Industrialization* (Princeton: Princeton University Press, 1990), p. 97.
16. "General Introduction, Coordinating Committee for the Application of Science and Technology to National Objectives, Executive Yuan, Republic of China," May 1977, AS-Li, A165–18, p. 2.
17. Wang, *K. T. Li,* chaps. 2–4.
18. See Wu, *A Political Explanation,* pp. 250–254; Kang Ludao, *Li guoding koushu lishi: Huashuo Taiwan jingyan* (The oral history of K. T. Li: Talking about the Taiwanese experience) (Taipei: Zhuoyue wenhua, 1993).
19. Wu Yongping has argued that the success of economic policy in the ROC has been dependent on the existence of bureaucratic strongmen, among whom he numbers both K. T. Li and Y. S. Sun. These men, according to Wu, were able to implement plans because of their authority and the respect they were granted by others in Taiwan (see Wu, *A Political Explanation*). A similar idea was conveyed to me by a STAG employee, who saw STAG's early success in coordinating government, industry, and academia as having been dependent on Li's personal power and charisma.
20. "Liushiwu nian shiyi yue ershiwu ri ben yuan di yiwulingsan huiyi" (Minutes from the 1503 meeting of the Executive Yuan), November 25, 1976, AS-Li, B-497, p. 2.

21. "Ben yuan yingyong jixu yanjiu fazhan xiaozu yici huiyi jilu" (Record of the first meeting of the Coordinating Committee for the Application of Science and Technology to National Objectives), December 9, 1976, AS-Li, B-497, pp. 5–7.
22. K. T. Li, "To Mark Shepherd, Jr.," December 17, 1977, AS-Li, B-491.
23. Materials from AS-Li, B-491.
24. "Minutes of the Meeting for Discussing ROC's Industrial and Technological Development Directions with Dr. Patrick E. Haggerty and Members of TI Mission," May 3, 1978, AS-Li, B-491–27, p. 3.
25. Patrick Haggerty, "Haggerty, Patrick, et al. to K. T. Li, et al.," May 17, 1978, AS-Li, B-491–5, p. 2.
26. Ibid., pp. 2–4.
27. Li, *The Evolution of Policy behind Taiwan's Development Success,* p. 107; Wang, *K. T. Li,* p. 201.
28. Frederick Seitz, *On the Frontier: My Life in Science* (New York: American Institute of Physics Press, 1994), p. 349.
29. Wade, *Governing,* pp. 277–278; Materials from AS-Li, B-485.
30. Wade, *Governing,* p. 277.
31. Excecutive Yuan, "Science and Technology Development Program of the Republic of China," October 1979, AS-Li, C4–85–29, pp. 1–2.
32. Sun, "Toward a Knowledge-Based Economy," p. 100.
33. Executive Yuan, "Science and Technology Development Program," pp. 18–19.
34. Ibid., pp. 23–31.
35. Ibid., p. 2.
36. The Executive Yuan, in fact, published a document to accompany the plan that provided diagrams explaining the roles to be played by the various ministries and committees involved. See "Kexue jixu fazhan fangan jianbao" (Brief report on the S&T Development Program), AS-Li, B-485–2.
37. "Ruhe jiji tuixing keji zhengti fazhan" (How to actively push the holistic development of S&T), AS-Li, B-493–8.
38. "Status Report on Implementation of Recommendations by Haggerty," May 1980, AS-Li, C-4–85, p. 1. See also Patrick Haggerty, "Letter from Haggerty to Li," August 6, 1979, AS-Li, A161–50.
39. "Status Report on Implementation of Recommendations by Haggerty," p. 1.
40. "Major Points of Science and Technology Advisory Group, Executive Yuan (Draft)," November 1979, AS-Li, C4–32.
41. Drafts of various STAG guidelines from AS-Li, C4–32.
42. Wade, *Governing,* p. 212; Wang, *K. T. Li,* p. 203, adds that K. T. Li "believed that a science and technology advisory group would greatly facilitate the transfer of American technology."
43. Wang, *K. T. Li,* p. 204.

44. "Guidelines for Discussion by Prime Minister's Board of Advisors on Science and Technology in January 1980 (3rd Draft, December 17, 1979)," AS-Li, C4–32.
45. Materials from AS-Qian, Box 36.
46. Y. S. Sun, "Address of Welcome to the First Board Meeting of the Advisors on Science and Technology," January 28, 1980, AS-Li, A166–3. Wang, *K. T. Li*, p. 202, also notes that Sun had risen through the ranks at Taiwan Power before entering politics and was especially supportive of Li's effort's to boost S&T.
47. Materials from AS-Qian, Box 36.
48. "Status Report on Recommendations of the First Science and Technology Advisory Board Meetings," AS-Qian, Box 36. The report makes specific responses to recommendations of the foreign advisers with subheadings titled "Progress Report on the Implementation of Dr. Wortman's Recommendations," for example. Still, at this early stage in the evolution of STAG, at any rate, the foreign advisers were playing a very prominent role, and their advice was being taken quite seriously.
49. "Performance Evaluation of Science and Technology Development Program," pp. 34–35.
50. Ibid., p. 36.
51. K. T. Li, "A Report on the Development of Science and Technology in the Republic of China, 1982–6," in Li, *Economic Transformation of Taiwan*, p. 238.
52. "Performance Evaluation of Science and Technology Development Program," pp. 42–44.
53. "Status Report on Recommendations of the First Science and Technology Advisory Board Meetings," p. 9.
54. Ibid., p. 2.
55. Ibid., pp. 3–4.
56. "Performance Evaluation of Science and Technology Development Program," 1–5.
57. Ibid., p. 7.
58. Ibid., pp. 21–24.
59. Ibid., p. 37.
60. Denis Fred Simon, "Taiwan's Emerging Technological Trajectory: Creating New Forms of Competitive Advantage," in Denis Fred Simon and Michael Y. M. Kau, eds., *Taiwan: Beyond the Economic Miracle* (Armonk, NY: M. E. Sharpe, 1992), p. 141.
61. Li, *The Evolution of Policy behind Taiwan's Development Success*, p. 108.
62. "Performance Evaluation of Science and Technology Development Program," p. 37.
63. Li, "Raising the Level of Science and Technology in Taiwan," p. 234.
64. "Performance Evaluation of Science and Technology Development Program," pp. 38–39.
65. Sun, "Toward a Knowledge-Based Economy," p. 99.

66. Wade, *Governing,* pp. 277–278. Only 15 percent of the 400 participants in the 1982 conference were from private industry.
67. Li, "A Report on the Development of Science and Technology in the Republic of China, 1982–6," p. 237; Hanna, Boyson, and Gunaratne, *East Asian Miracle,* p. 125.
68. Lin, "Science and Technology Policy in Taiwan," p. 195.
69. Li, "A Report on the Development of Science and Technology in the Republic of China, 1982–6," p. 245.
70. Ibid., p. 249.

Conclusion

1. Stephan Haggard, *Pathways from the Periphery: The Politics of Growth in the Newly Industrializing Countries* (Ithaca: Cornell University Press, 1990), p. 3; Wu Yongping, *A Political Explanation of Economic Growth: State Survival, Bureaucratic Politics, and Private Enterprises in the Making of Taiwan's Economy, 1950–1985* (Cambridge: Harvard University Press, 2005).
2. K. T. Li, *The Evolution of Policy behind Taiwan's Development Success* (New Haven: Yale University Press, 1988), pp. 108–109.
3. K. T. Li, "Strategy for Technological Development," in K. T. Li, *Economic Transformation of Taiwan, ROC* (London: Shepheard-Walwyn Ltd., 1988), p. 221.
4. K. T. Li, "A Report on the Development of Science and Technology in the Republic of China, 1982–6," in Li, *Economic Transformation,* p. 240.
5. Frederick Seitz, *On the Frontier: My Life in Science* (New York: American Institute of Physics Press, 1994), p. 352.
6. Science and Technology Advisory Group (STAG), "National Science and Technology Development" (Taipei: STAG, 1989), p. 4.
7. Ibid., p. 3.
8. Ibid., p. 28.
9. Otto C. C. Lin, "Science and Technology Policy and Its Influence on Economic Development in Taiwan," in Henry S. Rowen, ed., *Behind East Asian Growth: The Political and Social Foundations of Prosperity* (London: Routledge, 1998), p. 197.
10. National Science Council (NSC), *Indicators of Science and Technology, Republic of China (Charts)* (Taipei: Executive Yuan, 2002), p. 37.
11. Ibid., p. 43.
12. Ibid., p. 44.
13. Lin, "Science and Technology Policy," p. 197.
14. Ibid., p. 193.
15. Ibid., p. 197.
16. Sun Chen, "Toward a Knowledge-Based Economy: Taiwan's Experience in Developing Science- and Technology-Based Industries," *Industry of Free China* (March 1999): 98.

17. Lin, "Science and Technology Policy," p. 193.
18. Gee San, "Human Resources and Technological Advancement," in Chao-cheng Mai and Chien-sheng Shih, eds., *Taiwan's Economic Success since 1980* (Cheltenham, UK: Edward Elgar, 2001), p. 283.
19. Wang Huei-Huang, *Technology, Economic Security, State, and the Political Economy of Economic Networks* (Lanham, MD: University Press of America, 1998), p. 136.
20. *Taiwan Statistical Data Book, 1999,* p. 122.
21. Ibid., p. 124.
22. NSC, *Indicators of Science and Technology.* Taiwan's R&D expenditures as a percentage of GDP are slightly above that of the United Kingdom (1.88 percent in 1999) and slightly lower than France (2.18 percent in 1999).
23. STAG, "National Science and Technology Development," p. 8.
24. Executive Yuan, *Statistical Yearbook of the Republic of China, 2003* (Taipei: Executive Yuan, 2003), p. 97; NSC, *Indicators of Science and Technology,* p. 3. According to Lin, "Science and Technology Policy," p. 197, by the mid-1990s high-tech companies were investing about 5 percent of their sales revenue in R&D.
25. NSC, *Indicators of Science and Technology,* pp. 5, 18.
26. Ibid., p. 19.
27. *Taiwan Statistical Data Book, 1999,* p. 121.
28. Executive Yuan, *Statistical Yearbook 2003,* p. 49. It is not completely clear just how the Executive Yuan defines scientific and technical professionals. Overall population and total labor force statistics are on p. 43.
29. Executive Yuan, *Statistical Yearbook 2003,* p. 96; NSC, *Indicators of Science and Technology,* p. 8.
30. NSC, *Indicators of Science and Technology,* p. 59. Taiwan had 6.35 researchers per 1,000 in 2001, as compared to 9.7 in Japan in 2000, 7.9 in the United States in 1997, 6.8 in France in 1999, and 5.5 in the United Kingdom in 1998.
31. Ibid., pp. 24–27.
32. Heather Smith, *Industry Policy in Taiwan and Korea in the 1980s: Winning the Market* (Cheltenham, UK: Edward Elgar, 2000), p. 72.
33. National Science Council (NSC), "White Paper on Science and Technology: Vision for the Development of Science and Technology into the 21st Century Taiwan" (Taipei: National Science Council, 1997), p. i.
34. Ibid., pp. vi–vii.
35. Chang Chung-Hsiung, "A Green Silicon Island," *Geneva Diplomatic Magazine* 6 (June 2001): 8.
36. NSC, *Indicators of Science and Technology,* pp. 48–49.
37. Chu Yun-han, "Re-engineering the Developmental State in an Age of Globalization," *The China Review* 2:1 (Spring 2002).
38. Richard P. Suttmeier, "Science Policy and Organization," in Leo A. Orleans, ed., *Science in Contemporary China* (Stanford: Stanford University Press, 1980).

39. Leo A. Orleans, *Professional Manpower and Education in Communist China* (Washington, DC: National Science Foundation, 1961), p. 102.
40. Ibid., pp. 104–105.
41. Ruth Gamberg, *Red and Expert: Education in the People's Republic of China* (New York: Schocken Books, 1977); Hong Yung Lee, *From Revolutionary Cadres to Party Technocrats in Socialist China* (Berkeley: University of California Press, 1991).
42. Suttmeier, "Science Policy and Organization," p. 33.
43. Ibid., p. 35.
44. Tony Saich, *China's Science Policy in the 80s* (Manchester: Manchester University Press, 1989), p. 156.
45. See, for example, State Science and Technology Commission of the People's Republic of China, *Guide to China's Science and Technology Policy, 1987* (Oxford: Pergamon Press, 1987).
46. "Nankai daxue Taiwan jingji yanjiusuo: Ben suo gaikuang" (Nankai University Taiwan Economy Institute: About our institute), www.taiwansuo.com.
47. Richard P. Suttmeier, "Greater China and the Development of Science and Technology," in Zhiling Lin and Thomas W. Robinson, eds., *The Chinese and Their Future: Beijing, Taipei, and Hong Kong* (Washington, DC: AEI Press, 1994), p. 195.
48. Ibid., p. 208.
49. Wu Hongzhi, "Zhanhou Taiwan de jingji fazhan ruhe gei dalu jiejing: Yi Li Guoding wei li" (How Taiwan's postwar economic development serves as a mirror for the mainland: Taking K. T. Li as an example), www.japanresearch.org.tw, 4; Lou Jiwei, "Guoding xiansheng ersanshi" (Two or three things about Mr. K. T. Li), www.people.com.cn; Pieter Bottelier, "China and the World Bank: How a Partnership Was Built," Stanford Center for International Development, Working Paper No. 277, April 2006, pp. 20–21; Lutao Sophia Kang Wang, *K. T. Li and the Taiwan Experience* (Hsinchu: National Tsing Hua University Press, 2006), pp. 221–222.
50. Lou, "Guoding xiansheng."
51. Wu, "Zhanhou Taiwan," p. 5.
52. Wang, *K. T. Li*, p. 222.
53. Lyman Miller, "With Hu in Charge, Jiang's at Ease," *China Leadership Monitor* 13 (Winter 2005): 6.
54. H. Lyman Miller, "China's Leadership Transition: The First Stage," *China Leadership Monitor* 5 (Winter 2003): 60–61.
55. Cheng Li, "Educational and Professional Backgrounds of Current Provincial Leaders," *China Leadership Monitor* 8 (Fall 2003).
56. The CCP in its more Stalinist era had, of course, done something similar in the 1950s.

57. "Science and Technology Policy (14 May 2004)," www.chinaembassy-fi.org; "China's Science and Technology Policy for the Twenty-first Century—A View from the Top," Report from U.S. Embassy Beijing, November 1996, www.globalsecurity.org.
58. "China's Science and Technology Policy for the Twenty-First Century," pp. 1–2.
59. "Science and Technology Policy," p. 2.
60. Ibid., p. 2.
61. Keith M. Lewin, "Science Education in China: Transformation and Change in the 1980s," *Comparative Education Review* 31:3 (August 1987).
62. Ibid.
63. Ministry of Science and Technology, *2005 R&D Activities,* www.most.gov.cn.
64. Xinhuanet, "President Hu Joins Kids in Marking Children's Day (6 January 2004)," www.china-embassy.org.
65. "Beijing International Scientific Film Festival Begins (11 May 2004))," www.china-embassy.org/eng.
66. Cong Cao, "Strengthening China through Science and Education: China's Development Strategy toward the Twenty-First Century," *Issues and Studies* 38:3 (September 2002): 123.
67. Xu Guanghua, "A New Role of Science and Technology in Chinese Society" (speech at the World Economic Forum, Beijing, April 19, 2001), www.chinese-embassy.no, p. 2.
68. Ibid., p. 3.
69. Joseph Fewsmith, "Promoting the Scientific Development Concept," *China Leadership Monitor* 11 (Summer 2004): 2.
70. Ibid., p. 2.
71. Chua Chin Hon, "Hu Aiming to Be in Same League as Deng and Jiang," *Straits Times* (January 4, 2006).
72. Ibid.
73. "China to Promote Construction of College Technology Parks," May 11, 2000, http://english.people.com.cn; Wu Chong, "China to Build 30 New Science and Technology Parks" (April 19, 2006), www.scidev.net.
74. Dan Ilett, "China's Future—A Stroll in the Tech Park," July 7, 2006, www.zdnetasia.com.
75. "Top Transnational Corporations Set Up Research Centers in Shanghai (26 May 2005)," www.china-embassy.org/eng.
76. See Hu Jintao, "Hu Jintao zai quanguo kexue jishu dahui shang de jianghua (quanwen)" (Hu Jintao's speech at the National Conference on Science and Technology [full text]), January 9, 2006, http://news.xinhuanet.com; Edward Cody, "Chinese to Develop Sciences, Technology," *Washington Post* (February 10, 2006): A16.
77. Bruce Einhorn, "Blinding Science: China's Race to Innovate," *Business Week Online* (March 31, 2006), www.businessweek.com.

78. Cao, "Strengthing China," p. 125.
79. Many but not all of the articles in the *Nature* Chinese supplement had first been published in English in *Nature* 428 (March 11, 2004).
80. Hao Xin and Gong Yidong, "China Bets Big on Big Science," *Science* 311:5767 (March 17, 2006).
81. "Hu Urges Innovation in Science, Technology," January 9, 2006, http://english.gov.cn.
82. It has been argued that Taiwan "provided the leaders in the mainland with a model of success which they could not ignore and which has unquestionably caused them to introduce far more liberal policies." See Seitz, *On the Frontier*, p. 353.

Bibliography

Archives and Abbreviations

Nanjing Second Historical Archive

Academia Sinica (Nanjing–Academia Sinica)
Ministry of Education (Nanjing–Ministry of Education)
National Bureau of Industrial Research (Nanjing-NBIR)
National Resources Commission (Nanjing-NRC)

Academia Sinica, Institute of Modern History Archive

K. T. Li (AS-Li)
Ministry of Economy (AS-Jingjibu)
National Resources Commission (AS-Jingjibu-NRC)
Qian Siliang (AS-Qian)
Wang Shijie (AS-Wang)
Zhu Jiahua (AS-Zhu)

Abbreviations for Serials

FCR *Free China Review*
FRUS *Foreign Relations of the United States*

Books, Articles, and Documents

Aberbach, Joel D., David Dollar, and Kenneth L. Sokoloff, eds. *The Role of the State in Taiwan's Development.* Armonk, NY: M. E. Sharpe, 1993.
Academia Sinica with Its Research Institutes. Nanjing, 1929.

Albright, David, and Corey Gay. "Taiwan: Nuclear Nightmare Averted." *Bulletin of the Atomic Scientists* 54:1 (January–February 1998): 54–60.

Altbach, Philip G., et al., eds. *Scientific Development and Higher Education: The Case of Newly Industrializing Nations.* New York: Praeger, 1989.

Amsden, Alice H. "The State and Taiwan's Economic Development." In *Bringing the State Back In,* ed. Peter B. Evans, Dietrich Rueschemeyer, and Theda Skocpol, pp. 78–106. Cambridge: Cambridge University Press, 1985.

Arnold, Walter. "Bureaucratic Politics, State Capacity, and Taiwan's Automobile Industrial Policy." *Modern China* 15:2 (April 1989): 178–214.

———. "Science and Technology Development in Taiwan and South Korea." *Asian Survey* 28 (April 1988): 437–450.

Awokoya, Stephen. "Unesco's Science Education Experience in the Developing Countries." In *Science and Education in Developing States,* ed. Philip Gillon and Hadassah Gillon, pp. 73–87. New York: Praeger, 1971.

Bastid, Marianne. *Educational Reform in Early Twentieth Century China.* Trans. Paul J. Bailey. Ann Arbor: Center for Chinese Studies, University of Michigan, 1988.

Becker, C. H., M. Falski, P. Langevin, and R. H. Tawney. *The Reorganization of Education in China.* Paris: League of Nations Institute of Intellectual Co-operation, 1932.

Behrman, Jack N. *Industry Ties with Science and Technology Policies in Developing Countries.* Cambridge: Oelgeschlager, Gunn and Hain, 1980.

"Beijing International Scientific Film Festival Begins (11 May 2004)." www.china-embassy.org/eng.

"Ben yuan yingyong jixu yanjiu fazhan xiaozu yici huiyi jilu" (Record of the first meeting of the Coordinating Committee for the Application of Science and Technology to National Objectives). December 9, 1976. AS-Li, B-497.

Bian, Morris L. *The Making of the State Enterprise System in Modern China: The Dynamics of Institutional Change.* Cambridge: Harvard University Press, 2005.

———. "The Sino-Japanese War and the Formation of the State Enterprise System in China: A Case Study of the Dadukou Iron and Steel Works, 1938–1945." *Enterprise & Society* 3 (March 2002): 80–123.

Billings, Bruce. "The Republic of China and America: Seven Decades of Science and Technology Relations." In *R.O.C. and U.S.A. 1911–1981,* ed. Sun Tung-hsun and Morris Wei-hsin Tien, pp. 21–40. Taipei: American Studies Association of the Republic of China, 1982.

Bottelier, Pieter. "China and the World Bank: How a Partnership Was Built." Working Paper No. 277, Stanford Center for International Development, April 2006.

Boundy, R. H. "Science and Technology in the Republic of China, The Report of a Study." February 20–May 10, 1968. AS-Li, A161–2.

Bowers, John Z., ed. *Science and Medicine in Twentieth-Century China: Research and Education.* Ann Arbor: Center for Chinese Studies, University of Michigan, 1988.

Buck, Peter. *American Science and Modern China, 1876–1936.* Cambridge: Cambridge University Press, 1980.

Byerly, Paul R., Jr. "End of Tour Report, to AID/W from USAID/Taipei." August 6, 1963. AS-Qian, Box 77.

———. "Letter to K. P. Zi, Executive Secretary, NCSD." AS-Qian, Box 77.

Cao, Cong. "Strengthening China through Science and Education: China's Development Strategy toward the Twenty-First Century." *Issues and Studies* 38:3 (September 2002): 122–149.

Central Committee of the Kuomintang. "The Kuomintang Political Platform." Taipei: Department of Information, 1969.

———. "Outlines for Political Renovation." Taipei: Department of Information, 1969.

Chan, Steven, Cal Clark, and Danny Lam, eds. *Beyond the Developmental State: East Asia's Political Economies Reconsidered.* New York: St. Martin's Press, 1998.

———."Looking beyond the Developmental State." In *Beyond the Developmental State: East Asia's Political Economies Reconsidered,* ed. Steven Chan, Cal Clark and Danny Lam, pp. 1–8. New York: St. Martin's Press, 1998.

Chang, Cecilia S. T., ed. *U.S.-R.O.C. Relations: From the White Paper to the Taiwan Relations Act.* New York: Institute of Asian Studies, St. John's University, 1984.

Chang, Chi-yun. "Researches in Chinese Culture during Recent Years." In *China Yearbook 1957–58.* Taipei: China Publishing Company, 1958, pp. 404–409.

Chang, Chung-Hsiung. "A Green Silicon Island." *Geneva Diplomatic Magazine* 6 (June 2001): 5–8.

Chang, Pei-Chi. "Higher Education and Manpower Planning in Taiwan, the Republic of China." *Industry of Free China* 54:1 (July 1980): 10–21.

Chang, Peng-yuan. "Sino-American Scholarly Relations as Seen from Taiwan, 1949–1979." In *U.S.-R.O.C. Relations: From the White Paper to the Taiwan Relations Act,* ed. Cecelia S. T. Chang, pp. 35–87. New York: Institute of Asian Studies, St. John's University, 1984.

Chen, John Allen. "Higher Education in the Republic of China (Taiwan)." Ph.D. diss., University of Southern California, 1971.

Chen, Shiwei. "Legitimizing the State: Politics and the Founding of Academia Sinica in 1927." *Papers on Chinese History* 6 (Spring 1997): 23–42.

Cheng, Tien-fong. "Educational Developments and Reforms in Free China." In *Selected Speeches and Writings of Dr. Tien-fong Cheng,* ed. Ministry of Education, pp. 165–209. Taipei: Ministry of Education, 1954.

Cheng, Tun-jen. "Political Regimes and Development Strategies: South Korea and Taiwan." In *Manufacturing Miracles: Paths of Industrialization in Latin America and East Asia*, ed. Gary Gereffi and Donald L. Wyman, pp. 139–178. Princeton: Princeton University Press, 1990.

———. "Transforming Taiwan's Economic Structure in the 20th Century." *China Quarterly* 165 (March 2001): 19–36.

Cheng, Tun-jen and Chu Yun-han. "State-Business Relations in South Korea and Taiwan." In *Emerging Market Democracies: East Asia and Latin America*, ed. Laurence Whitehead, pp. 31–62. Baltimore: Johns Hopkins University Press, 2002.

———. "State-Business Relationship in Taiwan: A Political Economy Perspective." In *Taiwan's Modernization in Global Perspective*, ed. Peter C. Y. Chow, pp. 195–214. Westport, CT: Praeger, 2002.

Cheng, Tun-jen and Stephan Haggard. *Newly Industrializing Asia in Transition: Policy Reform and American Response.* Berkeley: Institute of International Studies, University of California, 1987.

Cheng, Tun-jen, Stephan Haggard, and David Kang. "Institutions and Growth in Korea and Taiwan: The Bureaucracy." *Journal of Development Studies* 34:6 (August 1998): 87–112.

Chiang, Jong-Tsong. "Development of Technology Management in Taiwan." In *Developing Technology Managers in the Pacific Rim: Comparative Strategies*, ed. Karen Minden and Wong Poh-Kam, pp. 122–136. Armonk, NY: M. E. Sharpe, 1996.

Chiang, Kai-shek. *China's Destiny.* Trans. Philip Jaffe. New York: Roy Publishers, 1947.

———. *Jiang zongtong yanlun lubian* (Collected speeches and writings of Chiang Kai-shek). Taipei: Zhengzhong shuju, 1956.

———. "President Chiang Kai-shek's Address to the National Assembly at the Closing of Its Fourth Plenary Session." *FCR* 16:5 (May 1966): 83–85.

———. "President Chiang Kai-shek's Youth Day Message." *FCR* 13:5 (May 1963): 94–96.

———. "President Chiang Kai-shek's Youth Day Message." *FCR* 15:5 (May 1965): 77–80.

———. "President Chiang Kai-shek's Youth Day Message." *FCR* 16:5 (May 1966): 86–89.

———. "President Chiang Kai-shek's Youth Day Message." *FCR* 18:5 (May 1968): 76–78.

———. *Xin shenghuo yundong* (The New Life Movement). 5th edition. Nanjing: Zhengzhong shuju, 1935.

Chiang, Monlin (Jiang Menglin). "JCRR as an Example of Effective Sino-American Cooperation." AS-Qian, Box 171.

China Handbook. Taipei: China Publishing Company, multiple years.

China Handbook, 1937–1945. New York: Macmillan Company, 1947.

"China to Promote Construction of College Technology Parks." May 11, 2000. http://english.people.com.cn.

China Yearbook. Taipei: China Publishing Company, multiple years.

"China's Science and Technology Policy for the Twenty-First Century—A View from the Top." Report from U.S. Embassy Beijing, November 1996. www.globalsecurity.org.

Chinese Ministry of Education, ed. *China Handbook, 1937–1943: A Comprehensive Survey of Major Developments in China in Six Years of War.* New York: Macmillan Company, 1943.

Chinese Year Book. Shanghai: Commercial Press, Ltd., 1936–1937.

Chow, Peter C. Y., ed. *Taiwan in the Global Economy: From an Agrarian Economy to an Exporter of High-Tech Products.* Westport, CT: Praeger, 2002.

———. *Taiwan's Modernization in Global Perspective.* Westport, CT: Praeger, 2002.

Chow, Tse-tsung. *The May Fourth Movement: Intellectual Revolution in Modern China.* Stanford: Stanford University Press, 1960.

Chu, Yun-han. "Re-engineering the Developmental State in an Age of Globalization." *The China Review* 2:1 (Spring 2002): 29–59.

———. "The State and the Development of the Automobile Industry in South Korea and Taiwan." In *The Role of the State in Taiwan's Development,* ed. Joel D. Aberbach, David Dollar, and Kenneth L. Sokoloff, pp. 125–169. Armonk, NY: M. E. Sharpe, 1993.

Chua, Chin Hon. "Hu Aiming to Be in Same League as Deng and Jiang." *Straits Times* (January 4, 2006).

CIECD. "Accomplishments under Science Education Project as from FY1959–FY1964." AS-Qian, Box 41.

———. "The Republic of China's Fifth Four-Year Plan for Economic Development of Taiwan, 1969–1972." Taipei: CIECD, 1969.

Clark, Cal. "Economic Development in Taiwan: A Model of a Political Economy." *Journal of Asian and African Studies* 22 (January–April 1987): 1–16.

———. *Taiwan's Development: Implications for Contending Political Economy Paradigms.* New York: Greenwood Press, 1989.

Cleverley, John. *The Schooling of China: Tradition and Modernity in Chinese Education.* 2nd edition. Sydney: Allen and Unwin, 1991.

Cody, Edward. "Chinese to Develop Sciences, Technology." *Washington Post* (February 10, 2006): A16.

Cohen, Wesley M., and Daniel A. Levinthal. "Innovation and Learning: The Two Faces of R&D." *Economic Journal* 99:397 (September 1989): 569–596.

Committee for Science Development. "Prospects of Industrial Development and Research Needs in the Republic of China." 1967. AS-Li, B490–44.

———. "Report on the Development of Science and Technology in the Republic of China." 1967. AS-Li, B490–42.

———. "Science Education and Research." 1967. AS-Li, B490–43.

Council for Economic Planning and Development. *Taiwan Statistical Data Book, 1999.* Taipei: Council for Economic Planning and Development, 1999.

"Culture, Science and Education." *FCR* 15:6 (June 1965): 74–75.

"Culture, Science and Education." *FCR* 15:12 (December 1965): 67–69.

"Culture, Science and Education." *FCR* 16:7 (July 1966): 73–76.

"Culture, Science and Education." *FCR* 16:10 (October 1966): 83–85.

"Culture, Science and Education." *FCR* 17:9 (September 1967): 86–88.

"Daxue ji zhuanke xuexiao zhi zuzhi fa" (Organizational law for universities and vocational Schools). In *Shinian lai de zhongguo* (China's last ten years), ed. Zhongguo wenhua jianshe xiehui. Changsha: Shangwu yinshu guan, 1937.

Daxue Yuan Gongbao (University Council report). Shanghai: Daxue yuan gongbao bianzhuan chu, 1928.

Deyo, Frederic C., ed. *The Political Economy of the New Asian Industrialism.* Ithaca: Cornell University Press, 1987.

Di er ci zhongguo jiaoyu nianjian (The second China education yearbook). Nanjing, 1948.

Di sici zhonghua minguo jiaoyu nianjian (Fourth education yearbook of the ROC). Taipei: Zhengzhong shuju, 1974.

"Di yi jie kexue huiyi: Yian shangyao lubian (di yizu)" (First National Science Conference: Record of discussions of proposals in the first session). AS-Li, B-489–3.

Ding, Wenjiang. "Zhongyang yanjiu yuan de shiming" (Academia Sinica's mission). *Dongfang zazhi* (Eastern Miscellany) 32:2 (January 16, 1935).

Einhorn, Bruce. "Blinding Science: China's Race to Innovate." *Business Week Online* (March 31, 2006). www.businessweek.com.

Elman, Benjamin. *On Their Own Terms: Science in China, 1550–1900.* Cambridge: Harvard University Press, 2005.

Evans, Peter, Dietrich Rueschemeyer, and Theda Skocpol, eds. *Bringing the State Back In.* Cambridge: Cambridge University Press, 1985.

Evenson, Robert E., and Gustav Ranis. *Science and Technology: Lessons for Development Policy.* Boulder, CO: Westview Press, 1990.

Executive Yuan. "Science and Technology Development Program of the Republic of China." October 1979. AS-Li, C4–85–29.

———. *Statistical Yearbook of the Republic of China, 2003.* Taipei: Executive Yuan, 2003.

Fairbank, Wilma. "A Study of Chinese Educational Needs and Programs of U.S.-Located Agencies to Meet Them." Report to UNESCO, 1948.

"Fazhan guofang kexue ji peiyang jishu renyuan xunlian jishu renyuan jihua dagang" (Outline plan to develop national defense science and cultivate technical personnel and train technical personnel). AS-Jingjibu 18–22–114.

Fewsmith, Joseph. *Dilemmas of Reform in China: Political Conflict and Economic Debate.* Armonk, NY: M. E. Sharpe, 1994.

———. "Promoting the Scientific Development Concept." *China Leadership Monitor* 11 (Summer 2004): 1–10.

Fields, Karl. *Enterprise and the State in Korea and Taiwan.* Ithaca: Cornell University Press, 1995.

Freyn, Hubert. *Chinese Education in the War.* Shanghai: Kelly and Walsh, Ltd., 1940.

Furth, Charlotte. *Ting Wen-chiang: Science and China's New Culture.* Cambridge: Harvard University Press, 1970.

Gamberg, Ruth. *Red and Expert: Education in the People's Republic of China.* New York: Schocken Books, 1977.

"General Introduction, Coordinating Committee for the Application of Science and Technology to National Objectives, Executive Yuan, Republic of China." May 1977. AS-Li, A165–18.

Gereffi, Gary, and Donald L. Wyman. *Manufacturing Miracles: Paths of Industrialization in Latin America and East Asia.* Princeton: Princeton University Press, 1990.

Gibert, Stephen P., and William M. Carpenter, eds. *America and Island China: A Documentary History.* Lanham, MD: University Press of America, 1984.

Gillispie, Charles. *Science and Polity in France at the End of the Old Regime.* Princeton: Princeton University Press, 1980.

Gillon, Philip, and Hadassah Gillon, eds. *Science and Education in Developing States.* New York: Praeger, 1971.

Gilpin, Robert. *France in the Age of the Scientific State.* Princeton: Princeton University Press, 1968.

Gold, Thomas B. *State and Society in the Taiwan Miracle.* Armonk, NY: M. E. Sharpe, 1986.

Graham, Loren R. "The Development of Science Policy in the Soviet Union." In *Science Policies of Industrial Nations: Case Studies of the United States, Soviet Union, United Kingdom, France, Japan, and Sweden,* ed. T. Dixon Long and Christopher Wright, pp. 12–58. New York: Praeger, 1975.

"Guidelines for Discussion by Prime Minister's Board of Advisors on Science and Technology in January 1980 (3rd Draft, December 17, 1979)." AS-Li, C4–32.

"Guojia anquan huiyi kexue fazhan zhidao weiyuanhui di yi ci huiyi jilu" (Records of the first meeting of the Committee for Science Development). March 29, 1967. AS-Li, B-493.

Haggard, Stephan. "Business, Politics and Policy in East and Southeast Asia." In *Behind East Asian Economic Growth: The Political and Social Foundations of Prosperity,* ed. Henry S. Rowen, pp. 78–104. London: Routledge, 1998.

———. *Pathways from the Periphery: The Politics of Growth in the Newly Industrializing Countries.* Ithaca: Cornell University Press, 1990.

Haggerty, Patrick. "Haggerty, Patrick, et al. to K. T. Li, et al." May 17, 1978. AS-Li, B491–5.

———. "Letter from Haggerty to Li." August 6, 1979. AS-Li, A161–50.

Hanna, Nagy, Sandor Boyson, and Shakuntala Gunaratne, eds. *The East Asian Miracle and Information Technology: Strategic Management of Technological Learning.* Washington, DC: World Bank Discussion Paper 326, 1996.

Hao, Xin and Gong Yidong. "China Bets Big on Big Science." *Science* 311:5767 (March 17, 2006): 1548–1549.

Hawkins, John N. "Higher Education Reform and Science and Technology in China." In *International Handbook of Education and Development: Preparing Schools, Students and Nations for the Twenty-First Century,* ed. William K. Cummings and Noel F. McGinn, pp. 375–391. Kidlington, UK: Pergamon, 1997.

Hayhoe, Ruth. "Cultural Tradition and Educational Modernization: Lessons from the Republican Era." In *Education and Modernization: The Chinese Experience,* ed. Ruth Hayhoe, pp. 47–72. Oxford: Pergamon Press, 1992.

Higher Education in China. Joint Office of the Educational and Cultural Organizations of China, 1936.

Ho, Samuel P. S. *Economic Development of Taiwan, 1860–1970.* New Haven: Yale University Press, 1978.

———. "Economics, Economic Bureaucracy, and Taiwan's Economic Development." *Pacific Affairs* 60 (Summer 1987): 226–247.

Hobday, Michael. *Innovation in East Asia: The Challenge to Japan.* Aldershot: Edward Elgar, 1995.

Hornig, Donald F. "Taipei News Conference Arrival Remarks by Dr. Donald F. Hornig." September 17, 1967. AS-Li, B490–18.

Hou, C. M., and G. San. "National Systems Supporting Technical Advance in Industry—The Case of Taiwan." In *National Innovation Systems,* ed. R. Nelson, pp. 384–413. Oxford: Oxford University Press, 1993.

Hsiao, Frank S. T., and Mei-chu W. Hsiao. "Taiwanese Economic Development and Foreign Trade." *Harvard Studies on Taiwan* 1 (1995): 199–270.

Hsieh, H. Steve. "University Education and Research in Taiwan." In *Scientific Development and Higher Education: The Case of Newly Industrializing Nations,* ed. Philip G. Altbach, pp. 177–214. New York: Praeger, 1989.

Hsu, Kao-yuan. "Blueprint for Science Education." *FCR* 12:3 (March 1962): 36–38.

Hu, Jintao. "Hu Jintao zai quanguo kexue jishu dahui shang de jianghua (quanwen)" (Hu Jintao's speech at the National Conference on Science and Technology [full text]). January 9, 2006. http://news.xinhuanet.com.

Hu, Shih. "Social Changes and Science." *FCR* 12:3 (March 1962): 39–41.

"Hu Urges Innovation in Science, Technology." January 9, 2006. http://english.gov.cn.

Hwang, Y. Dolly. *The Rise of a New World Economic Power: Postwar Taiwan.* New York: Greenwood Press, 1991.

Ilett, Dan. "China's Future—A Stroll in the Tech Park." July 7, 2006. www.zdnetasia.com.

"Industrial Technology Research Institute." AS-Li, B502–6.

Jacoby, Neil H. *U.S. Aid to Taiwan: A Study of Foreign Aid, Self-Help, and Development.* New York: Praeger, 1966.

James, Jeffrey. *Globalization, Information Technology and Development.* New York: St. Martin's Press, 1999.

Jen, C. K. (possibly). "The Planning of Science Education and Science Research in the Republic of China: A Preliminary Proposal for Cooperation and Assistance in Providing Advisory Services." 1963. AS-Wang, Box 7.

Jiang Tingfu. "Diary." Widener Library, Harvard University.

Johnson, Chalmers. "The Development State." In *The Developmental State,* ed. Meredith Jung-En Woo-Cumings, pp. 32–60. Ithaca: Cornell University Press, 1999.

———. *Japan: Who Governs? The Rise of the Developmental State.* New York: W. W. Norton, 1995.

———. "Political Institutions and Economic Performance: The Government-Business Relationship in Japan, South Korea and Taiwan." In *The Political Economy of the New Asian Industrialism,* ed. Frederic C. Deyo, pp. 136–164. Ithaca: Cornell University Press, 1987.

Jones, Graham. *The Role of Science and Technology in Developing Countries.* Oxford: Oxford University Press, 1971.

Kang, Ludao. *Li guoding koushu lishi: Huashuo Taiwan jingyan* (The oral history of K. T. Li: Talking about the Taiwanese experience). Taipei: Zhuoyue wenhua, 1993.

Kennedy, Patrick J. *Republic of China: A Study of the Educational System of the Republic of China and a Guide to the Academic Placement of Students in Educational Institutions of the United States.* Washington, DC: U.S. Department of State, 1977.

"Kexue jixu fazhan fangan jianbao" (Brief report on the S&T Development Program). AS-Li, B-485–2.

Kidd, Charles V. "The Loss of Scientist from Less to More Developed Countries." National Institutes of Health, Bethesda, 1961? AS-Qian, Box 41.

Kirby, William C. "Continuity and Change in Modern China: Economic Planning on the Mainland and on Taiwan, 1943–1958." *Australian Journal of Chinese Affairs* 24 (July 1990): 121–141.

———. "Engineering China: Birth of the Developmental State, 1928–1937." In *Becoming Chinese: Passages to Modernity and Beyond,* ed. Yeh Wen-hsin, pp. 137–160. Berkeley: University of California Press, 2000.

———. *Germany and Republican China.* Stanford: Stanford University Press, 1984.

———. "Technocratic Organization and Technological Development in China: The Nationalist Experience and Legacy, 1928–1953." In *Science and Technology in Post-Mao China*, ed. Denis Fred Simon and Merle Goldman, pp. 23–43. Cambridge: Harvard University Press, 1989.

Kuo, Cheng-tian. "Private Governance in Taiwan." In *Beyond the Developmental State: East Asia's Political Economies Reconsidered*, ed. Steve Chan, Cal Clark, and Danny Lam, pp. 84–95. New York: St. Martin's Press, 1998.

Kuo, Shirley W. Y. "Government Policy in the Taiwanese Development Process: The Past 50 Years." In *Taiwan's Development Experience: Lessons on Roles of Government and Market*, ed. Erik Thorbecke and Henry Wan, pp. 43–93. Boston: Kluwer Academic Publishers, 1999.

Kwok, Daniel W. *Scientism in Chinese Thought, 1900–1950*. New York: Biblo and Tannen, 1970.

Kwong, Kai-sun, Chau Leung-chuen, Francis T. Liu, and Larry D. Qiu. *Industrial Development in Singapore, Taiwan, and South Korea*. Hackensack, NJ: World Scientific, 2001.

Lau, Lawrence J. "The Role of Government in Economic Development: Some Observations from the Experience of China, Hong Kong, and Taiwan." In *The Role of Government in East Asian Economic Development: Comparative Institutional Analysis*, ed. Masahiko Aoki, Kim Hyung-ki, and Masahiro Okuno-Fujiwara, pp. 41–73. Oxford: Clarendon Press, 1997.

Lee, Bih-hearn. "State and Socio-economic Development in Taiwan, 1950–1989: The Transition from Early Industrialization to Postindustrialism." Ph.D. diss., Temple University, 1991.

Lee, Hong Yung. *From Revolutionary Cadres to Party Technocrats in Socialist China*. Berkeley: University of California Press, 1991.

"Letter from V. Bush to Ku Yu-hsiu." AS-Jingjibu 18–22–104.

"Letter to Dr. Ku and Co-workers from Wm. Han-chu Lee, et al, January 1945." Nanjing-NBIR 448–540.

Lewin, Keith M. "Science Education in China: Transformation and Change in the 1980s." *Comparative Education Review* 31:3 (August 1987): 419–441.

Li, Cheng. "Educational and Professional Backgrounds of Current Provincial Leaders." *China Leadership Monitor* 8 (Fall 2003): 1–11.

Li, Cheng, and Lynn White. "Elite Transformation and Modern Change in Modern China and Taiwan: Empirical Data and the Theory of Technocracy." *China Quarterly* 121 (March 1990): 1–35.

———. "The Fifteenth Central Committee of the Chinese Communist Party: Full-Fledged Technocratic Leadership with Partial Control by Jiang Zemin." *Asian Survey* 38:3 (March 1998): 231–264.

Li, Hongzhang, and Zeng Guofan. "The Proposal of Tseng and Li in 1871." In *China's Response to the West: A Documentary Survey, 1839–1923*, ed. Teng Ssu-yu and John K. Fairbank, pp. 91–93. Cambridge: Harvard University Press, 1961.

Li, K. T. "Address on 'Development of Human Resources and Its Relation with Science Education.'" Address to JCRR, November 7, 1961. AS-Li, A-175.

———. *Economic Transformation of Taiwan, ROC.* London: Shepheard-Walwyn Ltd., 1988.

———. *The Evolution of Policy behind Taiwan's Development Success.* New Haven: Yale University Press, 1988.

———. "Industrial Development and Industrial Research Activities in the Republic of China." April 15, 1964. AS-Qian, Box 41.

———. "Memo to Eugene R. Black on Cooperation in Science and Technology Development in the Republic of China." October 11, 1968. AS-Li, A161–5.

———. "To Mark Shepherd, Jr." December 17, 1977. AS-Li, B-491.

———. "Welcome Address to Hornig Mission." AS-Li, B490–19.

Lin, Ching-yuan. *Industrialization in Taiwan, 1946–72: Trade and Import-Substitution Policies for Developing Countries.* New York: Praeger, 1973.

Lin, Eric, Xu Bingyan, Yang Meiping, and Xue Wenzhen. "Chinese with an American Education and Taiwan's Scientific and Technological Development." *Chinese Studies in History* 36:3 (Spring 2003): 22–37.

Lin, Otto C. C. "Science and Technology Policy and Its Influence on Economic Development in Taiwan." In *Behind East Asian Growth: The Political and Social Foundations of Prosperity,* ed. Henry S. Rowen, pp. 185–206. London: Routledge, 1998.

Lin, Zhiling, and Thomas W. Robinson, eds. *The Chinese and Their Future: Beijing, Taipei, and Hong Kong.* Washington, DC: AEI Press, 1994.

Liu, Alan P. L. *Phoenix and the Lame Lion: Modernization in Taiwan and Mainland China, 1950–1980.* Stanford: Hoover Institution Press, 1987.

Liu, Paul K. C. "Science, Technology and Human Capital Formation." In *Taiwan: From Developing to Mature Economy,* ed. Gustav Ranis, pp. 357–393. Boulder, CO: Westview Press, 1992.

"Liushiwu nian shiyi yue ershiwu ri ben yuan di yiwulingsan huiyi" (Minutes from the 1503 meeting of the Executive Yuan, November 25, 1976). AS-Li, B-497.

Lo, Ming-cheng M. *Doctors within Borders: Profession, Ethnicity, and Modernity in Colonial Taiwan.* Berkeley: University of California Press, 2002.

Long, T. Dixon, and Christopher Wright, eds. *Science Policies of Industrial Nations: Case Studies of the United States, Soviet Union, United Kingdom, France, Japan, and Sweden.* New York: Praeger, 1975.

Lou, Jiwei. "Guoding xiansheng ersanshi" (Two or three things about Mr. K. T. Li). www.people.com.cn.

Maheu, René. "Introduction." In *Science and Education in Developing States,* ed. Philip Gillon and Hadassah Gillon, pp. 3–10. New York: Praeger, 1971.

Mai, Chao-cheng, and Chien-sheng Shih, eds. *Taiwan's Economic Success since 1980.* Cheltenham, UK: Edward Elgar, 2001.

"Major Points of Science and Technology Advisory Group, Executive Yuan (Draft)." November 1979. AS-Li, C4–32.

Manpower Development Committee. "Manpower Development in Republic of China." Executive Yuan, CIECD, June 1972. AS-Qian, Box 34.

Martin, Thomas L., Jr. "Report on Technical Manpower and Education." May 7, 1981. AS-Li, B-492.

———. "Report to the Honorable K. T. Li, Minister without Portfolio, on the Visit to the Republic of China–Taiwan." March 1980. AS-Li, C26–2.

McCord, Edward A. *The Power of the Gun: The Emergence of Modern Chinese Warlordism.* Berkeley: University of California Press, 1993.

McCusker, Henry F., Jr., and Harry J. Robinson. *Report on Education and Development: The Role of Educational Planning in the Economic Development of the Republic of China.* Menlo Park, CA: Stanford Research Institute, October 1962.

Meaney, Constance Squires. "State Policy and the Development of Taiwan's Semiconductor Industry." In *The Role of the State in Taiwan's Development,* ed. Joel D. Aberbach, David Dollar, and Kenneth L. Sokoloff, pp. 170–192. Armonk, NY: M. E. Sharpe, 1994.

"Memo on FY 1960 Science Education Grant Project from Y. C. Chu, CIECD to Howard Parsons, Director US AID/C." AS-Li, A120–6.

"Memorandum Prepared in the Department of State." December 30, 1958. *FRUS,* 1959–1960, vol. 19, China, pp. 509–510.

Miller, H. Lyman. "China's Leadership Transition: The First Stage." *China Leadership Monitor* 5 (Winter 2003): 54–68.

———. "With Hu in Charge, Jiang's at Ease." *China Leadership Monitor* 13 (Winter 2005): 1–10.

Ministry of Science and Technology. *2005 R&D Activities.* www.most.gov.cn.

"Minutes of Meeting with Dr. Hornig and His Colleagues on Science Development in the Republic of China." AS-Li, B490–24.

"Minutes of Meeting with US S&T Advisory Team." AS-Li, B490–20.

"Minutes of the Meeting for Discussing ROC's Industrial and Technological Development Directions with Dr. Patrick E. Haggerty and Members of TI Mission." May 3, 1978. AS-Li, B-491–27.

Myers, Ramon H. "The Economic Development of the Republic of China on Taiwan, 1965–1981." In *Models of Development: A Comparative Survey of Economic Growth in South Korea and Taiwan,* ed. Lawrence J. Lau, pp. 13–64. San Francisco: Institute for Contemporary Studies Press, 1986.

———. "The Economic Transformation of the Republic of China on Taiwan." *China Quarterly* 99 (September 1984): 500–528.

"Nankai daxue Taiwan jingji yanjiusuo: Ben suo gaikuang" (Nankai University Taiwan Economy Institute: About our institute). www.taiwansuo.com.

National Council for Scientific Development (NCSD). "Promotion of Science and Technology in Taiwan." December 1964. AS-Wang, Box 14.

National Science Council (NSC). *Indicators of Science and Technology, Republic of China (Charts).* Taipei: Executive Yuan, 2002.

———. "White Paper on Science and Technology: Vision for the Development of Science and Technology into the 21st Century Taiwan." Taipei: National Science Council, 1997.

Needham, Joseph. *Chinese Science.* London: Pilot Press Ltd., 1945.

"On Proposed Visiting Professorships to Help Stop Brain Drain in Taiwan." July 19, 1967. AS-Wang, Box 17.

Orleans, Leo A. *Professional Manpower and Education in Communist China.* Washington, DC: National Science Foundation, 1961.

———, ed. *Science in Contemporary China.* Stanford: Stanford University Press, 1980.

Pan, Shih. "Boom in Higher Education." *FCR* 14:10 (October 1964): 21–26.

Pang, Chien-kuo. *The State and Economic Transformation: The Taiwan Case.* New York: Garland, 1992.

"Performance Evaluation of Science and Technology Development Program." AS-Qian, Box 36.

Pietz, David A. *Engineering the State: The Huai River and Reconstruction in Nationalist China, 1927–1937.* New York: Routledge, 2002.

Platt, Joseph B. "Emigration of Scholars and the Development of Taiwan: Chinese-American Cooperation." *Development Digest* 4:1 (April 1966): 42–46.

———. "Joseph Platt to Wang Shijie." August 8, 1964. AS-Qian, Box 78.

Pong, David. *Shen Pao-chen and China's Modernization in the Nineteenth Century.* Cambridge: Cambridge University Press, 1994.

Porter, Jonathan. *Tseng Kuo-fan's Private Bureaucracy.* Berkeley: Center for Chinese Studies, 1972.

Qian, Changzhao. "Qian fuzhuren weiyuan xunci" (Vice Head Qian's Lecture). In *Ziyuan weiyuanhui Weng Wenhao, Qian Changzhao yanlun* (Speeches by the NRC's Weng Wenhao and Qian Changzhao). Nanjing-NRC 28(2)–314.

Qian, Siliang. "A General Report on the National Council on Science Development." AS-Qian, Box 41.

———. "New Patterns of Inter-University Cooperation in the Natural and Physical Sciences." AS-Qian, Box 191.

———. "Recent Development of Science Education and Research in Taiwan." Address to the Rotary Club of Taipei, February 9, 1961. AS-Qian, Box 157.

Quester, George. "Taiwan and Nuclear Proliferation." *ORBIS: Journal of World Affairs* 18:1 (Spring 1974): 140–150.

Ranis, Gustav, ed. *Taiwan: From Developing to Mature Economy.* Boulder, CO: Westview Press, 1992.

Reardon-Anderson, James. *The Study of Change: Chemistry in China, 1840–1949.* Cambridge: Cambridge University Press, 1991.

"Report of the Committee on Natural Sciences." In *Sino-American Conference on Intellectual Cooperation Report and Proceedings*, pp. 123–125. Seattle: University of Washington, 1960.

Rosenberg, Nathan. "Science and Technology Policy for the Asian NICs: Lessons from Economic History." In *Science and Technology: Lessons for Development Policy,* ed. Robert E. Evenson and Gustav Ranis, pp. 135–155. Boulder, CO: Westview Press, 1990.

Rostow, W. W. "Some Reflections on Taiwan: The Next Ten Years." Memo to K. T. Li, June 6, 1980. AS-Li, C4–85.

"Ruhe jiji tuixing keji zhengti fazhan" (How to actively push the holistic development of S&T). AS-Li, B-493–8.

Saich, Tony. *China's Science Policy in the 80s.* Manchester: Manchester University Press, 1989.

San, Gee. "Human Resources and Technological Advancement." In *Taiwan's Economic Success since 1980,* ed. Chao-cheng Mai and Chien-sheng Shih, pp. 275–311. Cheltenham, UK: Edward Elgar, 2001.

Science and Technology Advisory Group. "National Science and Technology Development." Taipei: STAG, 1989.

"Science and Technology Policy (14 May 2004)." www.chinaembassy-fi.org/eng.

"Scientific Manpower Development Program." January 1965. AS-Wang, Box 11.

Seitz, Frederick. *On the Frontier: My Life in Science.* New York: American Institute of Physics Press, 1994.

Shen, T. H. *The Sino-American Joint Commission on Rural Reconstruction: Twenty Years of Cooperation for Agricultural Development.* Ithaca: Cornell University Press, 1970.

Shieh, Milton J. T., ed. *The Kuomintang: Selected Historical Documents, 1894–1969.* New York: St. John's University Press, 1970.

Shive, Chi, and Hsien-Feng Lee. "Public Policies in the Taiwan Economy: The Nurturing of a Market Economy." In *Public Policies in East Asian Development: Facing New Challenges,* ed. F. Gerard Adams and William E. James, pp. 93–109. Westport, CT: Praeger, 1999.

Simon, Denis Fred. "Taiwan, Technology Transfer, and Transnationalism: The Political Management of Dependence." Ph.D. diss., University of California, 1980.

———. "Taiwan's Emerging Technological Trajectory: Creating New Forms of Competitive Advantage." In *Taiwan: Beyond the Economic Miracle,* ed. Denis Fred Simon and Michael Y. M. Kau, pp. 123–147. Armonk, NY: M. E. Sharpe, 1992.

Sino-American Conference on Intellectual Cooperation Report and Proceedings. Seattle: University of Washington, 1960.

Smith, Heather. *Industry Policy in Taiwan and Korea in the 1980s: Winning the Market.* Cheltenham, UK: Edward Elgar, 2000.

"St. Louis, George to Martin Wong (CUSA Secretary General)." AS-Zhu, Box 185.

State Science and Technology Commission of the People's Republic of China. *Guide to China's Science and Technology Policy, 1987.* Oxford: Pergamon Press, 1987.

"Status Report of Science Education." AS-Qian, Box 77.

"Status Report on Implementation of Recommendations by Haggerty." May 1980. AS-Li, C-4–85.

"Status Report on Recommendations of the First Science and Technology Advisory Board Meetings." AS-Qian, Box 36.

"Summary of Meeting with CKS." AS-Li, B490–23.

Sun, Chen. "Toward a Knowledge-Based Economy: Taiwan's Experience in Developing Science- and Technology-Based Industries." *Industry of Free China* (March 1999): 93–110.

Sun, Y. S. "Address of Welcome to the First Board Meeting of the Advisors on Science and Technology." January 28, 1980. AS-Li, A166–3.

Suttmeier, Richard P. "Greater China and the Development of Science and Technology." In *The Chinese and Their Future: Beijing, Taipei, and Hong Kong,* ed. Zhiling Lin and Thomas W. Robinson, pp. 195–209. Washington, DC: AEI Press, 1994.

———. *Research and Revolution: Science Policy and Societal Change in China.* Lexington: Lexington Books, 1974.

———. *Science, Technology and China's Drive for Modernization.* Stanford: Hoover Institution Press, 1980.

———. "Science Policy and Organization." In *Science in Contemporary China,* ed. Leo A. Orleans, pp. 31–51. Stanford: Stanford University Press, 1980.

Tang, Tong B. *Science and Technology in China.* London: Longman, 1984.

Taylor, George E. "Report on the Conference." In *Sino-American Conference on Intellectual Cooperation Report and Proceedings,* pp. 7–9. Seattle: University of Washington, 1960.

Teng, Lee C. "Thoughts on Sino-American Intellectual Cooperation." In *Sino-American Conference on Intellectual Cooperation Report and Proceedings,* pp. 290–291. Seattle: University of Washington, 1960.

Teng Ssu-yu and John K. Fairbank, eds. *China's Response to the West: A Documentary Survey, 1839–1923.* Cambridge: Harvard University Press, 1961.

Tien Hung-mao. *The Great Transition: Political and Social Change in the Republic of China.* Stanford: Hoover Institution Press, 1989.

Tipton, Frank B. *The Rise of Asia: Economics, Society and Politics in Contemporary Asia.* Honolulu: University of Hawaii Press, 1998.

"Top Transnational Corporations Set Up Research Centers in Shanghai (26 May 2005)." www.china-embassy.org/eng.

"Topics Discussed at Dinner Meeting, June 2, 1961." AS-Qian, Box 75.

Tozer, W. "Taiwan's 'Cultural Renaissance': A Preliminary View." *China Quarterly* 43 (July–September 1970): 81–99.

Tsiang, Grace Ren-juei. "Human Capital Creation and Utilization in Taiwan." In *Taiwan's Development Experience: Lessons on Roles of Government and Market,* ed. Erik Thorbecke and Henry Wan, pp. 249–267. Boston: Kluwer Academic Publishers, 1999.

Tsiang, Y. S. "The Role of Engineering Technological Education in the Economic Development of Taiwan." Speech delivered November 4, 1972, in New York City. *St. John's Papers in Asian Studies,* no. 20 (1972).

Tsurumi, Patricia. *Japanese Colonial Education in Taiwan, 1895–1945.* Cambridge: Harvard University Press, 1977.

Tucker, Nancy Bernkopf. *Taiwan, Hong Kong, and the United States, 1945–1992: Uncertain Friendships.* New York: Twayne Publishers, 1994.

UNESCO. *Science, Technology and Development in Asia and the Pacific.* Paris: UNESCO, 1983.

———. *Science and Technology in Asian Development.* Paris: UNESCO, 1970.

"United States–Republic of China Cooperative Science Program, January 23, 1969 through June 30, 1971." AS-Qian, Box 43.

USAID. "Status Report of Science Education." August 6, 1962. AS-Li, A-175.

Wade, Robert. "East Asia's Economic Success: Conflicting Perspectives, Partial Insights, Shaky Evidence." *World Politics* 44 (January 1992): 270–320.

———. *Governing the Market: Economic Theory and the Role of Government in East Asian Industrialization.* Princeton: Princeton University Press, 1990.

Waley-Cohen, Joanna. "China and Western Technology in the Late Eighteenth Century," *American Historical Review* 98:5 (December 1993): 1525–1544.

Wallerstein, Immanuel. *Unthinking Social Science: The Limits of Nineteenth Century Paradigms.* Cambridge: Polity Press, 1991.

Wang, Fan-sen. *Fu Ssu-nien: A Life in Chinese History and Politics.* Cambridge: Cambridge University Press, 2000.

Wang, Huei-Huang. *Technology, Economic Security, State, and the Political Economy of Economic Networks.* Lanham, MD: University Press of America, 1998.

Wang, Lutao Sophia Kang. *K. T. Li and the Taiwan Experience.* Hsinchu: National Tsing Hua University Press, 2006.

Wang, Shijie. "Address by Dr. Wang Shih-chieh at the Opening of Sino-American Conference on Manpower in Taiwan, June 26, 1972." AS-Wang, Box 12.

———. "Kexue shamo de luhua" (The greening of the scientific desert). Written in memory of Professor Liu Dazong, October 20, 1975. AS-Wang, Box 11.
———. "Kexue zai Taiwan" (Science in Taiwan). December 10, 1966, speech to the Zhonghua nongyehui. AS-Wang, Box 12.
———. "Letter to Walter Whitman." December 7, 1964. AS-Wang, Box 7.
———. "Shuqi kexue yantaohui kaimushi: Wang Shijie yuanzhang baogao" (Summer science seminar opening session: A report by Wang Shijie, president of Academia Sinica). June 29, 1964. AS-Wang, Box 12.
———. "Sino-American Science Cooperation." 1965. AS-Wang, Box 11.
———. "Some New Concepts in Free China." May 4, 1965, speech to the Chinese Writers and Artists Association. AS-Wang, Box 12.
———. "Time for Scientific Take-off." *FCR* 13:12 (December 1963): 9–13.
———. "27 October 1963 Address to the Sino-American Cultural Society in Washington." *FCR* 13:12 (December 1963). AS-Wang, Box 11.
Wang, Yijun, ed. *Zhujiahua xiansheng yanlunji* (Dissertations of Dr. Zhu Jiahua). Taipei: Institute of Modern History, Academia Sinica, 1977.
Wei, Wou. *Capitalism: A Chinese Version: Guiding a Market Economy in Taiwan.* Columbus: Asian Studies Center, Ohio State University, 1992.
Weiss, Linda. "Developmental States in Transition: Adapting, Dismantling, Innovating, Not 'Normalizing,' " The *Pacific Review* 13:1 (2000): 21–55.
———. *The Myth of the Powerless State.* Ithaca: Cornell University Press, 1998.
"Weng Wenhao to Ambassador Clarence Gauss, 7–25–1944." Nanjing-NBIR 448–544.
White, Gordon, ed. *Developmental States in East Asia.* London: Macmillan Press, 1988.
"White House Press Release." October 6, 1967. AS-Li, B490–30.
Wissing, J. A. "Industrial Education and Training in Taiwan." *Industry of Free China* 24:5 (November 1965): 12–26.
Wong, John, and Nah Seok Ling. *China's Emerging New Economy: The Internet and e-Commerce.* Singapore: World Scientific, 2000.
Woo, Jennie Hay. "Education and Economic Growth in Taiwan: A Case of Successful Planning." *World Development* 19:8 (August 1991): 1029–1044.
Woo-Cumings, Meredith Jung-En, ed. *The Developmental State.* Ithaca: Cornell University Press, 1999.
———. "National Security and the Rise of the Developmental State in South Korea and Taiwan." In *Behind East Asian Growth: The Political and Social Foundations of Prosperity,* ed. Henry S. Rowen, pp. 319–337. London: Routledge, 1998.
Wright, Mary C. *The Last Stand of Chinese Conservatism: The T'ung-chih Restoration, 1862–1874.* Stanford: Stanford University Press, 1957.
Wu, Chong. "China to Build 30 New Science and Technology Parks." April 19, 2006. www.scidev.net.

Wu, Dayou. "Duiyu 'guojia changchi fazhan kexue weiyuanhui' wenti zhi jianyi" (Recommendations on the problems of the NCSD). April 10, 1969. AS-Qian, Box 81.

———. "Fazhan woguo kexue de xin jueci" (New plans for developing China's science). New Year's 1967. AS-Li, B488–8.

———. "Kexue fazhan zhidao weiyuanhui" (Committee for Science Development). AS-Qian, Box 81.

———. "Science Development in Taiwan and Sino-American Cooperation." *Industry of Free China* 32:1 (July 1969): 2–10.

———. "Science Education and Research." 1967. AS-Li, B490–37.

———. *Woguo de kexue fazhan* (China's scientific development). Taipei: Xin shidai, 1968.

———. *Zhongyang yanjiuyuan shi chugao* (A historical sketch of Academia Sinica). Nankang: Zhongyang yanjiuyuan zong banshi chu, 1988.

Wu, Hongzhi. "Zhanhou Taiwan de jingji fazhan ruhe gei dalu jiejing: Yi Li Guoding wei li" (How Taiwan's postwar economic development serves as a mirror for the mainland: Taking K. T. Li as an example). www.japanresearch .org.tw.

Wu, Yongping. *A Political Explanation of Economic Growth: State Survival, Bureaucratic Politics, and Private Enterprises in the Making of Taiwan's Economy, 1950–1985.* Cambridge: Harvard University Press, 2005.

Wu, Yuan-li. *Becoming an Industrialized Nation: ROC's Development on Taiwan.* New York: Praeger, 1985.

Xinhuanet. "President Hu Joins Kids in Marking Children's Day (6 January 2004)." www.china-embassy.org/eng.

Xu, Guanghua. "A New Role of Science and Technology in Chinese Society." Speech at the World Economic Forum, Beijing, April 19, 2001. www.chinese -embassy.no.

Yager, Joseph A. ed. *Nonproliferation and U.S. Foreign Policy.* Washington, DC: Brookings Institution, 1980.

———. "Telegram from the Embassy in the Republic of China to the Department of State" (Taipei, December 31, 1959). *FRUS,* 1958–1960, vol. 19, China, 1959–1960, pp. 643–646.

———. *Transforming Agriculture in Taiwan: The Experience of the Joint Commission on Rural Reconstruction.* Ithaca: Cornell University Press, 1988.

Yang, Shuu-Jane. "The Role of the Ministry of Education in the Governance of Higher Education in Taiwan, the Republic of China." Ph.D. diss., University of Kansas, 1987.

Yang, Tsui-hua, ed. *Yuan Weizhou xiansheng fangwen jilu* (The reminiscences of Mr. Veichow C. Juan). Nankang: Institute of Modern History, Academia Sinica, 1992.

———. *Zhongjihui dui kexue de zanzhu* (Patronage of sciences: The China Foundation for the Promotion of Education and Culture). Nankang: Institute of Modern History, Academia Sinica, 1991.

Yang, Tsui-hua and Huang Yi-long, eds. *Jindai zhongguo kejishi lunji* (Science and technology in modern China). Nankang: Institute of Modern History, Academia Sinica, 1991.

Yen, C. K. "Address at the Fourth Joint Conference on Sino-American Science Cooperation." August 30, 1968. AS-Qian, Box 42.

———. "Premier C. K. Yen's Oral Administrative Report to the 1st Meeting of the 37th Session of the Legislative Yuan." *FCR* 16:3 (March 1966): 83–90.

———. "Prime Minister C. K. Yen's Oral Report at the First Meeting of the 42nd Session of the Legislative Yuan." *FCR* 18:10 (October 1968): 74–80.

———. "Prime Minister C. K. Yen's Oral Report at the First Meeting of the 43rd Session of the Legislative Yuan." *FCR* 19:3 (March 1969): 70–76.

———. "Prime Minister C. K. Yen's Oral Report to the 41th Session of the Legislative Yuan on the Administrative Policy of the Executive Yuan." *FCR* 18:3 (March 1968): 67–72.

———. "Prime Minister Yen Chia-kan's Oral Report on the Administration of the Executive Yuan at the First Meeting of the 44th Session of the Legislative Yuan." *FCR* 19:10 (October 1969): 74–80.

———. "Science, Technology and National Policy." Address to the Sino-American Workshop on Industrial Innovation and Product Development, Taipei, August 11, 1975. *Sino-American Relations* 2:1 (Spring 1976): 1–10.

———. "Text of Address by Vice President C. K. Yen to the Sino-American Conference on Manpower in Taiwan at Its Opening Ceremony Held in Taipei, June 26, 1972." AS-Qian, Box 34.

———. "Yen yuanzhang yu diyijie kexue huiyi kaimu" (Opening Address to the First Science Meeting). November 2, 1965. AS-Li, B489–1.

Yen, Chen-hsing. "Dui fazhan woguo yuanzi neng de zhanwang" (My views and hopes in relation to our development of atomic energy). *Yuanzineng weiyuanhui lubao* (Chinese AEC Bulletin) 2:3 (June 1966): 1.

Yip, Ka-che. *Health and National Reconstruction in Nationalist China: The Development of Modern Health Services.* Ann Arbor: Association for Asian Studies, 1995.

Yu, Q. Y. *The Implementation of China's Science and Technology Policy.* Westport, CT: Quorum Books, 1999.

Yum, K. S. *Successful Economic Development of the Republic of China in Taiwan.* New York: Vantage Press, 1968.

Zanasi, Margherita. "Nationalism, Autarky, and Economic Planning in 1930s China." Ph.D. diss., Columbia University, 1997.

Zheng, Youkui, Cheng Linsun, and Zhang Weihong. *Jiu zhongguo de ziyuan weiyuanhui: Shishi yu pingjia* (Old China's National Resources Commission:

Fact and evaluation). Shanghai: Shanghai Academy of Social Sciences, 1991.

Zhongguo wenhua jianshe xiehui, ed. *Shinian lai de zhongguo* (China's last ten years). Changsha: Shangwu yinshu guan, 1937.

Zhongguo xiandai shi cidian (Dictionary of modern Chinese history). Taipei: Jindai zhongguo chuban she, 1987.

Zhonghua minguo yanjiu jigou minglu (List of research organs in the ROC). Taipei: zixun zhongxin, 1994.

Zhongyang yanjiuyuan gaikuang (minguo shiqi nian zhi sishiwu nian) (Academia Sinica [1928–1956]). Taipei: Academia Sinica, 1956.

Zhu, Jiahua. *Guoli zhongyang yanjiu yuan jianshuo* (A brief sketch of Academia Sinica). Taipei: Academia Sinica, December 23, 1953.

———. "Kexue shijie yu jianguo qiantu" (A scientific world and the future of nation-building). In *Zhu jiahua xiansheng yanlunji* (Dissertations of Dr. Zhu Jiahua), ed. Wang Yijun, pp. 29–37. Taipei: Institute of Modern History, Academia Sinicia, 1977.

———. "Quanguo xueshu huiyi zhaoji yiyi" (The significance of calling together a meeting of scholars of the entire nation). In *Zhu jiahua xiansheng yanlunji* (Dissertations of Dr. Zhu Jiahua), ed. Wang Yijun, pp. 5–6 Taipei: Institute of Modern History, Academia Sinicia, 1977.

Index

Printed in the USA
CPSIA information can be obtained
at www.ICGtesting.com
JSHW020917030824
67307JS00005B/139/J